KT-102-679

Organic

Organic

Sophie Grigson and William Black

With photographs by
Georgia Glynn Smith

HEADLINE

Photographs © Georgia Glynn Smith
(except page 67, © Doug Houghton, courtesy of Orkney Salmon Company)
First published in 2001 by HEADLINE BOOK PUBLISHING

10 9 8 7 6 5 4 3 2 1

British Library Cataloguing in Publication Data
Grigson, Sophie
Organic: a new way of eating
1. Cookery (Natural Foods)
I. Title II. Black, William, 1954-641.5'637
ISBN 0 747272204

Edited by Susan Fleming
Designed by Maggie Town and Beverly Price
Home Economist Jacqueline Clarke
Stylist Penny Markham

Printed and bound in Great Britain
by Butler & Tanner Ltd, Frome

HEADLINE BOOK PUBLISHING
a division of Hodder Headline
338 Euston Road
London NW1 3BH
www.headline.co.uk
www.hodderheadline.com

*To our mums, your mums –
not forgetting Mother Earth*

Sophie's Acknowledgements

Thank you to everyone who has helped me to put together
these recipes and answer queries about what is and what isn't
organic. Particular thanks must also go to William, for putting
me right on so many things, Jennine Bierton and Michele King
for support and research, Wendy Malpass, Vanessa Jones and
Nicky Deeley for helping to test recipes, all at Headline,
especially Heather Holden-Brown and Doug Young, to Georgia
Glynn Smith, Jacqueline Clarke and Penny Markham for
conjuring up such gorgeous photos, to Bill Pack for keeping
the vegetables happy, to Florence and Sidney for their
forthright comments on the food, and finally, to all those
people who have pioneered and furthered the organic
movement and are finally being vindicated. Give us more!

William's Acknowledgements

My thanks to the many people who have put up with my
questions and patiently explained organic matters, especially
Helen Browning, and Francis Blake who generously spent time
checking the text. To all at Headline for helping to give birth
to the book. Big thanks to Susan Fleming for making order
out of chaos. To Georgia Glynn Smith for the photos and her
admirable ability to be cheerful when surrounded by alien
vegetables. To Sophie for even more yummy recipes. To
Florence and Sidney for teaching me about recycling and
being brutally honest about food . . .

All farm photographs in the book were taken on organic or biodynamic farms

Contents

Key to symbols

Ⓥ vegetarian
Ⓦ wild and therefore not strictly organic
 * not yet available organically

Part 1 Organics

Introduction

When aliens finally land on this strange little planet of ours, I'd like to think that they will be struck by its incredible beauty. We've all seen those spacey shots of Planet Earth, marvelled at the swirls and wisps of cloud, and the deep, dark blue of the oceans, and it may just be this that attracts our alien comrades. But I have a nagging suspicion that they will be simply delighted to have found a possibly unique member of the universe, a planet whose inhabitants seem to be intent upon self-destruction.

An impeccably democratic alien focus group will as sure as (organic, salmonella-free) eggs are eggs look at how we feed ourselves, and the conclusion that the business of producing food appears to be carried out in a completely unsustainable way would be quite justified. *Homo* is quite evidently not being very *sapiens* here. Might they have heard on the astral grapevine that we in the UK have perfected a most unnatural way of raising cattle – feeding over-bred herbivores minced-up sheep brain? Might they be curious about why we are adding such a vast array of toxic substances to our food?

When the idea of this book was first put forward, Sophie and I were both of the opinion that organic food just hadn't really made it. There seemed to be too little around, and much of it was worthy, a little tired, and grubby. That was in 1998. It's now 2001, and an awful lot has changed in those few short years. Organic food is now one of the fastest growth areas in the UK. In fact it has been quite difficult to keep up with things. Sainsbury's have seen demand for organic milk increase 60-fold. Organic food sections in all the major supermarkets are flourishing, and there are even organic supermarkets springing up all over Europe.

The Soil Association, one of the arbiters of what can and cannot be called organic over here, are frantically processing applications left, right and centre from farmers who see the future and it is green! When we finally agreed to writing this book, I dutifully went into supermarkets, and the one organic supermarket around at the time, Planet Organic in west London, and was amazed at how good the selection of food had become. OK, some of them were pathetically offering a few grim-looking tomatoes, and a tired-looking cucumber or two, but in Planet Organic particularly, there were gorgeous beetroot, exquisite potatoes, meat, fish – tricky one – teas, coffee, wine, ice-cream and spices, all certified as organic produce. It was clear that you *could* now go organic and have a varied and interesting diet. Organic is ready to go mainstream.

While supermarket shelves are being emptied for organic produce, and buyers are desperately trying to find enough to supply this spiralling demand, here in the UK we are being characteristically short-sighted about encouraging farmers to go organic. The Government is happy to help the period of transition from non-organic to organic production by means of a per-hectare subsidy, but after that the farmer's pretty much left to get on with it. That's all fine and dandy from a theoretical standpoint, all very laissez-faire, but meanwhile our fellow Europeans are subsidising organic production with a generosity quite unknown over here. The result? Over 70 per cent of organic food in the UK is imported, according to Soil Association figures. When we see organic mangoes and bananas that's quite acceptable, but it would seem good sense for each country to produce most of its own organic food.

Organics is not really about buying organic food, it is about producing it. It is about respect. Respect for natural ways of production, fertility, pest and weed control. It is about preserving our biodiversity, that richness of species and genes that makes up so much of our natural heritage. It's about sustainability as well – one of organic farming's strongest attractions is that it doesn't harm, damage or pollute the land on which it functions. A saying I think is just right is this: it's about the best of the old, and the best of the new.

I have to admit to my own cathartic experience when writing this book. Having had to talk and read organics intensively for the best part of the year, I was dreading a sort of green *ennui*. But luckily it never came, and I can really say that the organic way of producing food represents a sensible and viable alternative to the far from sensible ways of what is now called conventional production. And a word on that word 'conventional'. It wasn't always thus. In times gone by the use of manure, the complete lack of synthetic chemicals – they had yet to be invented – and the emphasis on maintaining soil fertility to make plants strong and disease resistant, was the way things were. Something somewhere has gone horribly wrong. I look forward to the day when conventional farming becomes organic.

What Are Organics All About?

Organics are really about how we grow and produce our food. In theory, an organic prune in France should be grown according to similar, if not identical, rules and principles as an organic ear of wheat in Canada. In other words, there is an organic method of production which works within some very tightly controlled guidelines. Although the word may still have a slight touch of the lentil about it, in reality organics represent a radical, dynamic approach to farming, to eating, even to living. This book is not intended to be a blindly uncritical tract of organic navel-gazing, but if you're an enthusiast, or a sceptic, whether you are excited, or just plain curious about organics, we'll try and clarify what they are all about.

The Four 'S' Words

Perhaps the best way to look at organics is to focus on what we can call the four 'S' words – all absolutely crucial to the understanding of what organics are all about:

sustainability
stewardship
stakeholding
soil

Sustainability

At the heart of organics is a set of principles that, refreshingly, has a clear and absolutely central objective, which is this: to promote, support and to help establish a system of production that neither degrades, nor destroys, the world we live in. This really is what both **sustainability** and organics are supposed to be all about. One of the main concerns we all have about what we can call 'conventional' farming – in other words the predominant method of farming – is that it has become over-industrialised, that it is polluting, excessively dependent upon toxic chemicals, and causing grievous damage to the environment. It is a classic example of a process that is simply *un*sustainable; in other words if we carry on producing food along those lines, the world and all who live in it will pay a heavy price. The soil will become ever more barren; antibiotic resistance will continue to allow increasingly virulent and uncontrollable bacteria to rampage; and we will all continue to endanger our own health by eating excessive amounts of toxic synthetic chemicals. Modern agriculture is in a sense killing the goose that lays the golden eggs, while organic production offers a viable alternative, something positive, something hopeful.

Stewardship

For far too long now there has been a slow tumorous distance developing between us as members of society and the world we live in. In the UK, Mrs Thatcher famously told us in the 1980s that there was no such thing as society. The individual reigned supreme, and blow the consequences. Thankfully, this deeply unattractive way of organising things seems to have lost its appeal, and a new sense of responsibility appears to have taken root.

The idea that we should really be acting as the guardians and protectors of the planet may sound a little dreamy and idealistic – maybe it is – but it now seems to be a perfectly respectable goal, one with its own clear logic. And this is essentially what **stewardship** is all about. So as far as organic farming goes, we have a duty to keep the land in good working order. We have a duty to preserve the environment, and to protect species from extinction. This moral aspect may be too much for some, but it is also simply good business sense, the old golden goose syndrome again. It's also an essential genetic building block for the future. Genetic variety – or biodiversity – is the world's greatest richness. We destroy it at our peril.

A basic principle of the world organic governing body, IFOAM (the International Federation of Organic

Agricultural Movements), is the maintenance of genetic diversity, and the protection of plant and wildlife habitats. It is one of the great attractions that eating organic food, and living organically, should actively contribute towards its preservation. Good stewards do not destroy their charges.

Stakeholding

Before we get down to the organic nitty-gritty, there is another 'S' word, **stakeholding**, that needs to be mentioned. It's equally over-used and fuzzy, but vital for the understanding of organics. I know these 'S' words are irritating. I have sat through endless meetings – mainly about fisheries, I have to admit – where they are bandied about with the laxity of an incontinent chicken. But again, it all really does warrant a thought or two. Stakeholders have a direct involvement in a process, they have a stake in it in other words, a little like shareholders in a business. We are all, as consumers, stakeholders in the process of producing food. It is we who buy, and we who eat. We are all linked to this process, just as we are all part of the same planet. This interconnectedness between us and the planet, as between us and all the animals and plants who live in it, is another fundamental of the organic movement. It is often called a holistic approach.

The organic movement recognises the role of the stakeholding consumer, and the need to address *our* concerns and desires. And these can then be reflected in a set of principles, written down in the form of a rather long and turgid document known as *The Standards*. Despite its turgidity, ideally *The Standards* should be freely available to those who feel like looking at it, but this is not as yet always the case. Often money has to change hands (in an entirely honourable way, I may add), but you can get a gist of what *The Standards* is all about from the Soil Association or IFOAM. Just about every country in the world now has an IFOAM-accredited national body that represents organic growers and producers countrywide, but there is confusingly no agreement internationally as to what constitutes organic production between all IFOAM members. What really differentiates organic produce in the shops is that it is clearly labelled, and this label is in a way the concrete evidence of the business of you

being a stakeholder in this process of production (see pages 248-9).

If consumers feel that certain welfare issues are not properly addressed, then *The Standards* can be changed accordingly. In most of the EU, with the exception of the UK, it is still technically possible for conventionally reared piglets to be fattened off and finished organically to achieve organic status, which is one of the loopholes that consumer action can address.

Soil

'S' word number four hardly needs any definition. It's the **soil**. Many years ago, in the 1940s, the marked increase in soil erosion began to alarm a number of farmers and thinkers. A battered and rapidly expanding post-war population had needed cheap and plentiful food, and governments eagerly promoted and subsidised a level of intensity in agriculture that had never been seen before. Hedges were grubbed up, fields became bigger, and tractors more powerful as the age of industrial agriculture began in earnest, and this all led to an alarming rise in soil erosion. The Soil Association, formed in 1946, began its long haul to evolving a comprehensive alternate system of agricultural production that avoided these problems, which over the decades became increasingly acute. And at centre stage was the soil. Healthy soil encourages healthy plants, plants which are strong and disease-resistant, which of course means that there is less need for artificial pesticides in organic production. 'Feed the soil and the plants will look after themselves' has been a popular organic *bon mot* since those early days.

As you'll see later on in the book, far from being a mundane brown sludge, soil is in reality highly complex and utterly fascinating. For the organic farmer, a healthy soil provides the backbone for a properly functioning organic farm, and it embodies the fundamental principle of using natural rather than artificial systems to create a sustainable way of farming. Many natural systems can be used to keep soil fertile, by adding animal manure, for example, or by using variations of crop rotation. This is why many organic farms tend to be mixed, both growing crops and rearing livestock, rather than the conventional type of farming called monoculture, where only one crop, or one type of livestock, may be farmed. And the principles again are equally clear when it comes to rearing animals. They should be treated in such a way that allows their natural behaviour to express itself: pigs should rootle, chickens should be allowed to scratch and forage, cows should eat grass. And lo and behold, when animals are treated with due respect, they actually tend to thrive. Remember we're still talking about soil here: a healthy soil will produce the plants that become feed for livestock, and grass for dairy cattle, whose milk will provide whey which feeds the pigs, etc. It's all very interconnected.

To sum up, the aims of organic farming are all centred upon these fundamentals, the four S's of sustainability, stewardship, stakeholding and the soil. Organic farming is a long-term sustainable method of production, that encourages a sense of responsibility towards the world, something which is lacking in modern agriculture. As well as this, it actually needs a direct link to the consumer for it to be truly successful and representative, and is dependent upon the continued maintenance of the good health of the soil for it to exceed its own and our expectations.

Questions and Answers

Every discipline has a selection of the most frequently asked questions, and organics is no exception.

Can Organics Feed the World?

One of the fundamental questions about organic food is whether organic agriculture could feed us all. It seems pretty crucial to me. At the moment, in 2001, some of the targets for organic production are to supply 10–15 per cent of the total market. But if it is such a good system, then why don't we pitch it much higher and go for the full 100 per cent? This second question is often asked as well, and can get a somewhat tetchy reply from die-hard organophiles. The reason is that organics have many enemies – vested interests at work here – busily trying to prove that it is actually fundamentally incapable of feeding the world, and this very question has become a stick to beat the organic movement with.

Briefly, the answer is a yes, organics could feed the world, but there's a 'but'... Since yields from organic farming tend to be lower, logically you are going to need more land to get the same amount and balance of food if you switched entirely to organic farming. And the critics then say, so, that means you'll have to destroy thousands of hectares of virgin land and forest to feed the world, and loudly portray themselves as the environment's greatest friend. Not only is this particularly ironic, it is really the wrong way of looking at things. The organic movement is changing fast, and will continue to do so. As far as yields are concerned, yes it is true, they are lower. But bear in mind these points. Firstly, particular varieties and techniques will be developed that improve the yield. Secondly, what is the sophisticated western model of agriculture actually producing at the moment? Huge surpluses of food, and huge environmental problems, so self-evidently we have an agricultural policy which is hopeless. Globally, enormous swathes of land are devoted to producing animal feed. It takes about eight times more land to produce 1000 kcal of beef than wheat. So if we were to change, or maybe just tweak our eating habits a little – eat less meat and more cereals, for example – then it could well be possible to feed us all organically. Yes, it may seem naïve and yes, there are many other factors to take into consideration, but fundamentally it is true. The world could go organic. But working against the gradual expansion of the hamburger culture is going to be tricky. It truly is a battle of David and Goliath proportions. Do you like a challenge?

Costing the Earth?

If we ever were to reach this state of global organic nirvana, with citizens from Lhasa to Lesbos munching happily on organic produce, then it would be an impressive achievement. But what would it all cost? There is already a justified concern that many people simply cannot afford organic food however much they would like to. Organic food often does cost more and we can look at quite why this is.

Firstly, it costs more to produce. Yields from organically produced crops are often lower, because organic farms simply do not use highly intensive methods of production, supported by quick-fix chemical fertilisers, fungicides, pesticides and

herbicides. Livestock fed extensively and naturally according to organic standards will take longer to reach marketable size, since growth-promoting hormones and protein-rich feeds are totally against organic principles. On the plus side, there are no massive agrochemical bills thudding on to the organic farmer's floor in the post each morning. But using people to remove weeds in a carrot crop, for example, will add vastly to the overall costs. Organic farming is a more labour-intensive business. At the moment, the problem with organic produce is really one of under-production, which contrasts starkly with the global surpluses produced by intensive farming. But as more land is brought into the organic equation, price differentials will fall. They already have to some extent.

In the UK the forward-looking frozen food group, Iceland, has vowed to sell only organic vegetables, which is of concern to some in the organic movement because of worry that big business will take over. Some producers feel that this pressure from larger organisations will put a long-term squeeze on the prices paid for the produce – which, of course, is what has happened in conventional food retailing. Organic farming has to be just as preoccupied by the market and its forces as farming elsewhere, and will no doubt be hectored and cajoled by businesses large and small over the years. But we have all to some extent begun to think seriously about finding alternate ways to buy food, and to forge direct links to producers, be they through farmers' markets or box schemes.

Another problem for the UK is that much of the organic produce sold actually comes from abroad – as does most of Iceland's – which is of little benefit to our own domestic agriculture. What we need is a brilliantly forward-looking policy directive from the Government which encourages and helps conventionally farmed land to move to organic introduction. The period of conversion is always a difficult one for farmers – yields can go down, and until you actually achieve organic status you cannot benefit from the higher prices organic produce can command.

Costs are all an unavoidable part of running a business, and trading profitably is a tricky game. A further point within *The Standards* – that mass of words that sets out what you can and cannot do – decrees that the social lives of farmers and everyone

involved in production have to be taken into account, and paying low or unjust wages is against organic practice. This may answer some of the concerns people may have about workers in the non-industrialised world. In other words, since *The Standards* states that paying fair wages is part and parcel of being organic, then we should be reassured that problems of exploitation have been addressed. If they haven't been, then any stakeholder, consumers included, would have every right to draw attention to the problems and demand that practice is brought into line according to fundamental organic principles. This interaction is one of the most distinctive characteristics of the organic movement.

The complaint that organic food is too expensive may be familiar, but the converse may not be, that the true cost of conventionally produced food is not represented by the selling price. For what are called external costs, or externalities, have to be brought into the equation. In conventional agriculture, these may include environmental costs, such as water and air pollution, or damage to the health of people involved in the production, distribution and use of chemicals. These, if added to the cost of what you buy in the shops, would hike the price up to the level of, and even above that of, its organic version.

A recent study by the Centre for Environment and Society at the University of Essex in England has estimated that these costs may be as much as £208 per hectare. This is not only far higher than many previous estimates but is considered by the authors to be a conservative figure. In 1996, for instance, water companies in the UK spent over 200 million pounds in cleaning up chemicals, nitrates, pesticides and herbicides that had run into the water system from farmland. And you can add to this the loss of biodiversity and habitat destruction which also represent unaccounted costs. 'Green accounting' is a growing discipline, which tries to take all these factors into account. We can already put a rough cost to the BSE crisis in the UK: a sum of 4.5 billion pounds has been calculated as representing the approximate cost of controlling BSE to date.

But, there's even more to think about. When you next tuck into a plateful of imported organic sugar-snap peas, even if the organic bit eases your conscience, think about the cost – in its broadest, ecological sense – of getting those peas to your plate. 'Food miles' represent another external cost, where transporting exotic fruits and vegetables in particular add to global pollution. In cold northern Europe you would of course be hard pressed to eat locally grown organic mangoes and bananas, but the issue of food miles is one that should be addressed. Food supply has become a truly global affair and greater fuel efficiency and non-polluting forms of transport need to be invented, together with a huge reduction in ghastly film-wrapped and plastic-covered sugar-snap peas. Until they are, a thoughtful consumer would be well advised to buy locally produced food wherever possible, and get away from the pernicious 365-day-a-year strawberry syndrome.

Where Can I Buy Organic Food?

Where does all this lead the consumer on a tight budget, keen to go organic but not so keen on paying more for an organic tomato? Well, just as an organic farmer will be laudably intelligent, so you the consumer should be. Find out where you can buy organic food locally; there is now an extensive network of organic suppliers countrywide. Many of them will offer local box schemes or may take specific orders, but you will need to sit down and really think about what you can and cannot afford. Eat less meat, balance your diet, and shop locally wherever you can. Just about every supermarket in the country now has a perfectly adequate and at times quite exemplary selection of organic food available, so supply is really no longer a problem.

Does Organic Food Taste Better?

Yes and no! Organic food is quite capable of tasting as nasty and insipid as conventionally farmed food, but in expert hands it can taste quite wonderful. The basic rules about food buying obviously still apply. With fruit and vegetables, buy them as fresh as possible. A freshly picked apple will taste a thousand times better than one that has been sitting on the supermarket shelf for too long. While researching for the book I ate a Discovery apple that was outrageously tasty, plucked from the tree on a biodynamic farm in Sussex. If there is a local farmers' market, or an organic producer near you, seek them out, and buy what's good and in season. I've had some bland and boring organic chickens from a supermarket, but some that were delicious from a farm in Cornwall. Meat should be properly hung, and well looked after, whether organic or not, for it to taste right. Fish should be as fresh as possible. Food should always be about taste, and neither Sophie nor I would be happy if all organic food was woolly and bland. It's interesting to know that there is now quite a lot of very good-quality wine being made from grapes grown either organically or biodynamically. Not all of them are labelled as such – early efforts were so abysmal that many producers are still wary about using the 'O' word. However, both these systems help the character of the wine to develop, as well as preserve the land from increasing sterility.

Is Organic Food Good For You?

Yes. Firstly, with little or no chemical residues there is an obvious appeal from the health angle. It's not that every non-organic lettuce, sausage or bottle of wine in the world is riddled with chemicals, they aren't, but you never as a consumer have even the vaguest idea as to what really went into the whole process of growing and producing the food you are eating – unless, that is, it's either organic or biodynamic. Just as you have no idea as to whether you or your children have a particular sensitivity to possible carcinogens. It strikes me as simply good sense to go for produce that you know has been produced without the use of chemicals, and this is essentially why many of you do indeed choose organic food. You know how it has been produced.

Of course it's also good for us all to support a system of production which as we have seen majors on sustainability. And how ludicrous it is for us in the UK to read of Sir John Krebs of the Food Standards Agency saying that organics aren't worth the money. Such comments are not worthy of anyone in a position of responsibility towards our health. Think, Sir John . . .

Biodynamics

If organics strike you as dreamy, biodynamics may well seem just plain barmy. But there is good ancestral sense here. Biodynamics are a variation on the organic theme, or perhaps it should be the other way round, since the biodynamic movement predates the organic by about twenty years or so. It owes much to Rudolph Steiner, who was born in 1861 in what is now Slovenia, then the Austro-Hungarian Empire, but these days Austria seems to have claimed him. Growing up in the middle of the last century, and being forced to study science, seems to have created a weird hybrid brain infused with both scientific logic and spiritual ideas from his past. In 1902, while on a visit to London, he became involved with the Theosophical Society, and was appointed to be their representative in Germany. This long-established sectarian group – 'a body of the seekers after Truth who endeavour to promote Brotherhood and strive to serve humanity' – inspired Steiner to form the Anthroposophical Society, which was a variation on the Theosophical theme.

It was Steiner's lectures that proved to be the most effective way of spreading his thoughts, and although the stroke of Steiner's brush was very broad, his views on agriculture were formulated in the early 1920s, and offered an alternative model to concerned farmers, with an added spiritual layer that has proved difficult for many to grasp. Theory of course is all very well, but the ideas were actually put into practice when a group of farmers established the *Versuchsring* (experimental circle) in a Swiss research institute founded by Steiner. Planting according to lunar cycles is a part of the ancient wisdom of farming in many cultures, and biodynamics places much importance on the timing of a whole range of activities according to either lunar or planetary cycles. BD farmers will use one of several charts available as a guide – Maria Thun's is the most popular in Europe – which dictates the best time for sowing and spraying for instance, but there can be real problems if the theoretically ideal time conflicts with bad weather. Sometimes the farmer has to be a little flexible.

There are really two sides to biodynamics, as the word would suggest, the biological and the dynamic. The biological bit is really the same as organics: with a clear emphasis on healthy soil, holism, and encouraging disease resistance in plants and animals through soil fertility. It is the dynamic part which is really different. Here the idea is to try and work with and harness spiritual energy and this is done in ways not too dissimilar to homeopathic medicine, where minute amounts of a potent substance have an ability to effect a huge mass in ways that science cannot as yet explain. Creating special biodynamic brews and preparations along these lines are intrinsic parts of the whole process and when combined with the organic production they do seem to give some excellent results.

Watching a preparation being made is fascinating. Using rainwater and a wooden water-butt, the water and a tiny amount of the required substance is stirred vigorously, fast enough to create a vortex, which is a crucial energising force. This stirring goes on for an hour, and then the preparation is ready to be used, sprayed on to a field by tractor or by hand.

The soil preparations are all made to quite specific formulae, and are numbered 500 to 508. The most commonly used preparation 500 is a mixture of silica and dilute fermented manure that has been buried in a cow's horn under ground. Even fresh cow manure can be made into its own form of preparation where small amounts are fermented, buried in a pit and then used three months later. All these preparations are used to increase the soil fertility and level of microbial life, and scientific studies seem to prove that they do actually succeed here. Biodynamic soil is often even richer in microbes than organic soil.

Cows play an important role in BD farms. There is much earnest discussion about the specific qualities of the various farmyard manures available, but cow is considered best, so you will almost always see a herd on a BD farm. You may even be able to get some lovely and rare green label unpasteurised milk. One of the problems that EU biodynamic farms now have is that they are not allowed to use their own horns any more in the light of the BSE debacle and are now forced to buy them in. This seems quite crazy to me. Compost as you would expect plays a crucial role on the BD farm, and both its shape and nature are proscribed with far greater rigour than under organics. You will find rows of manure rather than huge amorphous piles, and these are often injected with some BD preparations at specific places and depths along the row.

Not only is the farm developed to be a self-contained, self-supporting and sustainable unit, it should also place itself well and truly as part of a local community. What is called Community Supported Agriculture (CSA) is a logical extension of this holistic approach. Here local people effectively buy shares in the farm, and help to fund the whole business. In return they are entitled to a part of the harvest, and I have to say I really like this idea. Just think, you could take the kids down to a farm, in which both you and the community are involved, pick up some almost embarrassingly robust vegetables, farm-made cheese, even honey – bees by the way are one of the great unspoken heroes of the ecological cycle – and all without stepping into a supermarket.

Even if you are basically an old cynic like me, I suspect you can't fail but be impressed by the BD system, and if you try to accept the ethereal dynamic part without its linguistic whimsy, it is an intriguing form of organics plus. Just to add to all this, please note that some of the finest wines around can be made, and often are, along BD lines, although they won't always be shouting the fact loudly on their labels Biodynamic produce can be certified by the Demeter Association, fully part of the UKROFS/IFOAM network and can be recognised by the Demeter symbol (see page 249).

If you don't know the story of Demeter go back to your Greek myths. Demeter was Persephone's mother who celebrated her seasonal return from casa Hades with spring. What a pity we all became monotheistic... If you would like some clarification on the spiritual side I offer you this quote, taken from the website of the Anthroposophical Society in America, www.anthroposophy.org, which is virtually incomprehensible to me. The term anthroposophy has been coined by the biodynamic movement as representing their fundamental beliefs: 'Anthroposophy embraces a spiritual view of the human being and the cosmos, but its emphasis is on knowing, not faith. It is a path in which the human heart and hand, and especially our capacity for thinking, are essential. It leads, in Steiner's words, "from the spirit in the human being to the spirit in the universe", because only if we first come to experience the spirit in ourselves can we know the cosmic spirit. But anthroposophy is more than self-development. Through it we recognise our humanity. Humanity (anthropos) has the inherent wisdom (sophia) to transform both itself and the world.'

Labels

In many countries, there are IFOAM-approved bodies that represent the organic movement. It is mostly governments who control the business of labelling, where an approved collection of certification bodies will look closely at farms and producers to see whether they comply to organic principles, as represented by *The Standards*. If they do, they are then allowed to label their produce as organic and use an appropriate label or logo. In the UK, the governmental agency applying EU regulations is called UKROFS (The United Kingdom Register of Organic Food Standards). You are most likely to see the Soil Association mark, but there are others. Look on your organic anything and you'll find a label (see page 248-249) which will tell you which body has inspected and certified the produce.

In other countries the labelling is even more complex. It's a great shame that despite the spirit of European harmonisation (admittedly not the most popular topic with the average Brit), there is such a plethora of marks and symbols. But despite all this, the higher, earth-bound authority, IFOAM, attempts to regulate and control matters, and our beloved EU has also stepped into the fray, by creating various unreadable documents that control when we Europeans are allowed to use the word 'organic'. I refer you to ruling 2092/9.

However, this label is the proof, the tangible evidence of a process that involves inspectors, checks, and systematic monitoring. And behind all of this lies *The Standards*, the lengthy document against which the checking is carried out. It is a way of showing that the product before you has been produced according to organic principles. Just to emphasise how important this is, you will not, I suspect, see mass-produced, conventionally reared chickens being proudly and loudly labelled as being 'Intensively Reared'. And it's the label that provides the consumer with some much-needed reassurance. Eating and buying food post-BSE has become somewhat fraught. The natural home for the concerned consumer has become organic food.

Working with Nature

One of the clearest distinctions between conventional and organic farmers can be found in their approach to nature, and in particular how they go about keeping crops and animals in good health. Mr Intensivefarmer takes a preventative approach to controlling disease and will have a host of chemicals to hand, routinely spraying against bacteria, moulds, pests and even weeds, as well as adding nitrogen in the form of a synthetic chemical fertiliser to get as high a yield as possible from the land. The same sort of thing goes on with conventional livestock farming: there is a routine use of antibiotics, anti-wormers, anti-this, and anti-that, which all lead to a farmyard peppered with chemicals, and animals that are fundamentally incapable of resisting disease. Ms Organicfarmer's approach is different. The organic way is to encourage crops and animals to become bloomingly healthy, and strong enough to be able to resist disease. And this they do by working with and using nature rather than trying to control it. So, by both creating and maintaining soil fertility, through the judicious use of animal or green manure, through crop rotation or by planting varieties that are naturally disease resistant, the organic farmer allows nature to work on her behalf rather than trying to suppress it. Animals are allowed to behave naturally – pigs form social groups, chickens lay eggs in nesting boxes, cows graze on grass in fields – and the animals not only thrive under these conditions but are better equipped to resist disease.

When problems do occur, there are several permitted options available to treat disease, but prevention through good health is still the basic principle here. For example, at the organic farmer's disposal are a range of biological controls, such as the bacterium *Bacillus thuringiensis* (Bt) which, when sprayed on plants, acts against a number of potentially damaging pathogens – the various living things that cause disease. Importantly it is both natural and biodegradable. Again, this is using nature to her own advantage. When animals are seriously sick and antibiotics are called for, they must be treated to relieve suffering; they are then kept apart from the rest of the herd for an agreed period of time before they can be brought back into the organic equation.

While Mr Intensive's indiscriminate approach to farming may well be killing pathogens, it may just as well be killing a lot of soil microbes and creatures that are actually quite useful. He may well be encouraging quick growth in his crops, but will be creating a weak, showy plant that has little innate resistance to disease. He will also be adding synthetic and complex chemicals, often highly toxic and long lasting, into the soil and water systems of the farm, where they will join the estimated 1 billion litres of chemicals used in the UK each year. Canny Ms O will be aware that, by encouraging a healthy soil, many of the numerous pathogens' natural enemies will be in good supply, so she will devote a lot of energy to creating and maintaining soil fertility. For an organic farmer, the soil really is the organic nitty-gritty.

Remember that organic farming isn't simply a matter of avoiding using chemicals altogether, that is a popular misconception. The real issue is whether they are synthetically manufactured or not, and whether as a result they alter or degrade the environment. However, their use is strictly proscribed and, as in all matters organic, record-keeping – a bureaucratic but necessary burden – will show the certifiers if any breach of *The Standards* has occurred.

Institutionalised bad practice is rife in agriculture, and conventional farming can, has and does cause profound changes to the environment at many levels. The opposite to organic farming is often called HEIA, High External Input Agriculture, which has been the role-model for so long now that any alternative tends to be initially derided as quirky and simplistic. Organic agriculture, however, has got past this stage, and is now widely recognised as being the closest to a sustainable form of production. But it is a complex and

highly localised form of agriculture where global solutions – so easy with the HEIA way of chemical control – may well be inappropriate. It calls therefore for a far greater degree of thought and planning, and understanding of local conditions.

What's in a Healthy Soil?

Since in English we use the word 'organic', it may help to think of a farm as an 'organism', which, like all organisms, has a life of its own and needs to feed to survive. The food is the soil which, combined with energy from the sun, is the heart that beats within our theoretical organic organism. With neither healthy soil nor sun, crops won't grow, and the farm cannot function efficiently. Plants combine the energy of the sun with the mineral richness of the soil to grow, and can be eaten directly or can in turn provide food for animals that are themselves then eaten. But what exactly is a healthy soil?

One of the lasting legacies of the organic movement

is that it has begun the process of liberating the soil from years of chemical misuse, which have left it in a state of virtual sterility, compacted and lifeless. For the organic movement, the soil is the way, the life and even the truth. It needs to be mollycoddled, for the luscious brown mass that is healthy soil is positively buzzing with life. Soil is a densely inhabited, almost living organism whose health is so crucial to an organic farm. One vital component of the soil is called humus.

Humus

Humus is decomposed organic matter. Those of you that have lovingly nurtured a compost heap and noticed the miraculous transformation that comes from a pile of leaves, grass clippings and a good dose of household waste, will acknowledge that it's a fascinating process. Actually, humus, strictly speaking, is what happens after the initial, rather foetid stage, when it begins to take on – in theory at least – a positively edible, sweet, and crumbly texture. The process of decomposition gives rise to what are called

humic compounds whose presence in humus – and
then in the soil – allows plants to take up nutrients in
the form of positive ion, or cation nutrients. Many of
these – calcium, potassium and magnesium, for
example – are crucial to the growing plant and,
although they are highly soluble, can be held in place
in the soil by negatively charged sticky substances
called colloids, which are found in great numbers in
humus. Humus has many roles to play,
and it also improves the physical make-up of the soil,
making clay more workable and allowing sandy soils to
retain more water.

The opposite of a cation is a negatively charged
anion. Anion nutrients – such as nitrogen, carbon and
phosphorus – are also found in the soil, and are highly
soluble, but nitrogen, which is absolutely essential for
plant growth, can't be taken up directly by the plant.
Conventional farming adds it to the soil in the form of
a chemical fertiliser, which in its soluble form is acidic.
Nitrogenous run-off is one of the big pollutant
problems that result from using fertilisers whether they
are organic or not. But, by using nitrogen-fixing plants
in crop rotation, organic farmers can supply the plant's
needs in a different way.

Rhizobia

Hoping that this is still fairly clear, let us introduce you
to a curious group of soil microbes, some highly useful
bacteria called rhizobia, which are found around the
roots of plants in an area called the rhizosphere. The
rhizosphere is a narrow zone – it's about 3mm (⅛ in)
wide – of intense and complex activity, essentially
made up of the finest outer edges of the roots and the
soil that surrounds it. Oozing from these outer edges is
another biological complexity, a substance called the
mucigel, rich in both nutrients and microbes, that
feeds these rhizobia bacteria among others.

Rhizobia are important because they fix valuable
nitrogen from the air and enable the plant to take it
up in the form of protein, so a soil rich in humus and
therefore also rich in rhizobia, both indications of a
healthy, well-balanced soil, will enable a plant to grow
strongly.

The complex inter-relationship between organisms is
an area where more research is needed. Conventional
agriculture seems to be virtually cutting itself off from
many of the possible advantages of a healthy, microbe-
rich soil. Symbiosis is when two organisms benefit
each other, so in the case of the rhizobia bacteria,
although the symbiotic relationship is between the
plant and the bacteria, the farmer also benefits directly
from the overall increase in the health of the soil.
There are other symbiotic relationships to be found in
the soil. Take a look at mycorrhizae, for example.

Mycorrhizae

If you ever go mushrooming, you'll probably be after
the fruiting spore that appears above ground. For the
purists, these are known as ectomychorrhizal fungi,
but underneath them is a network of ultrafine
filaments collectively called the mycelium, and
individually, hyphae. What we are looking at here are
VAMs, standing for – and you'll have no trouble
remembering this – vesicular arbuscular mycorrhizae.
These VAMs are subterranean mushrooms that
essentially feed off the soil, and in so doing help to
break down organic matter into nutrients that can be
absorbed by a plant through its roots. Mycorrhizal
fungi are always present in a healthy soil and weave
their filaments throughout its content, and in the case
of a plant's roots actually grow into their outer layer of
cells. In so doing they also help the plant take up
water from the soil, as well as helping them convert
some of the insoluble nutrients found in the soil into a
usable form. They are also known to offer the plant
some protection from disease. They can even help a
plant survive in soil polluted with toxic substances such
as heavy metals, so one day it may be possible to
manipulate them to detoxify heavily polluted industrial
sites. Not bad for an invisible fungus! The symbiosis is
this: the fungus feeds off the soil and the root, and in
turn allows water and nutrients to flow into the root
down the fine network of filaments or hyphae.

Actinomycetes

Another useful group of micro-organisms are the
actinomycetes, a sort of halfway house between
bacteria and mycorrhizae. Again there are good and
bad actinomycetes. On the plus side they are vital in
helping break down compost into humus, but on the
down side they are also responsible for some plant
diseases such as potato blight.

Worms Etc.

Then there are the array of odd little creepy-crawlies, many of which you will have seen if you've been digging in the garden recently. And again some of them are useful, and others completely irritating. Take eelworms for instance. They have played havoc with my root crops but have helped to decompose my compost. If you understand the conditions in which such creatures thrive, then it helps. If you know the life cycle of the carrot-root fly for instance, a simple physical barrier can solve the problem.

Moving up an evolutionary level or two, let's take a brief look at that magnificent and in this case widely appreciated creature, *Lumbricus terrestris*, the earthworm. Although the benefits of soil mycorrhizae are probably still to become public knowledge, the earthworm's role does seem to be widely recognised. An average worm chomps its way through about fifteen tons of earth a year, and in the process helps give the soil excellent texture.

You can see that if you know what the soil can do, what good it can offer a growing plant, then it will pay to look after it. And this is exactly what an organic farmer will do. Healthy fertile soil, rich in organic matter, provides a sounder basis for strong growth than soil farmed conventionally, where a quicker growing crop racing away, boosted by a nitrogenous fertiliser, is often inherently weak, liable to collapse, and susceptible to disease.

Keeping the Soil Healthy

Much of the business of organic farming is centred on keeping that soil in good condition, and managing its fertility by using natural rather than artificial systems. Understanding what exactly goes on in the soil will help anyone who feels like turning their own garden or vegetable patch into a mini organic farm. So start with getting the soil good and fertile and then see how your garden grows. If you've got any grazing animals around, they provide excellent material to increase soil fertility and its microbial population – good old farmyard manure, often called FYM. And don't forget the principles of green manuring and crop rotation, both of which are well tried and tested means of keeping the soil in good condition.

Manure

Using manure to fertilise the land is not exactly novel. It is a widely practised and venerable technique, and is used by both organic and conventional farmers alike all over the world. Without being too descriptive, it can vary in texture and content, can be high in readily absorbable nutrients or, in composted form, can add both nutrients and help improve the texture of the soil. One of the real problems with manure can be its sheer quantity. Intensive farms produce huge amounts of liquid manure or slurry, far too much for the farm itself to use which, if allowed to run off into the local water supply, will cause serious pollution. Called eutrophication, this is where excessive levels of nitrogen and/or phosphates lead to an unbalanced and rapid growth of weeds and plants that suffocate the local ecosystem. Organic farms, with lower stock densities, do not generally have such difficulties, and treat both slurry and manure in either fresh or composted form as a valuable resource. Nestling within these steaming piles of FYM are minerals and nutrients – nitrogen, phosphate and potash – which are all vital for the healthy growth of plants. So what could be simpler than this most basic natural system of all, good old muck?

Under *The Standards*, only well-rotted manure, rather than fresh, can be used in the process of managing soil fertility. This avoids any possible cross-contamination with harmful bacteria. A healthy organic soil will be able to combat these bacteria more effectively than a soil with a low microbe level, but correct manure management is important. Muck from intensively reared animals can have high levels of salmonella and *E.Coli*.

Crop Rotation

One of the best and most natural ways of maintaining soil fertility is by planting rhizobia-rich crops (see page 25) such as beans and clover that can 'fix' nitrogen and make it available for plants in the soil, and this is one of the principles behind crop rotation. It had fallen into disuse with the rise of monocropping, but has been revived and adapted to modern-day organic farming extremely successfully. It is now the subject of much experimentation to try and improve it still further.

One of the classic forms of crop rotation found on organic farms uses red or white clover mixed with ryegrass, which both feeds livestock and increases the soil fertility by using the nitrogen-fixing properties of the leguminous clover. This principle is also at work in undersowing. Here, a cereal crop, oats say, is planted with a crop of clover, and in this case not only is there the benefit of the clover's nitrogen-fixing ability but the ground-hugging clover protects the soil from erosion and controls the growth of weeds. Clever, eh? Following on after a crop of legumes the farmer might plant a crop that thrives on a nitrate-rich soil. Whatever system of rotation is used, it has to be carefully designed to suit the aims of the farmer and the conditions of the land. There is even a system that works for farms where there is no livestock at all, and so no animal manure is available. This is called a stockless rotation.

Another of the important principles behind crop rotation is that a deep-rooting plant, like red clover, will help improve the texture of the soil for a more shallow-rooting crop like wheat, so in an organic rotation the one may often follow the other. When you begin to grasp the complexities of organic soil management, you will begin to understand just how unsubtle adding nitrogen in the form of a chemical fertiliser is. It is also an expensive business, as well as being an unnecessary one. It is now perfectly possible to achieve a fertile and healthy soil, with a sustainable output, by using management systems almost entirely derived from nature itself.

You can probably sense the implications for the agrochemical industry here (sorry boys, but let's face it, it's adapt or die time), and may begin to understand quite why there is so much sponsored criticism of the organic movement doing the rounds right now. An alarmed agrochemical industry is trying increasingly desperately and entirely unsuccessfully to nip the organic movement in the bud.

Green Manuring

This is when a useful crop is grown – often for as little as four weeks – and then dug into the ground to add to the soil fertility. If the plant that's to be dug in has loads of nitrogen-fixing potential, then it will add greatly to the overall fertility of the soil. The best plants of all for this are legumes like clover, beans or lupins that have whole nodules stuffed full of rhizobia on their root systems. Even sunflowers, if grown for the foliage, can add some benefit to the soil's texture.

Organic Ways of Controlling Pests and Disease

Having a healthy microbe-rich soil is crucial since it provides an effective and natural way not only to control disease, but also to help plants grow into strapping young things capable of battling against the complex array of bugs and nasties that can cut them off in their prime. All bugs have a purpose and a role to play in specific ecosystems, and all have their predators and their prey too, come to that. Things only really get tricky when man creates an artificial ecosystem – a farm – with an unbalanced distribution of species. And, as we have seen, an organic farmer needs to understand the lifecycle of all the parts of the ecosystem to try and avoid the problems becoming too problematic.

There are many ways that an organic farmer can try and control and manage disease. I originally wrote that there were many ways the farmer can fight the great fight, but this is really the wrong way of portraying things on an organic farm, although it is perhaps a better description of the way conventional farms have been encouraged to look upon disease. However, some of the techniques available to the organic farmer are essentially preventative rather than curative and are not used systematically, this being against organic principles.

An Ecological Approach

The more you understand about the ecology of pests and plants, the easier it becomes to evolve intelligent and natural ways to combat disease. If you know about the life cycle of the carrot-root fly, for example, you can try and outsmart it, not always successfully, but there are several strings to your organic bow. Carrot-root fly larvae overwinter in nettles and hedges around the fields, so the less of either around a carrot field will be a good start. Carrot-root flies lay their eggs in the soil, and when the larvae hatch they begin to

TYPICAL CROP ROTATION ON AN ORGANIC FARM WITH LIVESTOCK

1) 2 year red clover ley
2) 1 year beans
3) 1 year potatoes
4) 1 year wheat
5) 1 year oats
   (then back to 1)

TYPICAL CROP ROTATION ON AN ORGANIC FARM WITHOUT LIVESTOCK

1) 1 year red clover
2) 2 year cereals
3) 1 year beans
4) 1 year cereal
   (then back to 1)

feed off the growing seedlings. If you can time your seed-sowing so that you avoid this first generation of maggots in early summer, some time between June and July, depending on location, then the problem should be avoided. In fact you can even get carrot-root fly advice and temperature forecasts from MAFF!

Another way you can outwit pests is to grow plants that in turn attract the potentially damaging bug, diverting them away from the principal cultivated crop. In some cases, green manures can be used as a diversionary plant, attracting the destructive bugs in question to target their own roots, particularly useful with nematodes that can destroy root crops.

The techniques of companion planting are quite well known, and can be used on the smallest of vegetable plots, but the principles also work on a larger scale. Sowing carrots and onions at the same time seems to mask the smell of the carrot, reducing carrot-root fly incidence by as much as 70 per cent. Another useful technique is called intercropping, where the virtues of one plant strengthen the weaknesses of another. Plant sweet potatoes and maize together and the increase in

parasitic wasps on the sweet potatoes counters the actions of leafhoppers on the corn. The combinations are endless.

There is obviously much that remains unknown, so the roles of research and experimentation will be crucial in the years to come. Knowledge really is essential, and an organic farmer has to enter into a continual learning process.

Plant Extracts

In one of my more inspired gardening moments I once dreamed of a wild, flowing flower meadow, mixed with wispy barley, cornflowers and poppies to replace the boring old green hegemony of grass. I duly bought some seed, dug and prepared the ground, sowed and waited. In the first year it worked well, but creeping into this pastoral bliss was a voracious colony of docks and try as I may I have been quite incapable of digging them up with sufficient vigour. There they remain, a pox on my meadow, gradually taking it over.

The dock is a fine example of a plant with few natural enemies, a rugged brute of a plant. Analysis

SOME EXAMPLES OF BIOLOGICAL CONTROLS

- The *Bacillus thuringiensis* (Bt) variety kurstaki is used as a spray against butterfly and moth caterpillars.
- The Bt variety israeliensis is used against mosquitoes and aquatic fly larvae.
- Parasitic insect nematodes (*Heterohabditis megidis*) kill vine weed larvae.
- The native British midge (*Feltiella acarisuga*) kills red spider mite.
- The mite *Hypoaspis miles* kills a variety of pests including thrip larvae, springtails, sciarid and shore flies.
- The wasp *Encarsia formosa* kills whitefly larvae.
- The parasitic wasp *Banagrus atomus* destroys leafhopper eggs.

has shown that it contains over forty different substances that may act in varying ways to protect it from disease. Actually, the very strength of such plants can often be used on an organic farm to great effect. It has long been known that a mush made of minced up dock root can prove extremely effective against powdery mildew.

There is a whole host of plants that provides useful and entirely natural ways to control disease pathogens in their various forms. Diluted nicotine from tobacco plants is an effective pesticide. Horsetail extracts, rich in saponins, act against fungi and aphids, and even mixtures of fresh garlic can be used as a fungicide (mix 10g fresh garlic per litre of water, and spray). Garlic can even be administered to sheep as a wormer . . .

There's one tree that is a real star performer, and a brilliant biological pest-control role-model. The neem tree, *Azadirachta indica*, grows in arid conditions, and is native to India. It performs the following functions without a single word of discontent: it provides shade and oil from its seeds. This oil in turn gives fuel for lamps, can be used as soap, and protects against various pests that eat into stored seed. Neem oil solutions repel mosquitoes and nematodes, and help prevent scabies. Neem seed cake enriches the soil, and neem tea made from the leaves relieves the symptoms of some fevers. Not bad for one tree. Recent attempts to patent the neem tree's chemical properties have luckily fallen foul of legislation, but the attempt to take what is and has been common property away from us to become private property is of great concern. This bio-piracy is discussed later on (see page 31). The versatility of neem has encouraged the search for other natural stars, a search which goes on.

Biological Controls

This is a clever but at times expensive way of combating disease, where you introduce a specific organism which is a known predator of another one, and let it get on with its natural job of killing the pest that you, the farmer, want to control. These are generally called biological controls, and they are particularly useful in growing fruit and vegetables under glass where the steamy heat can encourage rapid growth of troublesome pathogens in their many guises. Although they are slightly against the whole principle of organic production, in that the proper ecological balance could be seen to be upset, and the principle of encouraging natural resistance is self-evidently not effective, they have become an important non-chemical solution to the many problems that can occur when so many of a single species are grown in close proximity.

In order for biological controls to work, the pest has to be present to some degree. The aim here, as so often in organics, is to control rather than annihilate the pest, and to avoid any substantial damage that would make the crop commercially unviable. Although many of the predators are native species, some are not. *Encarsia*, for example, introduced to control white-fly, only flourishes in greenhouse conditions – it will not overwinter in cool temperate climates.

One of the most popular species that can be used, and has been for over fifty years now, is the bacterium *Bacillus thuringiensis* (Bt), which produces toxins that will kill caterpillars. In spray form, it degrades very quickly but is very effective and entirely natural. Recently, this toxicity has been genetically transferred into various commercial crops – maize and potatoes, for example – the idea being that these genetically modified, or transgenic, plants will have then gained the ability to destroy any caterpillar that eats its leaves. Genetic engineering is a classic case of misguided science (see page 35), and if allowed to continue will have significant environmental effects that we are incapable as yet of calculating. As far as transgenic Bt plants are concerned, the continued exposure of pests to Bt can build up their resistance to this vital form of control. This is of major concern to organic farmers. Since a Bt spray degrades so quickly, resistance does not develop in the same way.

Homeopathy

Modern science can be very dismissive of things it doesn't quite understand and while organics now has a fair amount of science and research giving it legitimacy in certain minds, homeopathy is still considered to be alternative and slightly dodgy because it seems to be beyond objective explanation. To many of us, of course, that is one of its great attractions. It also works – crucial that. By administering very small doses of a substance that causes the symptoms in a healthy individual, it seems to stimulate the organism to cure itself. The problem comes in knowing what to administer and in what dose or form, so experts are called for both at human and animal level. The crucial point for organics, however, is that homeopathic remedies are from natural rather than artificial sources: plants and minerals.

Interestingly, the same sort of principle seems to be at work in the many biodynamic (BD) preparations used on BD farms. Here one of the most commonly used preparations is made by adding tiny amounts of silica to a vigorously stirred water-butt of rain or spring water. This is stirred so that a vortex is created, which energises the water with what I in my ignorance understand as the 'essence' of silica, an important constituent mineral of healthy soil. The water is said to take on an 'imprint' of the mineral. Just as intriguingly, this also seems to 'work' in that the whole gamut of techniques available to a biodynamic farmer, from preparations to crop rotation, give excellent results.

Another type of homeopathic remedy widely used is called nosodes, and these are proving to be an invaluable form of 'vaccination'. Here a preparation is made from the pathogen itself: in other words, rabies can theoretically be treated by a potentised preparation made from the saliva of a rabid dog. The principle here is that in some way this stimulates the body's complex defence system.

Weeds: Friend or Foe?

Whatever you have planted, one of the next problems to face is weeds which will appear, and need to be controlled, but not necessarily removed. Conventional farming wisdom is to go for the complete annihilation of weeds of every sort, by using chemical herbicides. Our organic farmer takes a different approach.

Not all of them actually need to be destroyed. Organic farming's rather cerebral approach places the emphasis firmly on control, rather than annihilation. Some vegetable crops, particularly carrots, do need to be protected from weeds, which can outpace them and seriously affect the crop yield, so in this case a lot of attention is paid to when the crop is sown. And a lot of money has to be spent on paying people to weed the crop, maybe once or possibly twice during

the plants' life cycle. One of the more bizarre sights I have seen on an organic farm was a machine which apparently worked with a line of Wellington boots at one end. On closer inspection it was actually a platform on which some twelve people were lying down and chit-chatting away while picking the weeds below them, being towed by a tractor.

Ideally, sowing should occur at a time that doesn't coincide with the germination of the local weed population. Hand and mechanical weeding may well be necessary with other crops, and will always add substantially to the cost of organic production. With some crops the technique of undersowing, often with a plant that actually contributes to soil fertility, is a useful one, but the idea that an organic field is a chaotic riot of weeds is very far from the truth.

No doubt mechanical solutions to weeding will be increasingly innovative over the coming years. A flame-thrower can work pretty well in a small area, and mulches serve as a blanket that prevent weed germination as well as giving a gradual seep-through of organic material. Undersowing can also attract pollinating insects and, by covering the ground, weed germination becomes more difficult.

But can these plants also be useful? The organic answer is yes. Many traditional farmers have also evolved ways of using weeds. In Mexico the *frijol tapado* is a technique whereby beans are planted in the middle of a field of weeds, and just before the beans germinate and send shoots up, the weeds are cut and left to act as a mulch.

Making a biodynamic preparation from rain water
and a minute amount of silica, energised by an hour's
hard stirring.

Working against Nature

Extolling the virtues of organic farming is all very laudable, but many of us are not entirely sure about what's wrong with the type of farming we all seemed to be perfectly happy with until recently. You don't have to look too far for the answer. Take a look at what we are actually producing at the moment: food with residues of highly toxic pesticides; meat from intensively reared, factory-farmed animals; chicken from birds that live a life of Mephistophelean misery; crops that grow on degraded and virtually sterile soil; crops that have been genetically modified; herbivores that have been fed on recycled meat; food coloured with possible carcinogens; lamb from animals dipped in organophosphates; food surpluses. Enough said.

What Farming Was Once All About

Before they became all mega and industrial, the average British farm was small, often raising livestock and growing crops side by side. They were probably what we would now call organic farms, all bar the certificate, where manure was used as a natural fertiliser, the soil was well looked after, and crops were duly rotated. OK, there were the occasional distinctly un-organic aberrations, largely born of ignorance – arsenic sprays on fruit weren't really a very sensible idea – but most of the farms produced food sustainably, their methods of farming recurring generation after generation, really with very little change, until the late eighteenth century.

In a heavyweight three-volumed handbook on farming published in 1844, Henry Stephens' *Book of the Farm*, you can get a refreshing sense of the importance attached to soil fertility. Hidden among the sketches of butter-makers, details on how to construct a hayrick, and passages extolling the virtues of the East Lothian turnip drill, Stephens writes that: 'The great object for which farming ought to be pursued . . . is the increase to the fertility of the soil. The object commonly kept in view . . . is constantly to derive the largest amount of produce from it.' A little further on he adds, and remember this was written in the middle of the nineteenth century: 'Not many years ago, cultivators were so irrational as to believe that they might continue to reap bulky and weighty vegetable crops from the soil without having to return to it an equal weight of vegetable matter.' He would no doubt be astonished to see that, over 150 years later, mainstream farming is being just as irrational.

Farmers were always masters of experimentation, testing crops, varieties, and techniques as a matter of course, and between the seventeenth and nineteenth centuries, innovation began to change the look of the British countryside. Crop yields increased fourfold without any help from the agrochemical industry, which didn't of course then exist. Quite why this increase occurred depends on the version of history you read. Some historians reckon that the changes were due to the inventiveness of a succession of agricultural geniuses. There was Charles 'Turnip' Townshend, whose work increased yields by encouraging the rotation of crops, Thomas Coke, the 'inventor' of the Norfolk four-crop rotation system, and of course Jethro Tull and his seed drill. Another view would be to see these changes in the context of a spirit of revolution worldwide. The latter part of the eighteenth century saw the French revolting and the Americans fighting for independence. It was a radical time for thought and action.

As the yields grew so could the population, which in Europe was becoming increasingly urbanised. And with the beginnings of the Industrial Revolution during the nineteenth century, producing food for these growing cities spawned a continual wave of innovations and inventions. Contemporary writers such as Arthur Young in the late eighteenth century, and the highly politicised William Cobbett in his *Rural Rides* (written in 1830), began to portray a rural world of real poverty and suffering. But the agricultural population, disparate and geographically isolated, never really achieved the radical power that some encouraged it to express. The Irish famine of the 1840s also showed the extreme price that could be paid by the increasingly unbalanced cultivation of a single crop, an imported and imperfect tuber, the potato. But it wasn't really until the end of the First World War that the chemical part of industrial agriculture began to rear its hideously ugly head. Being a war child probably hasn't helped it behaviourally either. Among the many lasting legacies of the First World War were toxic gases and tanks. From the people who created the first we learnt how to fix nitrogen chemically, and began to perfect the art of eradicating a wide variety of life, both small and large. And from tank technology emerged the tractor. Farming could, as we would say now, go large.

The understanding of how plants grew had increased considerably during the nineteenth century, and as soon as the vital nutrients were isolated it was only a matter of time before we began to manufacture them artificially. And this we did. As a result, there evolved a way to farm huge areas of land with the same crop, often year after year. The Canadian prairies became host to millions of acres of wheat and, in a smaller way, so did East Anglia. Idaho was plastered with potatoes. All this of course brought with it a golden opportunity for pests and disease to flourish on such a gorgeous feast.

And the solution here was also chemical. Sprays and toxins flowed and disease seemed to be well and truly conquered. But all was of course not at all well, and it didn't take long for this to be noticed. The chemicals did their job so well that they killed indiscriminately, and caused a seeping sterility in the soil. All very well for the developing agrochemical industry that provided the means to keep farming going – more chemicals – but not so good for Planet Earth. Not so good for birds, and insects either, nor farmworkers who suffered and continue to do so under such continued proximity to toxins. Farming had become industrial, and farmers were supposed to farm. Long gone were the days when they were innovators and experimenters. Research and innovation became the property of governments and scientists. And it all became very incestuous.

Many of the world's rulers were of course delighted at the way things were going. In post-war Europe, providing cheap food for a traumatised population was an urgent necessity, and food did indeed become cheap and plentiful. But in one absolutely crucial way,

the developed world took a huge leap backwards. It became, and regretfully remains, an agricultural junkie that simply couldn't survive without the grim attention of its dealer, agrochemistry. And it was in the light of all this that the organic movement emerged.

Indigenous Knowledge and Bio-Piracy

Just as early agricultural innovators learned from trudging around the countryside, so we could also learn by looking at the way people farm all over the world. What is called indigenous knowledge (IK) – you know it's important when it's got its own acronym – is a little like the social version of biodiversity, and it is an immensely valuable and largely underestimated global resource.

Indigenous forms of agriculture have evolved over thousands of years around a particular place and within a particular cultural context. With no artificial chemicals around, keeping the soil fertile and avoiding disease had to be addressed in more natural ways. So, unsurprisingly, there are common themes to be seen. Manure is always treated as a valuable resource. Monoculture is seldom practised, for there is a very practical understanding that spreading risk through growing many varieties is a more sensible – and sustainable – option. If we are to farm organically, some of these venerable and proven techniques could prove crucial. But although IK is a vital global resource, it is important that the 'owners' of this knowledge are properly rewarded for its use.

This is not always what happens. There have been many recent cases of what is called bio-piracy where agrochemical corporations have sought to patent genetic resources in some form. And in the case of the neem tree (see page 27) to patent a species, controlling its use and attempting to profit from its appropriation. This is plainly quite ludicrous. Any part of the range of life on the planet belongs to us all, and must not be allowed to be hijacked for any of the spurious reasons provided – which mainly concern the need to cover costs of marketing the hijacked project. There has been a lot of vigorous campaigning to draw everyone's attention to bio-piracy, much of it from the non-industrialised world, which emphasises the deep concern there is out there about the power of the corporate world.

Looking as we are on the global level, we should also take a sideways glance at the lumbering appropriation of land all over the world for feed to fuel our intensive farms in the West. Millions of hectares in Thailand are now used to grow cassava that makes cattle feed for the industrialised world's intensively reared cattle. Vast tracts of Brazil and Argentina are used in growing soya for feed. And where the land may once have been uncultivated the introduction of monocropping brings with it the chemical gang of herbicides, pesticides, fungicides, now surreptitiously pursued by genetic engineering.

What's Wrong with Farming Today?

At the root of farming these days is the primacy of economics, with its own logic and shortcomings. A logic which says that in order to produce food as cheaply as possible we must get as much out of the land as we can. A logic that says that to be as economically efficient as possible we should put as many animals as is workable on the farm and get them to market size as quickly as possible. To help this goal of maximising yields on its way, governments and agro-industry have funded research to find further ways to combat disease, to increase growth rates still further, and it has all become another closed system, self-serving, self-supporting and self-perpetuating.

Or at least it was. Both organic and biodynamic methods of production now offer a viable alternative, so it is hardly surprising that many concerned consumers are finding some comfort in organics. We have decided to focus in more detail on some of the key issues here. Understanding them will, I suspect, draw you still closer to the organic way . . .

Antibiotic Resistance

Antibiotic resistance is a growing problem that results from the long-term overuse of antibiotics not just in the doctor's surgery but on conventionally run farms where their use has become standard practice. This has contributed significantly to a growing problem of antibiotic-resistant bugs and superbugs.

In farming, antibiotics are not used just to control bacterial disease, they are also used to increase the rate at which animals grow, when they are administered at what are called sub-therapeutic levels.

This well-established technique has enabled conventional farmers to produce food more cheaply than an organic rival, one of the reasons, by the way, why organic meat is often more expensive. Routine antibiotic use is now seen by many to be overuse, and as a result of this many bacteria are developing resistance to antibiotics, leading to an alarming rise in diseases that are proving extremely difficult to treat. The organic movement has been pointing out the pitfalls of such antibiotic use for some time, and their routine use is not allowed in organic production.

There seems to be a link between the appearance of antibiotic-resistant superbugs and regular antibiotic use, but whether it's down to their use in farming or in general medical care is not yet entirely clear. Whatever the case, this is another significant problem that will lead us all to question standard practice on the farm, and even in the doctor's surgery.

One of these superbugs is called MRSA, or myocin-resistant *Staphylococcus aureus*, which is of great concern in hospitals. Staph, as it is more commonly known in the medical world, is a widely found bacterium that is a classic food-poisoning bug. The bacterium produces enterotoxins which cause the illness, and if you're sick, old or vulnerable, or even just plain run-down (a strong possibility in a hospital), then this can be dangerous. So you can see that if these Staph develop resistance, we have a major problem, and within a number of hospitals there does indeed lurk a population of bacteria that shows such multi-drug resistance. Ironically, hospitals are becoming places where you can actually pick up infections that in some cases are literally life-threatening.

To make it even more difficult, bacteria can also acquire resistance by transferring DNA from resistant to susceptible bacteria.

Agricultural antibiotics are less refined than those used on humans, and research has found that they contain relatively high levels of DNA from resistance genes. A paper published in Denmark in 1998 revealed that just under 80 per cent of all poultry carcasses examined contained bacteria, *enterococci* in this case, that were resistant to Vancomycin, a widely used antibiotic closely related to the growth promoter Avomycin that was used until recently – it was banned in the EU in 1997 – in the poultry industry. Vancomycin was one of the few drugs that could cope with MRSA, but surprise, surprise, there is now a new problem on the block: VISA, Vancomycin intermediate *Staphylococcus aureus*, and its more worrying relation, VRSA, Vancomycin-resistant *Staphylococcus aureus*. There have been cases of resistant tuberculosis, resistant *E.Coli*, salmonella, and campylobacter, all part and parcel of the developing problem of multi-drug resistance. Just one more alarming little thing here. Developing resistance does not stop when the antibiotic itself is no longer used. It goes on, through generations of bacteria that have learnt the process of adapting to what they perceive as their foe. Troubled times ahead, I suspect.

Bovine Spongiform Encephalopathy

BSE, the ominous acronym. You will, I suspect, be only too aware that bovine spongiform encephalopathy is a disease of cows, which apparently developed when they were fed on meal derived from poorly rendered cattle carcasses. Ruminants should eat only grass, certainly not each other. This entirely unnatural process evolved over years of increasing intensification in farming, when governments were continually encouraging farmers to maximise yields with little thought being paid to the how or the why.

A similar disease in sheep called scrapie has long been known. Like BSE in cattle, it makes sheep do odd things such as scraping off their wool, hence 'scrapie', and trembling, hence the French name for scrapie, *La tremblante*. They can also relentlessly move around which is why in German scrapie is known as *Traberkrankheit*, or 'trotting disease'. Scrapie is what's called a TSE, or transmissible spongiform encephalopathy, as is BSE and TME, or transmissable mink encephalopathy. When people liked to show how rich they were by draping dead mink around their shoulders, mink were farmed, in an intensive and lucrative way. As early as the 1970s, farmers began to notice the odd mink going uncontrollably berserk. Vets were called in to find out what on earth was happening. As you may have guessed, mink were being fed on meal containing material from animal carcasses, and the disease eventually called TME appeared, having crossed from one species to another. If, as appears to be the case, scientists had realised

then that these diseases could cross between species, then it is a great pity that this knowledge was not widely shared at the time.

What was quite astonishing was the incredible resistance to heat, chemicals, and even radioactivity shown by the disease. Material from infected animals was injected into healthy ones after blasting and treating to levels way above what would kill any other bacteria, and again and again it survived. In 1982, an American scientist, Dr Stanley Prusiner, suggested that the disease was transmitted by the prion protein, PrP, which had been identified in 1968, but whose importance at that stage wasn't quite clear. Prions are now known to transmit what are called conformational modifications between cells so that they are not recognised by the body's immune system as alien, and can thus reproduce, sometimes quickly, and in other cases more slowly. The result in all these TSEs is roughly the same. An area of the brain becomes spongy, movement becomes difficult, behaviour erratic, and in humans dementia occurs.

Recent research points to genetic mutation within cattle as being the most likely source of this epidemic of BSE, with infected material entering into the human food chain during the 1980s and 1990s. And the next stage of course, knowing that the prion can leap through hell and heat with ease, is that the disease arrived in humans. A fatal degenerative brain disease called CJD (Creutzfeldt-Jakob Disease) had been 'discovered' in a new form – nv or new variant CJD.

Despite the EU ban on feeding specified risk material (SRM) to cows or humans, the alarming news is that the disease has not disappeared. Animals that were born after the feed ban are developing BSE and the implications are significant. Cases in Germany, once one of the UK's most self-righteous critics, have now appeared, and we see the same ritual purging being carried out there, as happened in France, Portugal, Spain, and non-EU Switzerland. And as will no doubt occur in the few remaining EU countries to have avoided any cases of BSE. To date only Sweden and Finland seem to be BSE free.

Perhaps if there is to be a silver lining to the BSE cloud, it will be to convince our agricultural policy makers that we consumers really want to see a sane, transparant, sustainable food policy and active assistance to the organic sector. *A bas* deceit. Viva organics!

The story is a sorry one. The British have reacted with characteristic ineffectiveness and now moan constantly about the ban on British beef. There are many logical inconsistencies in the arguments put forward as to why British beef is now OK, but politics should be kept out of the equation. A simple answer is to avoid beef altogether. Another is to eat organic or extensively reared beef. There have been no cases of BSE reported in organic beef animals (i.e. those born and raised as organic).

Gender Benders

Technically referred to as EDCs or endocrine-disrupting chemicals, these are a whole host of different substances that disrupt hormone systems in unintended ways. They include a number of pesticides, wood preservatives, food-can linings, and even plastic mineral-water bottles, so they are not just a problem that relates to agriculture. You may have read of the increase in the incidence of testicular cancer and lower sperm counts. It seems that these gender benders may well be responsible, but we haven't yet been blessed with viable alternatives to many of those potentially harmful substances, so going organic would call for a great deal of vigilance and knowledge that would be beyond most of us. Finding less toxic alternatives to these substances may well come soon, as a sort of stage two to going organic.

Another sensational news item from the world of food and farming that may have passed you by is the story of the sex-change dog-whelks. EDCs are thought to be responsible for an unnatural change in their gender. A number of pesticides in general use can disrupt the hormone systems of many animals – us included. Carbendazim in particular has been experimentally proved to change the hormone system of laboratory rats, and this is present in many fruit and vegetables we eat. Although the recommended levels are not necessarily exceeded, they have been recorded as being on or above the permitted limit several times over the past few years. Of course, you may like me to be somewhat sceptical of these limits. The better option would be simply to ban Carbendazim. Common sense dictates that different people will have different levels of susceptibility to pesticides. High levels of this particular substance have been found in baby food, of all things. In a recent Government report 75 per cent of all yams for sale had excessive levels of Carbendazim, as did 6 per cent of conventionally produced baby foods. Pears also came in at a fairly thwacking 33 per cent.

Another area of concern is the use of soya-based foods and drinks, particularly when eaten by infants. These foods have high levels of phytoestrogens which, although naturally occurring in soya, are of concern since they may also cause a number of complaints including testicular cancer.

Genetic Engineering: GMOs and GEFs

There is a mighty battle going on for the hearts and minds of the consumer, but as we all desperately try to absorb the complexities and implications of genetic engineering, making a balanced and informed assessment is not easy. Recent 'advances' have enabled scientists to move genes across species so we can now cross a tomato with a fish. The results of such a seemingly bizarre process can be called GMOs, or genetically modified organisms, and these are no longer a scientist's dream but very much a reality.

The big chemical corporations such as Monsanto – recently transformed into Pharmacia – and Novartis (ex CIBA) have been well aware of the increasing resistance to chemical control shown by many of the world's crop pathogens, so new directions are needed not only to enable them to retain a market share of the huge global agrochemical business, but also to continue to offer 'effective' ways of controlling disease. As the chemical solution becomes increasingly ineffective and unsustainable, urgent attention to developing other solutions is needed.

One option of course is the organic one. If agrochemical corporations, governments and research institutes were to spend as much time and money looking for organic technological solutions to the problems as they do to finding biotechnological ones, considerable advances could no doubt be made. In theory, useful properties from one organism can be transferred to another by transferring specific genetic material, hence the recent experiment to transfer the flounder's ability to stay unfrozen into fruit such as tomatoes and strawberries so that they could be grown under more extreme climatic conditions. If resistance to certain diseases, chemicals or bacteria could be transferred then these corporations could potentially justify themselves by offering a seemingly environmentally sound, non-chemical means of disease control. This is essentially what has happened with maize and soya. And this is despite anyone really knowing what the implications may be and despite the outcry and concern shown.

But just because no-one can say incontrovertibly what's wrong with GMOs, or genetically engineered foods (GEFs), it doesn't mean that there *is* nothing wrong with them. One of the abiding principles of resource management these days is called the precautionary approach, and especially since the BSE fiasco, it seems totally unjustifiable for governments to be so irresponsible once again and not to take this principle on board in the complex and emotive arena of genetic engineering.

Informed scientific opinion has warned of possible dangers on many fronts. We have already seen what could happen if things went badly wrong. In the late 1980s a Japanese company, Showa Denko, used genetic engineering to increase the amount of one particular amino acid, tryptophan, that could be made from fermenting bacteria. Tryptophan had wide application as a food supplement and was known to counter depression in similar ways to Prozac. The introduction of new genetic material into the bacteria did indeed increase the amount of tryptophan produced, which was processed and exported to the US in the usual way, with no due process of licensing, specific labelling or assessment being required. Within a few months an outbreak of EMS (eosinophilia myalgia syndrome) had been traced to the Japanese tryptophan, and thirty-five people died, with a further 1,500 disabled to varying degrees. The genetic alteration appeared to have had some unforeseen effects, which in this case included the creation of some highly toxic contaminants probably caused by molecular reaction to the high levels of tryptophan within these modified bacteria. The explanation as to why the bacteria produced such toxicity has to remain a matter of informed conjecture since the corporation – which, by the way, insists it was all due to a fault in the filtration process – destroyed all the suspect

bacteria. Draw your own conclusions from that . . .

One area where we do have sufficient information to make an informed judgement is with genetically engineered Bt-resistant crops such as potatoes and maize. Bt spray is a well-tried biological control used extensively in organic farming (see page 27). The bacteria produce toxins, which in varying forms control a number of damaging insects. The advantage of the spray is that it breaks down rapidly in sunlight and is an entirely natural product. However, various crops – potatoes and maize – have been genetically engineered to produce this toxin, and thus acquire the ability to destroy susceptible insects, and all of this is done without the use of chemicals. On the face of it an excellent reality. The down side is this. The toxicity is not transient. It stays with the plant twenty-four hours a day. But what if this toxicity could be transferred to other plants by pollen from bees, for example? A recent German study (see www.psrast.org) has found herbicide-resistant genes in bees that had been feeding on pollen from GE oil-seed rape. Thus it's possible that long-term exposure could encourage all sorts of organisms to develop resistance which could substantially alter the effectiveness of one of organic farming's most valid means of pest control, Bt. There are other concerns regarding herbicide-resistant genes. Monsanto, the creator of one of the most widely applied herbicides – Roundup – has also been marketing genetically engineered Roundup-resistant soya beans for several years, much of it on the spurious environmental claim that this will mean lower herbicide use. The principle here of course is that the soya with resistance will survive when sprayed with Roundup when other plants will not. Quite why this ever suggested lower herbicide use beats me, for what is happening is that some farmers are spraying the crop with about three times as much Roundup as before, and Monsanto, a.k.a. Pharmacia, can happily profit from both seed and herbicide sales. As well as actually encouraging higher herbicide use, it has been shown that there are now higher residual herbicide levels in the resistant soya bean as well. Most of the GE soya and maize is used over here as animal feed, but can also be found in a number of processed foods where current EU and UK law allows up to 1 per cent GMO content before it has to be labelled.

Labelling is another crucial issue, for if we consumers are truly to be able to exercise free choice, then we need to know when and where GMOs have been used. Since many of them are used in animal feed it becomes very difficult, and there is no compulsory separation of GE maize and soya in place in any of the producer countries. Nor is there any agreement that the modified feed is safe for animals, especially since much of the research carried out by Monsanto and Novartis has been on single-stomach rats and mice with the results taken as being significant for ruminant and multigastric cattle.

Again in the US, a GE cow growth hormone (often referred to as recombinant rb GH) has been having unforeseen and unwelcome effects by sharply increasing the metabolic demands on the cow, causing increased illness and even death, and a greatly increased white-blood-cell count from higher levels of mastitis, which then leads to greater antibiotic use and antibiotic levels in the milk. Such hormone treatment is not allowed in the EU.

Although the actual process of adding genetic material is complex, there are certain principles that also provide cause for concern. When genes are inserted, a 'promoter' needs to be added in order for that gene to be read. There are also 'enhancers' that stimulate gene expression. These can alter the metabolism of the cell in totally unpredictable ways so that, for example, it could be possible for toxicity once confined to a pip or stone to be more widely distributed.

Recently, some GE soya was modified with a gene from a Brazil nut, which created a product that showed such high instances of allergic reactions it was promptly withdrawn. One of the promoters used is the gene for the cauliflower mosaic virus. Again, although the implications of its use are unclear, we know that it is by nature a virulent pararetrovirus similar to HIV. In GE maize, the ampicillin-resistance gene has been used as a genetic marker. What effects might this have?

Finally, there are ethical questions that need to be addressed. Should we be interfering with the processes of evolution, and should we be experimenting with the forces of nature in such a way? Bringing all this back to organics is relatively easy. The movement is unanimous and clear in the opinion that there should be no place whatsoever for GMOs, GEFs or GE in any form whatsoever. *The Standards* states that any land that has been growing GM crops will have to be in conversion for five years. Manure from cattle fed on GMO meal is forbidden, as is any other input containing GMOs or their derivatives. *The Standards* has to be a flexible living document, and it is refreshing to see it reflect the changes in agricultural reality so quickly.

Monoculture

The ills and problems associated with the state of the developed world's agriculture have been helped by the belief that monoculture, the cultivation of single species over large areas of land, has been the best, indeed only, way to feed the world cheaply and efficiently. Monoculture enabled some large-scale farms to become apparently highly efficient economic units, manned at low levels and easily worked by machines, although often subsidised by central governments. With disease and fertility closely controlled by chemicals, monoculture is the very antithesis of organic farming. It is now generally accepted that it is simply not a sustainable option, as the true costs of such production methods were never really taken into account. Since it is now becoming increasingly unprofitable, many farmers brought up on a college diet of mechanisation and chemicals are looking wistfully at farming methods where farm-gate prices are higher, and chemical bills are zilch. Organic farming, of course. Government assistance in the business of converting from one to the other is vital.

Pesticides

The World Health Organisation estimates that every year 3 million people suffer acute, severe pesticide poisoning. Over 20,000 may die.

Women and men working in the agricultural sector in developing countries make up 59% of the global working population.

Just over 3% of the three billion pounds spent on farm support in the UK is currently allocated to environmentally sensitive farming schemes.

Pesticides cause 14% of all known occupational injuries in agriculture and 10% of all fatalities.

The gas leak in Union Carbide's pesticide plant in Bhopal killed over 3,500 people at the time: registered deaths had reached 22,149 by December 1999.

Despite a tenfold increase in the use of chemical insecticides since World War Two, the loss of food and fibre crops to insects has risen from 7% to 13%.

75% of genetic resources for food and farming have been lost this century, mainly due to industrial agriculture.

Cotton production uses 11% of global insecticides each year. Overuse, misuse and abuse of pesticides has caused human ill health and suffering, and has exhausted soils and increased insect resistance to pesticides.

One tablespoonful of spilled pesticide concentrate could pollute the water supply of 200,000 people for a day.

Control in the industry is concentrating, with eight companies now supplying 80% of the pesticide market. Six of the top agrochemical companies control 24% of the seed market, representing about 95% of genetically modified seeds.

At least 530 species of insects and mites, 50 plant diseases and 113 weeds have become resistant to pesticides meant to control them.

Highly hazardous stocks of obsolete pesticides have reached over 20,000 tonnes in Africa and at least 100,000 tonnes in all developing countries. They threaten the health and environment not only of local communities but also of the globe.

60 pesticide active ingredients have been classified by recognised authorities as being carcinogenic to some degree. 118 pesticides have been identified as disrupting hormonal balance.

(The quotes above are from the Pesticide Action Network.)

The litany of problems associated with synthetic chemical pesticides has much to do with what's wrong with conventional forms of agriculture. The chemical approach is to nuke the problem, and to support it agrochemistry dutifully comes up with an ever-increasing range of chemicals to do the job, but the price is high. Many of the chemicals used become useless after a while as the target organisms – plants, bugs, etc. – build up resistance. All this is actually very good news for the industry, which then has to come up with a new alternative chemical to replace the defunct one.

Although residual pesticide levels are quite strictly controlled, it is not entirely clear whether these levels are valid for all of us, big and small, fat or thin. Common sense would seem to suggest that this is not the case, which puts them in a different light: i.e. are they reliable? There are particular concerns over the sensitivity of children and the unknown cocktail effects of combinations of different chemical pesticides and herbicides.

Many of the chemicals are highly persistent, and can enter into food chains, and the water we drink, and can be found in the sea as well as on land. Some of them are toxic, others are even capable of changing the sex of smaller organisms. These are the endocrine-disrupting pesticides (see Gender Benders, page 35). But remember that pesticides are also used in the home and garden. Fly sprays, flea collars and ant killers can all contain highly toxic chemicals, and alternative, non-chemical solutions to the problems should be found if possible. The basic principle behind using natural products as pesticides is that they can be broken down and assimilated without causing long-term toxicity.

Pesticide use in conventional agriculture is systematic and long-term. A conventionally farmed apple may be sprayed as many as forty times during its growth-cycle. Washing conventionally produced fruit and vegetables before use is recommended, which removes some but not all the chemical residues. With conventionally grown carrots, you are advised to cut off the tops and wash them as well. Eat organic and you don't have to worry about this at all . . .

Of the more toxic chemicals used, we should be aware of these in particular.

- Lindane, now being phased out in the EU, is an organochlorine (OC) widely used in agriculture to kill a range of pests. It disrupts animal hormone systems and causes breast cancer in humans. It has been found in analysis of human breast milk, along with over 300 other chemicals. In 1996, over 30 per cent of all cows' milk was shown to have varying levels of Lindane. Some studies have shown that the level of breast cancer in Lincolnshire is 40 per cent higher than the UK national average, Lincolnshire being of course one of the country's prime agricultural areas. Lindane levels in some non-organic chocolates has been found to be high. This type of OC accumulates in our bodies.
- Vinclozolin is another EDC (endocrine-disrupting chemical), and is used as a fungicide on a wide range of crops, particularly on peas and beans. It has been detected on imported fruit and vegetables.
- Carbendazim is a fungicide widely used on fruit and vegetables. High residues have been found on some pick-your-own farms, and in many fruits and vegetables, in baby food and fruit drinks. Experimental work has revealed that Carbendazim can damage the development of mammalian foetuses, and can damage sperm and testicle development. It is one of the chemicals thought to be responsible for the world-wide decline in sperm counts.

Growing Green

For most of us, going organic starts here. The lurking suspicion that conventionally grown fruit and vegetables may have nasty pesticide residues, and the fact that many crops are routinely sprayed with both pesticides and antibiotics, are issues of very real concern. And so many of us are turning towards organics, the refuge for the worried, the discontented, and the disillusioned.

Recent figures from the UK portray an alarming picture of pesticide residues on a wide range of crops. Some 26 per cent of all the food samples tested by the Government contained pesticide residues. One imported pear from Belgium and a pepper from Spain had enough pesticides on them to make a child ill. The figures helped the outgoing chairman of the UK Government's Pesticides Residues Committee to conclude that parents would be well advised to buy tinned baby foods rather than making their own from fresh vegetables. He failed to note, however, that it would make better sense, both nutritionally and environmentally, to carry on using fresh food, but to make it organic. But the biggest unknown here is what is called the cocktail effect. No-one really knows what can happen if you eat low levels of different chemicals over a long period of time, and whatever the effect is, it is almost certainly going to vary from person to person.

Not so long ago, the problem with organic produce was the lack of choice, but these days this is most definitely not the case. As I write, munching through a pack of the most delicious cherries I have eaten for a long time, I can gladly tell you that they are organic, and perhaps a little less gladly, that they are from Italy, for a huge amount of our organic produce, particularly fruit and vegetables, is imported. You could blame this on the lack of any real support from UK governments past and present, particularly in helping farmers through the difficult time of conversion. Or you could blame it on our climate, for growing large succulent cherries has never been that easy in the UK, and making the crop fit local conditions is an important and significant start for any organic farmer.

As you would expect, the key to good organic fruit and veg, be they organic bananas from the Dominican Republic or organic beans from Broadstairs, lies in the soil. Healthy plants are more disease resistant. On the conventional farm, disease control is all about eradication, spraying this and that in endless cycles. For example, to cope with fireblight, a bacterial infection that can affect fruit trees, a conventional farmer may spray his crop with antibiotics as many as five to six times between when the blossom opens to when the petals fall. Indeed it has been calculated that an average apple (not an organic one, of course) will have been sprayed over forty times with a variety of chemicals before it gets eaten. You really need to understand why disease occurs in the first place to be able to control it organically, but there isn't this blind determination to eliminate disease altogether. It's all about management and control, and encouraging natural strength and disease resistance in plants.

Organic farmers need to know every organic nook and cranny of their farm: the soil, its pH, and its type will dictate what can and can't be grown, and what needs to be done to create the best conditions for healthy growth. Looking at what was grown in days long gone may well help establish what will do well today. There are very good reasons why the Vale of Evesham is famous for asparagus – perfect light loamy soil, shelter and water. And wasn't Kent – fertile, warm(ish) and close to London – once called the Garden of England?

There is very little point in trying to grow or produce something that will be a struggle. Bananas don't grow on Dartmoor. But whatever and wherever crops are grown the fundamental organic principles, if not the way that they are applied, have to remain the same. IFOAM helps here, setting its global standard, but it is still up to the individual governments to implement and interpret the rules and regulations, usually after consultation with the representative organic bodies. We have become so used to having ready access to mangoes, melons and even mangosteens all year round, we should perhaps stop for a while and reflect on some of the issues that relate to this glittering array of fruit and vegetables.

Are we, for example, really helping things if we continue to buy imported certified organic produce

from far and wide? On the one hand the answer is almost definitely yes. Producing anything anywhere along sustainable organic lines will help reduce global chemical levels, will promote healthy soil, and protect the world's diminishing biodiversity. But when we air-freight beans halfway across the world we are inescapably adding to global pollution and the degradation of the planet (see Box below).

This is neither sustainable nor desirable and, what is more, it seems to go against one of the current themes that the organic movement supports, that the polluter pays. Are we paying the 'correct' or true price for our imported air-freighted organic produce? Basically, no. The cost of pollution hasn't always been allowed for, as this is far too radical and difficult to quantify at present. And it's not just imported food either. With the increasing number of central depots around, even our home-produced fruit and veg are travelling around far more than is good for them (and us). Without being too Luddite about buying food, and suggesting that we eschew anything that is grown abroad – remember that in the UK we import around 70 per cent of our organic food – we, and the organic movement, do really need to think this one through. Again, farmers' markets, growing your own where possible and using box schemes are some of the alternative ways of getting your greens and fruit to the table in a more sustainable way. It ain't easy, this organic business!

Are Organic Fruit and Vegetables Good for You?

The thought might have occurred to you that if these organic plants are so good at looking after themselves, could they look after us as well? Is there anything objectively better about an organically grown vegetable or fruit than a conventionally grown one? Our evolutionary past brought us to omnivory via an insectivorous group of early mammalian ancestors. As time wore on, our early hominid predecessors turned to highly nutritious proteins such as meat and fish, and so inevitably to hunting. Yet they never quite

Food Miles

- An aeroplane uses 15,839 kilojoules per metric tonne of goods transported per kilometre. Rail uses 677, boat 423, and road 2,890.

  - We imported 434,000 tonnes of apples into the UK in 1996, of which over 200,000 tonnes came from outside the EU. Meanwhile we have grubbed up over 60 per cent of our apple orchards since 1970.

- Over 2 million tonnes of conventionally grown soya is imported into the UK, which is used as animal feed and in food processing. Leaving aside the habitat loss involved in the massive amount of land being converted to agriculture, particularly in Brazil and Argentina, much of this and the US crop is from genetically engineered soya.

(Statistics supplied by SUSTAIN, see page 250.)

abandoned plant food altogether. The few hunter-gatherer communities that still exist today use over forty different underground roots and bulbs, and over 100 plants from what to us would seem a peculiarly inhospitable environment. Many of them would also be quite unpalatable for us to eat.

Our livers were once kept busy cleaning our blood of toxins from some of the more bitter fruit and veg we came across (nowadays they have to deal with alcohol and the toxins found in modern processed foods). Over time, though, we have selected plant varieties that are altogether milder – one might almost say bland – and now we eat a pretty pathetic selection of plants by comparison. Many of the more unpleasant tasting varieties are actually richer in plant chemicals, or phytochemicals, which as we will see are very good for us.

Phytochemicals

Organic foods appear to have higher levels of what are called phytochemicals, which are important for our health.

A rather weird process in our bodies, as a result of cell metabolism, causes some renegade oxygen atoms to combine in the form of unstable molecules known as free radicals. These race around our bodies looking for somewhere to offload the toxic oxygen atoms, which may be dispatched into human cells unless they are nobbled before they get there by a substance that can absorb the oxygen with no harmful effects. If they get into a cell they cause oxidation which can in turn affect neighbouring cells, which may then also turn into free radicals, and so on. When the oxidation process becomes too much, or when it is helped along by external factors – cigarette smoke, or pollution for example – cell growth can become cancerous. (This may change the way you look at oxygen; it always sounded quite benign and friendly to me.) Free radicals may also attack fat in the blood, causing it to accumulate as fatty deposits, a process which itself is responsible for heart disease. However, the body has evolved a system of keeping these free radicals in check, but we can help this along by eating food that is antioxidant in action, i.e. will counter or prevent the oxidation caused by free radicals.

The majority of phytochemicals are antioxidants, and

they can be found in virtually all fruit and vegetables to varying degrees. One group of phytochemicals, called flavonoids, are enzymes whose function in the plant is to help protect the plant against bacteria, fungal parasites and damage to its own cells from oxidation, caused perhaps by a break in the stem or damage on the plant. And flavonoids act as antioxidants in us as well. It may warm the cockles of your healthily beating heart to know that one of the best sources of these enzymes is red wine, and they are also present in citrus fruit and a nice cup of tannin-rich tea.

Other phytochemicals include Vitamins C, E and beta-carotene (which our body changes into Vitamin A), all of which are antioxidant as well. So too are lycopene (found in tomatoes), alpha-carotene, lutein (found in kale and broccoli, and which also appears to be an immunostimulant), and the impossibly named allyl isothiocyanates found in brassicas, particularly certain varieties of Brussels sprout.

The phytochemicals' ability to absorb oxygen can be measured and fruit and vegetables give what is called an ORAC (oxygen radical absorbance capacity). Blueberry farmers are absolutely delighted at the news that the blueberry is top of the ORAC charts. In an article nattily entitled: 'New Thrills for Those over the Hill' published on the North American Blueberry Council's website (and yes, it is www.blueberry.org), the thrilling news is that rats fed on blueberry supplements seemed to have reversed some of the normal ageing processes. Down to your local, quick, and buy up all the organic blueberries you can find.

Plant Vitality

Recent experiments in Switzerland have also suggested that organic produce may have a substantially higher level of phytochemicals. Dr Ursula Balzer-Graf of the Swiss Forschungsinstitut für Vitalqualität looked at the differences between organic and non-organic apples, and has been working on a more verifiable means of checking what is called the plant's 'vitality', which is basically its ability to grow in the environment. One of the most apparent differences between organic and conventional produce can be seen via the process of crystallisation, where small amounts of the fruit, or vegetable, are dissolved in copper sulphate and then crystallised. Of major interest is that the regularity of the crystal structure is significantly, and consistently, different between conventional and organic produce.

If for example you were to take a potato fresh from the Andean soil (a traditional plant grown in its native soil, not grown for mass-production), and compare it with a spud from a modern, conventional farm, you should see that the crystal patterns of the Andean variety are more regular and symmetric than the other. Interestingly, you would see the same sort of thing if you compared a conventional with an organically grown potato, the latter looking more like the traditional variety.

This is all deemed to be very exciting, but trying to be objective about quality is tricky, as is trying to assess whether this is really an indication of quality or vitality at all. However, here is the possibility of a verifiable difference existing between organic and conventional produce, even though what it all means is as yet unclear. But it is certainly being taken seriously: it is reported that a chain of German health-food shops is now rigorously checking the crystal structure of all their supplies.

The Plants We Eat

There's much common ground when we look at organic methods of growing the plants that we eat, from cereals to salads, fruit included. As there is with the plants we drink – tea, coffee, wine – and those that we use (cotton, for example). By now I am sure you will have an idea as to the importance of soil fertility, and the goal of sustainability. So whether you are eating an organic cherry or cherry tomato, or biting into an organic banana, the fundamental organic principles hold true.

Although we could take a detailed look at the whole range of fruits and veg, to avoid repetition we have decided to focus on a few rather than skate over them all. An organic artichoke after all is grown along similar lines as an organic yam. Yet, despite the voluptuous selection around we are actually eating only a very small percentage of the world's potentially edible crops and are missing out on some extremely nutritious possibilities that we just simply don't know about and therefore don't grow.

The focus on preserving biodiversity has been mentioned several times in this book. I have recently heard of a melon farmer in Eastern Uzbekistan who has systematically recorded and cultivated a unique collection of all the varieties of watermelon that had been grown in the area. The collection became his lifetime's work, and is proving invaluable. Over here, the potato collection that was amassed by Captain Townsend in Scotland in the 1980s inspired many others to start sitting up and taking note of all the varieties that were being rapidly pushed out of production by intensive agriculture.

Many of them, although quite possibly slower growing or less productive, may well have a genetic ability to resist disease, quite apart from tasting excellent. Modern agriculture has tended to select varieties that grow quickly and travel well, but it seems that the organic movement may well become a guardian to some of these more ancient varieties, not simply for sentimental reasons but because they may be better suited to organic farming. I continually mourn (well maybe that's a little strong) the demise of any strawberry other than the relentlessly bland Elsanta. This is definitely preferred by the multiples since it keeps its colour and shape far longer than any of those lovely strawberries that used to taste so fantastic – remember Cambridge Favourite? Elsanta is however susceptible to a disease called Verticillium and the UK crop is blasted with about 160 tonnes, yes 160 tonnes, of methyl bromide, which, although it is being phased out, contributes towards the destruction of the ozone layer. And by the way, while we are on the subject, can it be wise for us to import over 1,000 tonnes of air-freighted Californian strawberries every year?

One of the real pluses of the organic system is that if you see a product that has been grown abroad, and which carries, let's say, Soil Association certification, then you know that exactly the same standards have been reached. The certification process provides you the consumer with verifiable evidence that there is no deception. If there are problems or doubts, as indeed there are – take a look at the sugar section, page 53, for instance – then remember that not all certification schemes are equally rigorous and if the problem is of real concern then *The Standards* is a living document that can be changed. Pressuring pressure groups is great fun . . .

One thing that you will notice with organic produce is that it needs to be used up more quickly than a lot of the conventional equivalents where growth suppressant is quite widely used. Chemicals that stop spuds sprouting, for example, are not what we really want to eat when we tuck into a potato. When disease does occur in organic vegetable and fruit production, there are weapons available. Bordeaux mixture – copper sulphate – is still permitted as a fungicide, and Bt can be an effective pesticide against caterpillars. Biological controls are often used – nematodes against slugs is a favourite (see page 27) – and they are effective, if at times expensive, solutions that need to be used with care.

Grains and Cereals

A golden field of wind-swept wheat can be a magical sight, and will no doubt warm the cockles of many a city boy's heart as he speeds down to Gloucestershire at the weekend, but appearances can of course be deceptive. Many of those fields are full of weedy, weak plants supported by chemical crutches. When it comes to organic grains, it is of course the method of production that distinguishes them from the conventionally grown, but as we have seen elsewhere, yields can often be substantially lower, and you may well be paying more for your organic grains in whatever form.

However, on the plus side, you can buy just about any grain in organic form that you can imagine. Wheat, of course, and the closely related spelt, as well as barley, rye, oats, rice, corn, buckwheat and millet – you name it, they grow it. From the nutritional point of view we would be well advised to eat more cereals in their many guises and, as we have previously mentioned, less meat, which is often reared on intensively farmed crops.

If you reflect a while on what a grain actually is – nothing more than a seed – the process of milling, which removes the natural protection and a lot of the nutritional goodness that is found in the outer layers, may seem a little pointless. But this outer layer often makes the whole grain virtually inedible unless treated in some way, and if foods containing whole grains can still hint of macrobiotic stodge, mixing different types of flours when making bread or cakes may help lighten the load. We often make a quick and totally unkneaded wholewheat loaf at home, derived from an Irish recipe, that seems to work a treat and isn't at all heavy.

Occasionally I have spied packets of whole Italian farro, derived from the species *Triticum dicoccum*, which can be soaked overnight and cooked, as can spelt, *Triticum speltum*, but this is rarely found as whole grain in the UK. You may find it in its green form in Germany. Spelt is an interesting grain. It has been marketed over here as an ancient Roman type of wheat, which isn't far from the truth, but what is exceptional about it is its unsuitability to intensive agriculture so it has remained in cultivation only in isolated pockets of Italy, France and Northern Europe.

De facto, much of it is grown along organic lines, and much of it is hastily being certified as such. Spelt is also highly nutritious and, despite being a rather tough grain which is difficult to mill, makes excellent flour and delicious bread.

As for flour, although crops that are free of pesticides and all the other -cides will be better for us and the planet, a good miller working with organic grain will still have the same quality requirements – on gluten levels, moisture content and density – and will not, should not, ever accept second best. Every shipment will be checked and analysed to keep those standards high, and records will provide a ready means to compare data between shipments.

Another difference as far as running an organic mill is concerned is in the business of keeping it clean, for here too *The Standards* will permit only a few naturally derived substances. Much of the everyday cleaning on an organic mill is done by using a simple blast of air, but both 'fogging' – fumigating with a permitted substance – and treatment with the naturally derived insecticide Pybuthrin are permitted by the Soil Association to control pests.

We tend to forget this side of organics. When there is processing going on, as with milling, there are different problems that will also need sustainable solutions. It would be inconsistent, not to say completely hypocritical, for anyone involved in organics to be tipping cleaning fluids of varying toxicity down the drain, and we as consumers should also begin to think about some of the issues here . . .

Vegetables

Growing any vegetable organically relies upon the same principles and fundamentals, and doesn't necessarily vary that much according to variety or species. By focussing on just two – potatoes and carrots – you can get some idea of the problems and complexities involved.

Potatoes Push your garden fork under a potato hulm (marvellous word that) and lift. There is magic here. If things go well, neat and often surprisingly clean potatoes can be easily teased from the soil, and if you have never eaten a freshly dug spud, try one. Incomparable. But your pastoral dream may well have

a Stephen King tinge to it. What's that wiggling through the roots, a potato cyst nematode perhaps? Is that fungus I see on the leaves? Maybe a touch of blight, potato leaf roll, net necrosis, silver scurf, or even dry rot? Growing potatoes is not a relaxing form of farming, and with such huge demand and intensive cultivation, our conventional spuds are sprayed and treated chemically throughout from hulm to pot. To avoid this, the organic grower will use the by now well tried and tested techniques of growing strong plants that are disease resistant. Much of the organic response will be to use effective crop rotation, and to choose resistant varieties.

Potato blight when it does occur can be controlled by removing the plant's leaves but this will inevitably give a smaller crop. The best solution is to time the growing and the harvesting to avoid the peak blight periods – much is now known about the life cycle of this pernicious and devastating fungus – but there are years when blight is a real problem to organic growers. Organic potato yields are always lower and they may not have the same perfection about them as a perfect baking spud, but they are at least pesticide free. And one real advantage to growing spuds organically is that it is quite easy to run the whole thing mechanically. Hand weeding can be avoided by piling up the earth around the stem during the growing season, but potatoes are a hungry, exhausting crop and great attention must be paid to soil fertility. On my small-scale plot they are a right pain, but gastronomically immensely rewarding.

When you get round to harvest time, a new set of problems can keep you thinking, and the chemist happy. Potato crops are notoriously difficult to keep. If harvested when wet then they can rot and spoil, so chemicals have been used here too. An organic grower will pay great attention to how they are stored, ensuring they are kept cool and dark but well aired.

Carrots Carrot growing is not exactly a doddle either. They deeply resent being disturbed so must be treated with great care. Since an organic crop will brook no chemicals, you need to weed the rows of crops (so best not to start an organic carrot crop anywhere remote). They are choosy plants, preferring loose sandy soil. My attempts to grow carrots on thick

Growing under Cover: Polytunnels and Greenhouses

If you have never come across a polytunnel, let me say that they are the mainstay of much organic farming. Once upon a time they were very ropy and insubstantial affairs that very quickly became mad wind-flapping messes that scored no farmer any aesthetic brownie points. But they do serve a purpose: they enable us poor, climatically challenged northerners to grow a lot of vegetables (in particular) that are marginal up here. And even as far south as Crete, a grower using them can have an earlier and often bigger crop.

Tomatoes, sweet peppers, chillies, cucumbers, and herbs, in particular basil, all do well in polytunnels, and you will often see a few marigolds sensibly planted at the exit in order to deter aphids.

They do present a particular set of problems, in that they create a microclimate that is particularly susceptible to disease in various forms. And biological control helps enormously here, as it does for growers using greenhouses. To act against aphids there is a parasitic wasp, *Aphidius colemani*, that lays eggs in aphids' eggs. *Feltiella acarisuga* is a native UK predatory midge that will attack the red spider mite. And there are nematodes that eat slugs, nematodes that eat glasshouse scarid flies – the list is long and the variety wide and growing.

Northamptonshire ironstone have given a pathetic crop of bizarre two-pronged alien carrots that no-one really spoke very fondly of. (This reminds me to remind you that to avoid the two-pronged carrot problem not only should the soil be light and sandy but it should be stone free if possible.) But it's a fly that gives carrot cultivators their biggest worries. The carrot-root fly, *Psila rosa* – is not actually unique to the carrot as it also affects celeriac, celery and parsnips – will readily lay eggs in a crop of carrots, usually twice a year in May and August. The eggs become maggots, and they munch away into the carrot, giving it an unpleasant look; no one likes maggots with their carrots.

Much is now known about the habits of this creature, so avoiding the carrot-root fly is possible. Usually a simple, but expensive, physical solution works best: a net will prevent the flies laying their eggs on the growing carrots. On the down side, the warm microclimate of the tunnels and cloches is a happy home for slugs and snails so a vigilant cultivator is needed. For the really serious carrot grower, MAFF now offers regular carrot-root fly forecasts to help you decide when to harvest and sow throughout the year. The carrot-root fly has lost its secrets.

There are quite a few varieties of carrot now available that are resistant to the carrot-root fly. Though not necessarily the tastiest varieties, plant Nantes types if you can. But always be on the look-out. Vigilance is essential. Which is probably why my carrots are so pathetic – I'm hardly ever there!

Fruit

Trying a chalk-and-cheese approach, here we take a look at the apple and the banana, both high-profile everyday fruit that most of us consume in large quantities. Both have their story to tell.

Bananas Split Driving through a vast banana-growing region in the Pacific lowland of Ecuador will bring home just how big the banana business can be. This is monoculture gone mad. Mile upon mile of these fruit, covered in bits of blue plastic, is not a pretty sight, and what's more they all appear to grow upside down; I always expected a banana to grow pointing groundwards rather than skywards (forgive my banana ignorance, specialists). If you get the

chance, and if you happen to be passing by a roadside banana stall, don't miss the delectable little red ones that taste like 100 per cent banana perfection. (Don't bother to eat them over here, as they don't seem to take to travelling very well.)

Anyway, such intensive cultivation is the diametric opposite of what organic production should be about. There is little chance for any form of mixed agriculture, and little chance for any regular doses of locally produced brown gold, or compost, to keep the soil fertile and the plants strong and healthy. With the involvement of huge corporations in many of the traditional banana-growing areas, it is the Dominican Republic, with its band of small growers, that has become the centre for the burgeoning organic banana business. Following on is an increasing number of producers in Costa Rica and even some in mega banana land, Ecuador itself.

Inevitably there are serious disease problems in the intensive banana industry, and there are some areas where what is called black sigatoka, or black leaf streak (BLS for short), Panama disease, moko, and weevils can only realistically be controlled by chemicals. The soil has become microbe poor, and low in fertility – the same old story.

In the Dominican Republic a decline in the importance of sugar cane meant that alternative sources of income were urgently needed and organic banana production was first tried in 1989. The advantage was that it was new land that was being put into cultivation and it was already known that with good site location – a crucial point with bananas, by the way – there was a good possibility of entering into the niche European market with an organic Dominican banana. So with suitable sites duly chosen, the task of building up soil fertility was undertaken, and new techniques were tried and tested to fine-tune the organic system. Bokashi, a Japanese method of creating rapidly fermented fresh compost proved difficult to handle but green manures, crop rotation and mulches have now all become integral parts of the organic banana system. It was also important to find an area where there was relatively low rainfall, for the dreaded black sigatoka is easier to control where there is less than 700 millimetres of rain per year.

The banana is a political fruit. Social problems are

rife at many levels and as a result of consumer pressure, originally from the Netherlands, a movement that we haven't as yet touched on, Fairtrade, was begun. The links between the two movements, organics and Fairtrade, are on many levels. Firstly, and most obviously, they work on the principle of changing behaviour and production methods by harnessing consumer power, by creating a market for a product which is labelled and certified as conforming to fundamental principles. If we look at what Fairtrade means in the context of bananas you can get a feel for what it is all about. There are separate criteria for cocoa, tea, coffee, honey and orange production, but I think it is fair to say that the focus in all of them is on working conditions rather than the production method.

The start-off point should be the creation of a management structure which is both open and verifiable, and – importantly – controlled by its members. After that there are a series of goals and criteria that we can summarise as follows:

- **Avoiding discrimination**
- **Freedom of association**
- **Right to join any union**
- **Right to collective bargaining**
- **Fair wages**
- **Pension schemes**
- **Maternity leave**
- **Fairtrade premiums on prices should be allocated according to written business plans**
- **No forced labour**
- **No children under 15 years allowed to work, and only if there is no interruption to their education**
- **Safety at work**

Then there begins to be a distinct divergence with the organic system over pesticide use, which under Fairtrade is allowed, but controlled to some degree. Some products listed as seriously toxic by the Pesticide Action Network (PAN) are not allowed and when pesticides are used a re-entry period has to be applied, i.e. workers are not to be allowed into the area until the period has expired. Fairtrade criteria continue along the following lines:

- **No pesticides to be used by those under eighteen, pregnant, or nursing mothers**
- **Recommends a programme of pesticide reduction and a move towards organic production and biological control if possible**
- **Protection of the ecosystem – possibly contradicted by pesticide use**
- **Protection of water resources**
- **Ban on herbicides**
- **Use and recycling of organic waste**

That gives you a flavour of Fairtrade banana style; the criteria for organic production are virtually identical apart from the fact that synthetic chemicals are completely forbidden. Organic banana plants have a lower density with a maximum of about 600 plants per hectare. Shade is also important because, just as with coffee and cocoa, wild banana plants grow naturally in shade. Under organics the shade cover must be at least 40 per cent.

There is a vague echo of chickens here (see page 72), where the dominance of one variety has grown with the primacy of monoculture. The banana equivalent of the Ross chicken is called the Cavendish and is widely grown in the banana world. But as more work is being focussed on disease resistance, new types are beginning to be tried, some with deeply evocative names – try FHIA 18 – and the more exciting sounding African banana, Yangambi.

The success of the Dominican Republic's organic banana production has had a knock-on effect as well, so now farmers are busily developing cashew, cocoa, passion fruit and mango among other plant crops, all along organic lines. This is one of the best ways to get the reality of the organic method across – by example – and has definitely been behind the phenomenal success of another tropical product which we look at below, chocolate.

A brief word on ripening bananas. Bananas are shipped green and are ripened in huge depots throughout the world. There's none of the 'vine-ripened' syndrome yet with bananas for they are fragile and need to be expertly processed to avoid any major losses. Although it is an external input, organic bananas are allowed to be ripened using ethylene, which in fact does occur naturally as a result of an

creation of an annual Apple Day in October, largely as a result of pressure from an excellent pressure group called Common Ground (see Appendix, pages 248-249), has become immensely popular, and there you can relish some of the weirder but utterly delicious varieties that haven't been shipped halfway around the world, and actually taste of apple.

The story by now must be familiar. Many of them are disease-resistant but give small fruit. They are a legacy which we need to preserve and on a purely culinary level – this is a cookbook after all – if you ever get the chance to bake a Reverend Wilkes or taste a tiny Pitmaston Pineapple (which really does taste of pineapple), then take it. Many of these apples are from trees that simply get on with the business of producing apples without the use of chemicals. The theme of locality is as we've seen a strong one in organics. Buying locally produced food means lowering pollution levels, and supporting farmers' markets is one excellent way to do this. Many of these have sprung up because of local councils' commitment to Agenda 21 and they have proved to be phenomenally successful. Expect to see piles of apples and gallons of cider in your local farmers' market every autumn. Don't expect to see piles of Golden Delicious all year round.

Chocolate, Sugar and Honey

Of course not all the plants we use are eaten straight from the ground. Many of them, like chocolate and sugar, have to undergo a fairly complicated and lengthy process before they become edible. Honey of course is in a class of its own.

Chocolate Happily for chocolate lovers, organically grown cocoa beans give excellent quality chocolate. And since costs are generally higher, the product has found its own little organic niche, very much at the top end of the market. Indeed so successful has it become that the pioneer suppliers, Green and Black's – sadly no relation – have been joined by the rather larger Swiss company Lindt, and as organic cocoa supplies increase no doubt the range will broaden. Hopefully the high quality will remain.

What I take to be good chocolate is not the stuff that covers bars and biscuits and has high levels of

increase in temperature or the action of some banana-hungry pest. However, if only natural amounts of ethylene were allowed, then the whole ripening business would be very protracted and irregular, and losses would be too high to make the enterprise viable.

Apples A few years back we in the UK had one of our momentary bouts of being Little Englanders and decried the excessive amount of apples being imported. French and Italian Golden Delicious, woolly American Jonathans, as well as Jonagolds and Pink Ladies were all over the place, and we desperately tried to redress the balance. But it has proved to be too late. Our orchards were too small, too inefficient and grew some varieties that none of the big buyers were interested in. Conformity, size and price was what they wanted, and since there was not enough around domestically, supplies from abroad have continued to grow.

However, this ruction reminded us that an apple doesn't actually have to be dull and uniform. The

vegetable fat. It must have that borderline bittersweet lusciousness that you can get from a dark chocolate made with high levels of cocoa solids. About the highest level you can eat straight from the pack without it getting a little too bitter is 70 per cent cocoa solids, so look out for it.

Organic cocoa is grown at lower tree densities than usual, and in order to retain water and keep the plants in excellent health the usual tactics are used: green manures, mulches and biological control. The trees are also very carefully pruned and are often planted in shade, a more natural environment for many of the tropics' fruit trees. Taller trees attract birds that can add to the soil fertility by the regular addition of their droppings, and they can also draw up nutrients from the deeper ground via their roots. Spacing the trees at wider intervals, and the higher labour costs, all add to the actual cost of production, so this niche market is probably the only way to make organic chocolate viable at this early stage in its life.

Just as with sugar and coffee, which are discussed below and on page 58, there is quite a lot that has to be done to the beans when they are harvested. Making sure that the pods are neither under- nor over-ripe is a skill that needs to be practised systematically if the quality is to be maintained.

Perhaps most important is the process of fermentation. On smaller farms, this will be carefully monitored on site, possibly using a fermenting box, or more simply wrapping the pulp in banana leaves. The same attention to detail is devoted to the process of drying, but these are really quality issues and are not necessarily unique to organic chocolate.

Perhaps what has characterised Green and Black's company profile most is the very public almost messianic zeal that we come across so often in organics. Here is a company that holds the opinion that doing good (in its real rather than derogatory sense) is an important part of being in business. This is no longer considered to be either quirky or weird. Although just about every business trading is keen to be seen to be good honest capitalists, much of this is a spurious marketing exercise. Here is one company that has very much, and very publicly, put its money where its mouth is.

We consumers have very little idea about the working conditions on the conventional farms that grow cocoa worldwide – they are simply too distant and disparate. Reports appear occasionally about the gruesome, medieval conditions that occur – some have mentioned the Ivory Coast in this light – and this seems an area where we need to reflect, and buy thoughtfully. Organic or Fairtrade chocolate uses cocoa from farms where the conditions are known, and can be verified. Organic chocolate will contain no conscience-pricking surprises.

Sugar To date, most of the organic sugar you see is from sugar cane rather than sugar beet, so it is grown in the steamy tropics rather than the cold north. The amount of duty-free cane sugar being allowed into the EU is restricted by a quota, and there isn't as yet much organic product coming from the producers who are restricted under this quota. What is being produced comes mainly from smaller growers in Paraguay and Brazil, and since it is non-quota, it is subject to a fairly swingeing duty, which is one of the reasons why organic sugar is more expensive.

Cane sugar needs to be protected from weeds in its early delicate years and at this point a conventional farm will use a chemical herbicide. Since organic growers don't approve of this sort of thing, they use manpower, and although their bill with the agrochemical supplier will be lighter, their wage bill will be substantially heavier. Countries where labour is cheap and chemicals are not may therefore be increasingly tempted by organic production, but in fact cane sugar isn't one of the world's most chemically dependent crops (the cane's greatest enemy is actually drought).

However, the growing of sugar is only half the story and when it comes to refining, some commentators think that organics haven't quite got it right. The big European sugar beet industry is a powerful lobby with strong representation at EU level, and they are obviously well aware that organic beet sugar would be a key product for them. At present there is practically none being produced. Under current EU legislation, it is technically possible to produce organic sugar from organically grown sugar beet which is refined using substances like sodium hydroxide and sodium carbonate, and even sulphuric acid without losing organic status. Sugar beet always has to be completely refined as opposed to cane sugar, which does not.

By the way, sugar cane is by far and away the world's most cultivated crop, way ahead of wheat in second place, followed by rice, maize and the potato. So the impact of increasing organic production could be quite substantial.

Honey It was difficult to know where to slot honey in, for although it is very obviously bees that make honey, they, equally obviously, make it from flowers. But the rigorous Soil Association standard that is used for virtually all the organic honey for sale in the UK states that there must be no pollution or chemical use within the bees' working radius of four miles from the hive. Fine, but if you think about it, where are such places here in the industrial West? Answer, basically nowhere, and so all our organic honey is imported.

As the search for organic produce has expanded into every culinary nook and cranny over the past few years, pressure from one of the multiples led one of the country's prime honey suppliers to look for a reliable source of organic honey anywhere in the world that could work to Soil Association standards. Their search concluded that Mexico and Argentina were the most likely sources, and on taste the Argentinian honey won in both clear and set form. And now almost all the own-brand and branded organic honey comes from hives set in one of four Argentinian provinces: Cordoba, Santa Fé, Entre Rios and San Luis. Given our predilection for variety, however, you may also be able to source other types of organic honey from specialist shops. The exquisite Australian eucalyptus honey, Turkish pine, New Zealand clover and Mexican campanita are all being produced to Soil Association standard, and are worth trying.

One of the main problems with all honey producers is the Varroa mite, which is causing havoc with one of the two main honey-bee species, *Apis mellifera*, which has no means to combat this destructive little pest. And the solution has to be a chemical one. Under organic production, lactic acid and formic acid fumigation are both permitted, but anything else will result in the honey losing its organic status for a year. (Bee species number two, *Apis serena*, deals with it by vigorous preening, by the way.)

Bee welfare is also to the fore here. The hive is a complex social unit, which needs very little interference from man, and both organic and biodynamic standards keep this as a fundamental. In fact the BD view of honey is that it has unique healing properties because of the bees' natural tendency to mingle with the flowers and the air rather than the mucky old earth.

Bearing in mind that it is the surrounding flowers and nectar that feed the bees that make honey, organic status provides an assurance that there are absolutely no chemical residues or GMOs present. But a word in defence of 'conventional' honey: there is not really any such thing as intensively reared honey – blended, yes, but intensive, no. Much of it is a sound, first-class and thoroughly natural product.

As a postscript, I have tasted some wild forest honey from Zambia which was a Fairtrade product – very laudable but very nasty!

The Plants We Drink

Whiling the time away at the kids' school auction recently, I foolishly let my daughter go and buy a drink – she was six – and experience the joys of free choice. She came back with something so utterly nasty that I take my hat off to its creator. This Frankensteinian brew was blue, yet it was supposed to be raspberry flavour. It tasted as much like a raspberry as a pint of rancid milk. Many of these lurid drinks are emphatically not organic, positively brimming over with additives and sugars and, in the case of low-calorie drinks, some highly questionable artificial sweeteners. To avoid additives and preservatives, blue raspberries and other delights, once again common sense is called for. I need hardly remind you that neither additives nor preservatives are essential requirements for a healthy diet.

Fruit Juices and Cordials
Common sense might also suggest that the less mucked about a fruit juice is then the better it will be. With a wide range of organic juices of this and that available, it's easy just to be organic and worthy about juice, but bear in mind that some of the real

nutritional benefits come from really fresh juice, those ORACs (see page 46) and that vitality we looked at earlier. You could always make your own juice from organic fruit. An electrical juicer is a great idea, but in reality it does have its drawbacks. On the plus side, it can give you juice that tastes fresh and healthy, and it gives you the freedom to mix and match as you see fit. But the machine we've got takes tiny little bits of fruit, and you can spend ages just chopping. And about as long cleaning it afterwards. Mind you, a hand-held, old-fashioned juicer works far better with a pile of organic oranges. That's easy.

One thing everybody likes is elderflower cordial – we're a little spoilt at home as the gardens and local woods are full of elders – but a seasonal blast of cordial, iced, or just mixed with water, is not far from perfection. Organic cordials are now widely available to save you plucking elderflowers from the wild. Of course, organic drinks will all come from fruit that has been grown organically, but it's not quite so simple with wine.

Wine

Pedants may tell you that organic wine doesn't exist, but this legalistic nicety shouldn't worry you. Organic wine, or more correctly in Euro-ese, wine made from organically grown grapes, is doing very well, with sales leaping exponentially. In the early days, much of the stuff was barely drinkable, produced by committed but inexperienced wine neophytes. It has taken a while, but the quality and range has improved dramatically.

Not every wine-producing area finds organic production easy. Hot and dry areas – the South of France, Spain and parts of Italy – are well suited for organic production, where the nasty moulds and diseases of the colder, damper, northern wine-growing areas are not usually so problematic. The fundamentals are still just as fundamental. Feeding the soil, strict limits on additives, and for some obscure reason a ban on some physical treatments such as centrifugation, polyculture and homeopathic treatment – these are all the essence of organic viticulture, the cultivation of grapes. The highly skilful process of wine-making, or viniculture, doesn't get very far without good-quality grapes, and there is a recognition by many that organic and, perhaps more

interestingly, biodynamically grown grapes can in the right hands make some outstanding wine.

In the same way that people are often drawn to organic food in the belief that it's free of pesticides, there has been a lot of hot air flowing in from the land of the free about 'sulfites', or sulphites as we call them over here. About 0.25 per cent of the population has an allergy to sulphites and US Federal Law now states that wines should be clearly labelled to show that they are likely to have some sulphites within. For once both the US and Australia are being stricter than the EU, which doesn't require sulphite levels to be labelled at all. This of course raises the important issue that we never quite know what is inside the bottle. Sulphites are part of the armoury of wine-making, used as a preservative, and to prevent oxygenation, particularly of newly picked grapes. Since sulphites can also be naturally present during fermentation, the idea of a sulphite-free wine may seem a little contradictory, but they do exist, although they call for care and skill in their production and storage, since sulphite-free wine can be unstable. US Federal law allows any wine with less than 10 parts per million (ppm) to be called sulphite free. *The Standards* doesn't ban their use altogether but sets the limits much lower than the EU and US permitted minimum levels for conventional wine production. The Soil Association will permit 90mg per litre in red wine and 100mg per litre in white. EU levels are set at 160 and 210 respectively. But when all's said and done, sulphite levels are not really what organic wine is all about. What is worth knowing is that sulphites can give you a headache, so if you ever have a problem with this, try organic wine for a change and see if it helps you carry on drinking!

Routine chemical use has taken its toll in viticulture, and the soil, even in some of the classic wine-producing areas of France, has often become virtually sterile, bug free, as dead as the proverbial Norwegian blue parrot. Consumers are rightly concerned about drinking wine produced in this way which, combined with some deep thinking and analysis by a surprisingly diverse range of wine producers, has led to radical and very successful efforts to produce some excellent organic wine.

You may have heard of the French word *terroir*, a term that has become rather emotive in the wine

trade, and one which is rather difficult to translate. *Terroir* is defined in Jancis Robinson's excellent tome, *The Oxford Guide to Wine*, as 'the total natural environment of any viticultural site'. It encompasses the soil, the location, the grape and even the way the vines are pruned, all factors that help give a wine its unique character. Whether you look on this link between land and wine as something indefinable or scientifically verifiable will obviously depend upon what sort of mind lurks inside your head, but understanding *terroir* is at the heart of both good viticulture and in turn viniculture. Getting away from the corporate uniformity of industrial wines is probably the only way that many of the smaller producers can survive, and the attachment to the soil, the vine and the grape is all part of the complex business of creating quality. If the soil is dead, it doesn't hold much hope for the end product.

Organic cultivation encourages vines to root deeply, which not only gives them strength, and in turn a better ability to resist disease, but also adds to the character and individuality that many wine producers are trying to achieve. Ploughing between the rows, companion planting, and cover crops all encourage the plant to push its roots ever deeper, as the vine competes for water. Famously, John Williams of Frog's Leap in California once bought some land planted with vines he well knew were infected with phylloxera, and then decided to turn them over to organic cultivation. Out came the irrigation system, away went the chemicals. On went the green manure, and the vines survived, pushing their roots over fifty feet down. His neighbour stayed with the conventional ways and was forced to grub up the vineyard when disease became too much. And his roots were only a measly foot or so down, weakened by years of irrigation that encouraged shallow surface rooting. The top layer of soil is the very place where the phylloxera louse thrives so the deeper rooting vines outsmarted their natural enemy and all without using a drop of chemical.

The cerebral organic approach will always lead to a lot of experimentation. Plants that encourage predatory insects may well be planted around or even in and among the vines. On the down side, some broad-leaved weeds actually encourage populations of insects that can spread grape-vine yellow, a serious

disease that is difficult to control. Other plants – mustard and oats – discourage nematodes. One of the big differences here is that if you over-fertilise the soil for vines, you may not be creating the best conditions for top-quality wine. Great wines are not made in lush bucolic vineyards. If you are a gardener you may know that wisteria is rather perverted and enjoys being thoroughly abused (well, it encourages flowering anyway). The vine also appreciates a bit of abuse, perhaps not so much as wisteria, but needs to be in a condition called 'water stress' for it to make the best wine. Organic conditions, particularly when the vine is encouraged to root deeply, is just what is needed for a good bit of water stress, which probably helps to explain why organic methods seem to work quite well for non-irrigated dry Mediterranean vineyards.

Something else that can give wine character is wild yeast. Yeast is essential for the fermentation of the grapes and juice, and many organic producers like to use the local wild yeast population that builds up over years of wine production. It's found on the grapes, in the buildings and even in the air around the vineyard, and although it is not an essential part of organic wine production, the principle of minimising external inputs holds true in organic viticulture as well. It also gives Old World producers a distinct advantage over their New World colleagues, whose wild yeasts haven't had enough time to become usable, and cultured yeasts are bought in. Maybe New World wine-making is just too clean and wholesome.

Biodynamic Wine One of the most exciting areas of wine production is biodynamics. Despite Herr Steiner's strong disapproval of drinking alcohol, a surprising number of high-quality wines are made using this complex and strictly controlled method of production. Famously, Domaine Huet in Vouvray, Nicolas Joly at Savennières, and Ostertag in Alsace are all working successfully along these lines, but note that none of their wine is cheap. The highly respected Domaine Leflaive has gone 100 per cent biodynamic, producing a stunning range of fabulous Burgundies, but again, not cheap. As you would expect, BD preparations and working according to lunar and zodiac cycles govern much that goes on in biodynamic vineyards. I find the idea of biodynamics intriguing (see

pages 15-16) and if you want to be convinced that it can work try some BD wine.

Coffee and Tea
Although the supply of organic coffee is still small, it is growing. As with many other food and drink plants, coffee bushes prefer to be grown in the shade and when they are, they tend to be healthier than the bushes in direct sun. Most large-scale, non-organic plantations tend to cultivate bushes in full sun. Coffee originally came from Ethiopia where much of the crop is still grown along traditional organic lines. It won't always be labelled as such, as the growers can't easily afford the cost of certification. There are no huge estates in Ethiopia, small-scale farmers contributing the biggest part of the country's coffee output, so if you can't buy organic you could always buy Ethiopian. Just over the border in Kenya the situation is very different with coffee being grown mostly in the full sun along what are called high input/high output lines. Here yields are higher, but so is chemical use.

There's quite a lot of organic coffee being grown in Central America – in Costa Rica and Nicaragua, for example. Here going organic is easier because of a generally less problematic level of pests. In South America, Columbian coffee is often grown below the illegal coca crops; these have at times taken so much water from the mountainside that the coffee crop suffers as a result.

Generally, the quality of organic coffee is considered to be quite good. With tea the situation is somewhat different. Although there is some good-quality organic tea around – try Pussimbing or Chamong Darjeeling if you can get it – most of the crop is still grown along conventional lines. One of the reasons, so I've heard, is that the pickers actually prefer it that way because there are less bugs, rodents and snakes in tea treated with chemicals than with organic tea, which seems quite understandable to me. And as usual, the yields are substantially lower and so the price is higher.

Cider
Despite its rather rustic image, cider hasn't escaped the brush of conventional and chemical agriculture. The amount of pesticides sprayed on to an apple crop has achieved almost iconic status. Apples grown

organically make very good cider, but much of the art here is post harvest, with the drink's overall character closely governed by the variety of apples used. Not all the organic cider you will find on sale is actually made from British apples, and some is made from imported organic apple concentrate. This may not bother you at all, but it strikes me as a little off track, as English cider (British doesn't sound quite right) to me smacks of apples from England. For some, the commercial reality means that imports are the only way to get enough cider to make it a commercial proposition.

There tends to be a difference in the cider made on the east coast – typically made from sweet and dessert apples – and the West Country cider that uses a lot of bittersweet varieties, giving their cider its distinct character. Although much of the cider we buy in the UK is blended, there are moves to use some of the smaller more obscure varieties, with their marvellous names – Bloody Turk and Brown Snout to name but two – as varietal ciders. Many of these are grown without the use of pesticides, if not necessarily under organic status. Remember too that as with all these drinks that are essentially processed, there are clear regulations on the types of cleaning agents used which must comply with organic regulations.

Beer

Organic beer, as you would expect, is far from being laggardly in the face of the organic revolution, and is now quite widely available. But there are problems, particularly in the UK, primarily concerning the availability of sufficient organic hops. Hops are notoriously susceptible to disease, particularly mildews and other fungal infections, and there are very few growers in the UK who can get over this rather fundamental problem. In New Zealand the varieties grown seem to be easier to manage under organic standards, so quite a lot of the organic beer brewed in the UK is made from imported hops. (On a purely qualitative note, New Zealand hops are bitter, with high alpha acid levels and are not well suited to our more traditional ales.) However, the producers I spoke to were all of the opinion that organic hops are fundamentally an excellent raw material with an intensity of aroma that does not come easily.

As so often, there are real differences between the brews that can be found. Freedom make an excellent organic lager, and Brakspears a marvellous ale. Look out in particular for the latter's Live Organic ale, which is bottle conditioned, a process that gives beer real life through the addition of small amounts of yeast in the bottle. It will pay to look for that good old UK 5 (the Soil Association) label, for they do not allow any sulphur dioxide and do not, unlike Organic Farmers and Growers, allow any non-organic hops to be used in their beer-making process. I must say that I find it a little ridiculous that OF&G permit organic beer to be made from non-organic hops, on the fundamentally flawed logic that less than 5 per cent of the ingredients of beer are hops. That seems to miss the point. *Caveat* organic *emptor*.

The future for organic beer may not, however, be very bright. There is talk afoot of a European ban on the use of copper sulphate, the organic hop-farmer's only really effective means of fungal control. (The ban is being imposed because of fears over the level of heavy metals in the soil.) Watch out for developments.

Spirits

Writing can be a solitary and pretty thankless task at times, but there are those delightful moments of deep euphoria. And I am in euphoric mode right now as I have just discovered that round the corner from where I am writing, in Clapham, south-west London, is the world's only organic gin distillery. Being truly disciplined, I have resisted an immediate visit with empty glass in hand. The British of course famously love their gin, and the skills and fine art of distilling still has its practitioners here in deepest London. But organic gin in Clapham frankly surprises me.

Actually, the base spirit is made from organic rye and is imported, so sadly we cannot as yet see combine harvesters reaping organic grain on Clapham Common. But what has surprised all involved in the making of this gin is the excellent quality of the end product. And much of this seems to be due to the characteristics of the organic grain itself. Distillers look for a grain with a high carbohydrate level, which in turn gives a higher alcohol yield. With the intensification of agriculture over the past fifty years, these levels have indeed gone up substantially, but what has also happened is that the yeast used in the fermentation has had to become increasingly powerful to be able to act on the carbohydrate, making a harsher, less palatable spirit. The organic base is less demanding of its yeast, and it is possible to use less harsh yeasts, which give the gin its good character.

As well as gin, there are also small amounts of organic vodka around, again distilled over here in the deepest UK. And quality wise, for the same reasons, this is a winner – in fact both have been awarded medals in the coveted International Wine and Spirit Competition, a gold for the gin and a silver for the vodka. Very impressive for a new product. You should also be able to find organic Calvados, grappa and eau de vie. And expect organic white and gold rum soon. Now we can all eat and drink organic . . .

The Plants We Wear: Fabrics and Organics

It's bleak chemical-fact time! Did you know that about 300 grams of chemicals are used for every kilogram of cotton produced, some of them of acute toxicity? Or that about 25 per cent of all the pesticides used in the US are in cotton production? Further afield, recent outbreaks of serious cotton pests in Andhra Pradesh, India, have caused a sharp upswing in the level of chemicals being used, and of course willingly supplied. As a result the local pest population has been developing increasing resistance to those same chemicals. Cotton farmers are in despair and high rates of suicide have been reported. Cotton is a difficult, disease-prone crop, and one which is grown in many parts of the world where limits on chemicals, and the information provided about them, leave something to be desired. Cotton production is definitely part of the agricultural problem, and also has an organic solution.

It is easy to forget that organics is about much more than food production – but the basic principles can apply where any crop is grown. Although efforts are now being made to try and address the chemically voracious cotton-production system we have created, the percentage of sustainably produced cotton is low – but as you would expect by now, growing. Nike, like many of the big US multinationals, have tried to take on a green tinge and have set a 3 per cent level of organic cotton in some of their lines as a production target. This may sound pretty paltry, but they alone could actually swallow up the world's entire cotton crop fairly easily. With many producers aware that there is a possible niche market here, several of them are putting increasing areas of cotton over to organics.

And it's not all in the industrialised world. New Mexico, Egypt, Turkey and Uganda have some organic cotton production, but the majority of the vast cotton areas of the US, Uzbekistan and Kazakhstan still follow the conventional route.

Organic cotton is planted at a lower density first of all, and with no chemical control allowed. Choosing a suitable site is crucial, one where disease is relatively unproblematic, and where soil fertility can be easily improved. There is so much land put over to cotton cultivation which has become virtually sterile, that building up natural soil fertility can be a very long-term prospect. The US organic standard will allow bought-in chicken manure to be used, but a preferable solution would be to ensure that the farm itself provides the majority of the material that will help the soil produce vigorous disease-resistant plants. With no herbicides allowed, labour costs will obviously be higher, so areas with lower labour costs may actually be better placed to make organic cotton competitive.

Surrounding the fields by cover crops that allow natural insect predators to thrive helps create a balance to the pest problem, but it's really biological control that will provide the key to successful organic production. Much research is needed in this department, although there are already effective biological means of controlling spider mites, lygus – a bug that causes the boll to drop – and aphids.

One of the reasons why cotton is such a heavy chemical user is the need to defoliate the plants before picking the cotton. How this is best done along organic lines is still being fine-tuned. There is probably a place here for what is called IPM (Integrated Pest Management), where judicious use of biological control and an awareness of the importance of avoiding excessive use of kill-all insecticides can lead to substantial reductions in pesticide use. IPM is in a sense a halfway house to organic production.

So far as quality is concerned, most organic cotton is good, with a lot of the crop being mixed into conventionally grown cotton. There can be a degree of discoloration of organic cotton where the leaf matter has stained the lint, but it is early days, and the quality will assuredly improve over the coming years. Although natural dyes are permitted under some organic Standards – although not by the more monastic organic bodies – I suspect that we won't all accept that we should be walking around in monotones of beige and off-white, the predominant colours so far for organic cotton. Largely as a result of the diligence of one particular American researching for a PhD in Peru, a few varieties of coloured cotton were rescued from genetic obscurity and are now being cultivated on a commercial scale in the States. The colour range is not extensive, but there is potential here, and there is the possibility of a red, brown and green which can be grown organically.

Once again, we really need to remember that what is now called 'conventional' is in fact an innovation that has evolved over the past fifty years or so. Organic cotton will in part be returning to the days when the soil was as a matter of course kept fertile, and crop densities and yields were lower. We will most assuredly not see a return to the days of bonded slave labour, which in no way complies with the social side of the organic equation.

Getting from boll to the cotton we use involves a series of processes, which are also chemically greedy and dependent. Dyes, bleaches and a wide range of additives are used, and this is another important area that organic cotton addresses. No bleaches are allowed, although some Standards permit hydrogen peroxide.

With many of the big boys getting involved, expect to see more eco-friendly, or sustainably harvested, products appear over the coming years. We may soon be padding around on organic carpets, in hemp fibre clothes. My fabric informant tells me that hemp grows so readily that most of the growers never need to add any chemicals, and with its immense versatility hemp is an interesting crop. It is not, by the way, the same plant that many of you may remember smoking . . .

Organic linen, even a tiny amount of organic silk – produced rather surprisingly in the Hebrides – and organic wool, free from any organophosphates, are all beginning to appear on the market.

One of the more enlightened companies to tackle the problems is Patagonia. They are clearly committed to using sustainably produced material, and their sportswear range is quite extensive so you can even climb a mountain or two clothed in the colour green. There's progress for you.

Fish and Shellfish

Lean, mineral rich, easily digestible, almost embarrassingly easy to cook, does even an organic banana have a more perfect profile than fish? Perhaps not, but organically speaking, we have a slight problem here, for the EU in all its glory has decreed that nothing that is either captured or harvested from the wild can be called organic. The logic is clear. Organic food is about production, and wild food isn't really 'produced'. It is simply there, or at least should be if looked after properly. So fish could be a difficult area for the organic purist. So far, only organic salmon and trout are readily available, but watch out for organic cod, halibut and sea bass. Personally, I think it would be crazy to cut yourself off from all wild fish so, assuming you to be a thoughtful and interested consumer, look out for eco-labelled wild fish, or read on for guidance.

Farmed Fish

Fish farming isn't, as one might be led to believe, something dreamt up by clever Europeans. It has existed in various guises for thousands of years, chief of which is carp farming in the Far East, where fish are often cultivated alongside, even among, crops such as rice, a very holistic form of agriculture. This is an excellent role model for us to follow in the West, but of course we haven't. Instead, we have largely chosen the high-tech route, farming with an intensity and dependence on chemicals quite unfamiliar to these ancient mixed systems of fish farming. Sadly we eat very little carp.

Salmon and Sea Trout

Conventional fish farms have become increasingly intensive over the past few years. It is worth remembering that this type of aquaculture is still incredibly young. Scientifically speaking, farmed salmon are only about six generations old. Compare this against the lengthy and continued process of breeding cattle, sheep and pigs, and it's a mere nothing. Much of the salmon breeding stock comes from Norway, and fish farmers are endlessly selecting the right kind of fish that don't 'grilse' too soon, i.e. reach sexual maturity, for it has long been known that some wild salmon swim back to the rivers of their birth to spawn when they are only a year old. Sexual maturity in farmed salmon is not good news, for it gives thin and low-fat fish which are not what the market wants at all.

It was in the 1970s that *Salmo salar*, the Atlantic salmon, began its long leap from nobility to ubiquity when the Anglo-Dutch multinational Unilever began to rear young salmon to a marketable size with some success in Scotland. Soon the Norwegians followed suit, as did the Americans, Icelanders, Irish, Faroese, and latterly Chileans and even Tasmanians, who all began to farm salmon in distant places where previously business had often meant an occasional tourist, a touch of fishing and little else. And, almost as suddenly, the world was blessed with increasing quantities of a rather flabby fish called salmon, and many of us seem to have quickly forgotten that *Salmo salar* was once an exquisite but occasional delicacy. Because wild salmon have suffered so long from overfishing and habitat destruction, they will probably remain just that for the foreseeable future. Although there are some fisheries that are trying to adopt a righteous environmental profile, most are far from being sustainably managed, the crucial point when it comes to wild fisheries.

The boom in salmon farming has not been without its problems. The Norwegians in particular have been accused of producing so much that they have been dumping the fish worldwide, flooding the markets with vast amounts of surplus fish at less than cost price. While the Scots bemoan unfair competition, environmentalists have begun in their endearingly heroic way to draw our attention to the pitfalls and malpractice of salmon farming. The consumer is left with a product of dubious worth, and a practice of dubious value. Salmon really has become the chicken of the sea.

Huge amounts of waste, rampant sea-lice infections,

interbreeding with wild fish and excessive chemical control have given us much to think about when it comes to assessing conventional salmon farming. But it is still a relatively new business and has to some degree learned to mend its ways: sick and diseased fish are in no-one's business plan. As you would expect, organic salmon should answer many of the concerns. Working to characteristically strict guidelines, most, though not all, of the really serious issues have been addressed – chemicals aren't allowed, welfare issues are to the fore, and feed is from natural by-products, fishmeal and prawn shells. The supply, though, is still limited, and remains in the hands of a few dedicated producers. Much of the organic fish in the UK comes from the Orkneys which, despite or perhaps because of its remoteness, has a remarkable reputation for the quality of its food and the purity of its ingredients.

The salmon pioneers didn't initially put too much thought into where their salmon pens should be located. Sheltered fjords and lochs seemed ideal but with little tidal flow, waste inevitably built up and, with it, problems. Years of salmon droppings deposited on the sea floor have accumulated, altering the balance of life on the seabed beneath, particularly in some of the deeper sites where water may take as much as seven years to circulate fully. The art of choosing a site has moved on since the early days, and wise fish farmers accept that there must be a regular tidal flow to flush away the muck. Not only do fish excrete, but they don't exactly eat at table and finish every last pellet of feed. So added to this submarine lavatory is the food which falls to the river or seabed, and acts as an inappropriate and unnatural nutrient, altering the balance of life around the pens. And this encourages what are called algal blooms, where huge numbers of algae, fed by the nutrients and waste, create a suffocating miasma on the surface of the water. It can cover huge areas, starving both wild and farmed fish of oxygen, causing stress and death in some cases. Many of the more intensive mega salmon farms use computerised fish feeders that chuck out feed relatively indiscriminately, food that again enters into the eco-system nearby. This is an industrial solution to what should be a carefully controlled, skilful process.

The more intensive the salmon farm, then the

greater the density of fish in the pen, and disease thrives off this thick mass of fishy life. Salmon can suffer from complaints of positively medieval nastiness. Take *Lepeophtheirus salmonis*, the sea louse, an unpleasant little copepod which, if left unchecked, chomps its way through the protective mucus that surrounds the fish, even into the flesh itself, causing what is politely called death through osmotic imbalance or, more graphically, death through being eaten alive. In those glory days when salmon were only found in the wild, the odd sea louse or two was quite usual, but salmon farms have given them a new lease of life. Controlling them can be difficult, while the organic solution is simple. The fish are stocked at low levels, and constantly monitored. If there is an outbreak, then it is technically permitted to bathe the fish in hydrogen peroxide, which effectively washes the sea lice from the salmon's body. Low levels of sea lice are not really a problem, and in three years the Orkney Salmon Company, the pioneers of farmed organic salmon, have never had to resort to the stress, for both fish and humans, of a hydrogen peroxide bath. It sounds too Crippenesque to me anyway.

By contrast, the chemical solution on offer is a menu of extremely toxic substances. Even though Scottish regulations no longer permit unauthorised use, organo-phosphates such as Dichlorvos, Ivermectin and now Imermectin are still used as pesticides against sea lice, and any of these remain in the food-chain for long periods. This is of great concern.

One of the unfortunate results of an excessive sea louse population has been that they have moved on to attack wild fish, particularly younger, more vulnerable smolt. The problem is that it is a massive attack, beyond the levels of normal activity. Populations of wild sea trout, in particular, are suffering from the scourge of the sea louse. This is a sad state of affairs. Not only is the sea trout a beautiful fish, it is wonderful to eat.

And then there is furunculosis. This disease gives the poor salmon debilitating furuncles, a word I find particularly appealing (and means 'boils' or 'inflammatory tumours'). This poses a serious problem, and is controlled by antibiotics or vaccination. If there is an outbreak on an organic farm, the salmon are allowed to be treated for welfare reasons only, but again the location of the site is crucial for it seems that the wild population infects the farmed fish, not vice versa, and in the Orkneys, for example, there aren't many wild salmon to worry about.

The next in this catalogue of unpleasantness is the disease now known as ISA, infectious salmon anaemia. This viral infection causes salmon to haemorrhage and die. It is a serious, notifiable disease so any farm suffering from ISA will have to destroy all its stock, and abandon the site altogether. Despite all this it has spread from the west coast of Scotland right up to the Shetlands. Salmon farmers are rightly worried. No-one will buy the affected stock, so there aren't many options but to close the site down completely. Sites have to be left to regenerate, a practice called 'fallowing', and millions of fish have to be destroyed. As well as all this, the wild population seems to be at some risk, although may not actually get full-blown ISA. And why, you may ask, is all this happening? There is definitely a link with salmon farming, and it may well be that algae are transmitting the virus from one site to another.

One thing you may notice with organic salmon certified by the Soil Association is its colour, which is distinctly paler than conventionally farmed fish. I have to admit I find it off-putting. I know I shouldn't, but however much I reason with myself, it just doesn't seem quite right. Remember wild fish are naturally red from the keratin found in the crustaceans that the salmon like to eat. If farmed salmon were left untreated, its meat would range from an unappetising grey to a sickly pink, and since grey salmon isn't a hot seller, something has to be added to make it resemble what we expect salmon to be. Conventional salmon farms use colouring agents, another area of controversy. The two most widely used are Canthaxanthin and Astaxanthin, both highly effective, but forbidden under organic standards, and there have been some reports that Canthaxanthin is carcinogenic. Synthetic Astaxanthin has a natural equivalent, which is preferred by producers farming to the less rigorous chemical-free standard.

Orkney organic salmon are reared on feed made from prawn shells, the by-product of the tonnes of shelled prawns we eat. To me that is a crucial plus, and it's the meal from these shells that give organic fish their colour. But using industrial fish meal is a major concern. Millions of tonnes of fish are caught, mostly in the North Atlantic or off the fish-rich Peruvian coast, and processed into meal, to feed chickens and farmed fish the world over. If salmon farming is to be sustainable it's important that the fish that go to make this meal are also from a sustainable fishery, but as yet no such industrial fishery exists.

Confusingly, you may see some organic salmon with a brilliantly vivid colour which somewhat contradicts all of the above. As elsewhere, there are different standards that can be applied with fish and some of these allow the use of phaffia yeast, an effective colouring agent employed, for example, in the farmed salmon from Clare Island in Ireland. The Soil Association doesn't like the use of phaffia for two reasons: firstly, it is only added for cosmetic reasons, and secondly, it might have been grown on soya-based agar which could be derived from GMO soya. And while we're on the subject of GMOs, much of the feed supplied to conventional fish farms may well include US soya which until recently would almost certainly have been genetically modified. Complicated enough for you?

One of the trickiest problems to quantify is that of escapees. Every time a gale blows, a net is cut or a pen is damaged, there is a risk that the fish inside will escape into the wild. And inevitably, they do what salmon instinctively do: eat, migrate and reproduce. It may at first seem no bad thing: wild stocks are diminishing, and could do with a population boost. But what if this meant that the genetic variety of the wild fish was slowly being watered down? What if the very traits that a salmon farmer looks for are precisely what the wild stock does not need? And this indeed seems to be the case. Farmed fish have been selected to be unaggressive, slow to reach sexual maturity and uniform, but wild salmon show a genetic variety within quite small areas. The issues are complex. Adopting the good old fallback of the precautionary approach, I think that caution is needed until the full implications are clearer.

Freshwater Trout and Carp

Globally, two herbivorous fish, the carp and the tilapia, win the stakes for being farmed in the greatest quantity. You can stun your friends by telling them that carp actually provide more protein worldwide than cattle, and that this giant minnow is actually quite an ecologically sound fish. Being largely herbivorous, you don't need to catch a huge amount of fish to feed them. Figures for 1995 show that for an annual production of 10.3 million tonnes of carp, there was an input of 4.3 million tonnes of protein. Look at shrimp, on the other hand, and the figures are 1.4 million tonnes of protein to produce only .932 million tonnes.

The story of the carp's global expansion is an interesting one. Notoriously hardy fish, they can live out of water for hours, days even at the right temperature. Originally from China, carp slowly went westwards, taken along the Silk Road by traders in the Middle Ages, passed from pond to pond on into the Caucasus, and from there into middle Europe, where they remain popular.

Chinese traditions of fish farming are suitably ancient and of low intensity. The clever combination where carp are farmed under chicken, or even silk-worm, sheds, eating the natural waste, and thriving off the nutrient-rich water, is still widespread. Different carp species even play different roles: black carp eat snails, bighead and silver carp thrive on algae, mud carp eat detritus, common carp scavenge, and grass carp eat vegetation – and a fish pond might have all six species living together. The challenge comes when trying to make this work on a bigger scale. This is an important principle that should really become part of the organic principles behind fish farming. Just as on land, integration and mixed use is the name of the game, so it should be with fish farming.

Slowly, we are beginning to see alternate shrimp and rice production in Vietnam, and in the States there is an interesting attempt to grow lettuce and even basil alongside tilapia, where the plants convert and use the waste from the fish farm.

Although this principle may be ancient, it has now been blessed with its own little sobriquet, IFS, or integrated farming systems, which may of course mean it will be taken more seriously. Echoes of the redundancy of monoculture on land, perhaps?

The only other freshwater species we can actually buy that is farmed organically is the freshwater trout. I cannot honestly say that I am its greatest fan, but trout are popular and cheap, and that can't be all bad. Smoked it's another matter, and I can happily chomp through a fillet or two, and strongly recommend Sophie's smoked trout fish pie (see page 167) for a cold winter's day.

Wild Fish

Fish is the only wild food that we see consistently in our shops and markets, and is by far and away our most valuable wild food resource. You are probably well aware that fish stocks are severely over-exploited worldwide, and as well as this, habitat destruction and pollution are threatening some of the finest species ever known.

A recent ban on swordfish in the US – 'Give swordfish a break' – drew attention to the abysmal state of the Atlantic swordfish where juveniles are being caught at a completely unsustainable level, but a similar campaign hasn't taken off in Europe, as yet. Actually most of the swordfish we eat in Europe, with the notable exception of Spain, who still have a significant Atlantic fishery, is fished in the Indian Ocean or the Pacific (where there are similar serious problems which have yet to be highlighted so publicly). Tuna is also in the spotlight. This immensely popular, valuable species is hunted and pursued using just about every means available – spotter planes, radar, even submarines, I have heard. It may well be necessary to put the bluefin tuna on a CITES (Convention for International Trade in Endangered Species) list which will curb all commercial fishing. And if we want to see wild salmon survive in Europe, we will have to address some very serious issues. We need not only to control over-fishing, but to put in place measures that will preserve their spawning habitat, the rivers to which they migrate with such magic regularity, and, crucially with this species, those areas of the northern seas where the fish congregate to feed.

There are some initiatives spluttering a little fitfully into life, eco-labelling schemes that provide some comfort and a verifiable means to buy with confidence. The MSC (Marine Stewardship Council) is a global initiative which is beginning to gather momentum but, as yet, only West Australian rock lobster, Alaskan salmon and Thames herring have gained certification. The idea is that any fishery that has been independently certified as sustainable can then use the MSC logo, so that a consumer can recognise – just as with organics – that the bit of fish in front of them will have come from a well managed fishery. If it is to be received with real global gravitas, the scheme needs to work with some of the world's more important white fisheries, such as those in Iceland and Norway, where conservation of marine resources is relatively successful.

Using the power of the consumer has already proved to be a powerful tool in encouraging good practice, and is after all central to organics. For instance, the campaigns that have drawn our attention to the dolphin by-catch in tuna fishing have been highly successful in changing the way these fish are caught. There are now many campaigns that focus on the protection and good management of marine biodiversity, and again there are real links with organic philosophy. (Take a look at the National Audubon website,on www.audubon.org, and the WWF's Endangered Seas Campaign for more.) TEDs (turtle-excluding devices) are now widely available, although they're not always used where they should be. The problem of sea birds, particularly the rare and marvellous albatross, being caught up with long lines is another issue which could be addressed by having eco-labelled fish. Each time the industry is forced into changing the way it works, we should doff our hats to the many campaigners involved.

What Is a Well Managed Fishery?

The essence of a well managed wild fishery is that the level of fish being caught should not substantially alter the ability of the fishstocks to survive. Obviously, the process of fishing affects the fishery to some extent, so there is much reliance upon good-quality scientific data and a need for constant monitoring of the stocks. In some years climatic conditions mean that the level of reproduction is low, so at such times the amount of fish caught should be reduced. It is a complex business, and one which we have proved singularly useless at managing so far.

Preserving the marine biodiversity is another goal,

but the essence is simply good management. The MSC has a long list of principles and criteria which it uses to decide whether a fishery is sustainable, for here just as with organics the 'S' words hold true (except of course you can substitute 'sea' for 'soil'!) The MSC is after all the Marine *Stewardship* Council.

Iceland

Iceland has become a marine role model to many – authors included – and you'd do well to seek out Icelandic fish wherever possible. This tiny country of 270,000 people lives and breathes fish. It doesn't take a genius to realise how important good management of their seas has to be. During the 1980s, catches of some of the key species, such as cod, haddock and plaice, began to fall, prompting the Icelandic government to introduce a rigorous system of quotas and control. Despite some reservations from within Iceland, it has become a real success. Icelandic fisheries are doing well on this rigorous diet of strict control and a constant review of information and data. What is more, there are no subsidies in Icelandic fisheries.

The issue of subsidies is important, even if it may seem a little dull. European governments at all levels subsidise the fishing industry, which in turn helps the fleet become even more high-tech and efficient. Old boats are taken out of commission and grants given for newer ones; fishing gear can be upgraded; and money is even given to purchase the right to fish in non-EU waters. The net effect is that there are simply too many highly efficient boats chasing too few fish.

But things are changing fast. Even during the writing of this book, two new species, sea bass and gilt-head bream, have appeared on the markets, reared to the Soil Association standard. Also in the pipeline are organic cod and halibut, so watch out for developments.

Shellfish

Shellfish are actually very well suited to being reared organically, but a fully acceptable standard has yet to be developed. We are talking oysters, mussels and scallops here, which are all reared in sea water in enclosures, or on ropes in the case of mussels, and are

not subject to enormously intensive production methods. Disease-resistant, and almost entirely reliant upon the sea for food, shellfish seem to represent a neat and trouble-free form of farming. However, it is only relatively trouble-free.

In France the oyster industry, which is massive compared to that in the UK, has had outbreaks of a nasty virus that can't really be controlled, let alone by chemicals. Much energy has been expended on trying to find out what's going on, but there may be links with the intensive pig industries of Normandy and Brittany (both prime oyster areas), that pump huge quantities of noxious substances into and on to the

environment including the once pristine Breton coastline.

Just to reassure you, all shellfish sold for human consumption in the EU have to be either from the ultra-pure Category A waters (no filtration or treatment required here), or from a plant that is specifically designed to filter and clean the water, and the shellfish, if the waters are Category B. Category C waters are not allowed to be used for shellfish farming.

Fish and Shellfish **67**

Sweet and Sour Prawns

On October 4, 1997, two Honduran fishermen – Israel Ortiz and Marin Seledonio – were shot dead on a reserve in the Gulf of Fonseca, on the west coast of Honduras. To date, no-one has been prosecuted for their deaths. No-one probably ever will be. Both of them were involved in a bitter, violent dispute between local communities and prawn farmers.

Back in the 1930s, a keen Japanese graduate, Motosaku Fujinaga, adapted ancient ways of prawn farming to the twentieth century, spawning the native kuruma prawn in captivity and bringing the larvae up to market size. In the 1950s, a research laboratory in Galveston, Texas, developed a system that could feed the larvae with phytoplankton on a large scale, which liberated the process of farming still further.

There were three species that began to be cultivated. *Penaeus monodon*, or the black tiger prawn, was and still is the mainstay of Asian prawn farms, while in Latin and Central America it was the introduced species, the western white shrimp, *P. vannamei*, that became the mainstay of their industry. China worked very successfully with its own native *P. chinensis*.

Prawn farming requires land, quite a lot of it, and warm brackish water. In Honduras, as in Ecuador, the coastal zone includes ecologically rich, but economically unproductive, mangroves. With complex and sensitive eco-systems, mangroves act as a nursery ground for fish, and host highly adapted species of crabs and birds. They also protect the coast from erosion and often support a human population that fishes and farms on a fairly low level, using the wood for fuel, and in some places for building houses. Left to their own devices, these communities establish a successful balance between man and nature. Tourism in mangrove areas is similarly low key, because frankly mangroves can be smelly and impenetrable. But where they have been developed, there has to be some destruction before the construction. As with prawn farms. In Honduras, the coast is technically owned by the State which, with money from the US Government and the World Bank, began to plan for wide-scale development. Even if their intentions were honourable, many locals were unable to raise capital, and large corporations moved in to develop the area for prawn farming. Honduran prawn farming has become a cause célèbre, for where there was a sort of harmony before, there is now major disagreement on how, what and even why prawn farming should be organised. On the plus side, there are now over 10,000 people employed in the Honduran prawn industry. One group alone has the capacity to produce over 6,000 tonnes of prawns per year.

So what is the problem? Why the violence? It is really a very familiar conflict in prawn farming, but being so distant, we tend not to be as inquisitive about our prawn as we would be about our pig. As with any cultivation, prawn farms alter the existing balance between species. They pollute the local water supply with salt water and chemicals and can cause the gradual desertification of the coastal zone, where the salt water pumped into the huge artificial ponds built on the land gradually seeps into the land and makes it barren. The coastal zone, where it has been denuded of its protecting mangroves, becomes eroded by the wind and waves. Disease is often rife and can wipe out a prawn population in one season. What is really ludicrous is that on some farms after as little as five years' trading, the site becomes too diseased to use any more, and is simply abandoned, a sterile wasteland. But, here comes the cavalry. With admirable

'we tend not to be as inquisitive about our prawn as we would be about our pig'

doggedness, the environmentalists have niggled and protested, informed and educated, so it is now becoming an issue.

And it's not just the usual green dramatis personae. In 1988, the local Honduran population, increasingly concerned with the violence and conflicts, formed their own pressure group, the impossibly named CODDEFFAGOLF (Comite para la Defensa y Dessarralo de la Flora y Fauna del Golfo de Fonseca) to represent them and their interests. They are not against prawn farming. They are simply against the way it is carried out. And the deaths? Ortiz and Seledonio were both local fishermen, caught up in this conflict. Business has power. Land that had been used by the local population became out of bounds, and fishermen, well aware that their falling catches and polluted water were due to the prawn farms, decided to fight back, seeking to reassert their own rights and their own vision for the future.

'prawn farming... takes more protein in the form of feed than you will ever get out as prawns'

Thousands of miles away, in the Indian subcontinent, things are little better. The industry there is vast, producing over 60,000 tonnes of prawns each year. It's also in deep trouble. Many of the farms are diseased, both polluting and polluted. Drinking water and local paddy fields are badly affected by salinisation. The Thai prawn industry has been badly hit by disease, and a depressed Japanese economy. The Malaysian industry has disease, habitat destruction and financial losses to deal with, and over in East Africa a huge development in the environmentally sensitive Rufiji Delta has a ring of familiar problems. In 1992, not far away from Guayaquil in Ecuador, in the Taura Estuary, a particularly virulent virus known as TSV (Taura Syndrome Virus), caused catastrophic losses in local prawn farms, before moving up through Central America and on to Texas where, in 1995, mortalities of up to 80 per cent were recorded. And another virulent virus, white spot disease, is working its way through prawn farms the world over.

To crown all this, the process of prawn farming is fundamentally wasteful. It takes more protein in the form of feed than you will ever get out as prawns, much of the protein used being fishmeal made from the ever-diminishing pool of wild marine fish. Fishing for wild prawns is equally wasteful and unsustainable because of its unselectivity. Recent legislation in the US has insisted that any wild prawns imported into the country had to be fished with turtle-excluding devices (TEDs) after campaigners revealed the sorry saga of turtle by-catch.

Actually, what most of us eat in the UK are cold-water, North Atlantic prawns – *Pandalus borealis* – which are fished far away off Greenland and Iceland. And here also there are some major problems, principally to do with sheer waste. Much of the catch is too small for eating, so has to be used for meal, but the industry is now trying to design trawls that let juveniles escape without getting squashed, thus preserving a percentage of the potential breeding stock.

So the primary question is whether we should be buying prawns at all. If you are concerned about the environment and good management, the answer has to be no. But there has to be a 'but'. Since the theme of the book is so tied up with the way food is produced, let's emphasise that there is considerable room for improvement. There is already an eco-labelling scheme on the books started by the GAA, the Global Aquaculture Alliance. It is a step in the right direction. I have even heard talk of an organic prawn farm. You can be sure that activists, scientists and experts the world over will be looking at all the claims with intensity. If any claims of good practice are made, look into them. Nag, inquire and interrogate. All power to the consumer! Over to you.

Animals

Leonardo di Caprio, the American Adonis whose gravitas sank with the *Titanic*, bravely, and in the end rather ineptly, chose the first Earth Day of the new Millennium to draw our attention to his new cause, the problem of cows' farts. A typical cow will emit a massive 48 kilograms of methane per year, so you can imagine that the global total is a truly staggering amount of gas. For cows, because they eat cellulose-rich grass which is difficult to digest, have evolved a highly effective gut system, full of microbes and bacteria that break down this cellulose into more easily digestible food, and this troublesome gas. Why should this concern us? Well, methane is a greenhouse gas, contributing to the alarming, and inexorable, rise of the earth's temperature. Cows of course are not the only guilty party, but for this and other reasons we need to closely examine whether we are eating too much meat.

Animals, especially cows, are particularly inefficient at converting food into meat. There are millions and millions of hectares devoted to feed production, mostly farmed conventionally and destined primarily for intensive farms. But if we were simply to say, right, we should all eat organic meat, then a lot more land would be needed to grow the crops to feed the animals that we eat. That land is simply not always available. As we have seen, one of the biggest question marks to hang over the organic food industry – kid yourself not, it truly is an industry now – is whether it can actually feed the world. Something has to give.

We have given less emphasis to meat than you may have expected in this book, for the simple reason that a thoughtful organic consumer may well want to eat less meat. Make it good, make it organic and if you haven't already, move on from your daily dosage of meat and two veg.

Raising Stock Organically

Organic farming needs healthy animals for it to work, so letting them eat what they would do naturally helps them function properly. Having animals around, along with the brown gold that flows from their rear ends, is important for a truly self-contained and holistic organic farm, and cows are considered to be absolutely essential on a biodynamic farm. Both organic and BD farms take careful note of what animals do to the ground. The pig's tendency to make a complete pig's ear of any patch of ground can be useful, and the broken fertilised ground can then be made part of the cycle of rotation. Rotation is also used to keep animals from grazing the same land for long periods of time, for this allows pests and diseases a chance to establish themselves, which is not what an organic farmer wants at all. So pigs often follow sheep, and crops follow pigs. Cows and sheep also crop the fields in different ways, sheep being far better at keeping the grass in control, so all of this can be used by our thinking organic farmer as tools for the proper management of the farm. The organic production system works best with this mix of livestock and crops as part of a self-contained unit. Animal manure provides essential fertility to the system, and the animals themselves should be largely fed on feed and crops grown on the farm. All very cyclical and holistic.

As you would expect there are strict dos and don'ts in *The Standards* relating to livestock production. The fundamentals are these. Firstly, just as a healthy soil gives a healthy crop, the system needs healthy animals for it to work, and everything centres around this point. Where they live, how they live, and what they eat are all part of the same business of keeping the animal healthy. Organic production rears animals on the land rather than intensively inside, and their 'natural' behaviour is allowed to express itself. Pigs rootle, chickens forage, and cows and sheep are allowed to eat grass, so they must have access to outside pasture during the grazing season. That's not to say that they all stay outside all year round. Pigs and chickens have shelter, and cows and sheep will be brought in during the winter when necessary.

Although ideally feed should be entirely organic, as things stand this isn't always possible. There are specific percentages of non-organic feed allowed: 10 per cent for beef herds, and up to 20 per cent for pigs and poultry, according to the UK's Soil Association. This will only apply until 2005 when the derogation, the specific exception, will be discontinued and all feed will have to come from certified organic sources.

Welfare

An added dimension, which is crucial to organics, is that of animal welfare. Although *The Standards* directs the farmer towards certain practices which should give you a healthy animal, if you accept, as I think you must, that animals are sentient beings, capable of feeling pain, and maybe even emotion, then we have a moral obligation not to cause them suffering. We are entering highly subjective ground here, but we can try and clarify what we mean by looking at the Farm Animal Welfare Council's Charter that lists the rights that all farm animals should have:

- **Freedom from malnutrition**
- **Freedom from thermal or physical discomfort**
- **Freedom from injury and disease**
- **Freedom to express most normal, socially acceptable patterns of behaviour**
- **Freedom from fear**

Organic systems have to take these into account, and *The Standards* states quite categorically that: 'the general conduct of animal husbandry should be governed largely by physiological and ethical considerations, having regard to behavioural patterns and the basic needs of animals.' You might also like to check out the more detailed standards that clearly limit the density and stock levels of each type of farm animal. So if this reassures you, and if you think that this is the right way to go forward, then you may well be tempted to go organic, yet remain a meat-eater.

With fewer animals per square metre, longer maturation times, no growth promoters, no high protein feed, the raison d'être of intensive livestock farming, organic meat will cost more, another reason perhaps to eat better meat less often. This issue about costs comes up again and again, but like many questions you need to look at it closely. Remember that the true cost of conventionally produced food is far greater than the price you pay in the shops – the cost, that is, of the continual harm to the environment that results from seriously misguided policies.

Antibiotics

There's another, more complex reason why we should all seriously think about eating less meat and buying organic, and it's to do with antibiotics. We all know that antibiotics have helped us in the battle against disease, and many of us, myself included, would probably be dead without them. But bacteria are canny, complex organisms that have an admirable ability to survive. By their very nature, they are continually adapting to the world around them.

And one of their adaptations is to develop a resistance to these very antibiotics. It's not difficult to see how reliant on them we've all become. If you've got children, it seems entirely natural to take them to the doctor when they develop those nasty infections. And the doctor duly prescribes an equally nasty Barbie-pink concoction that tastes of bitter almonds, just the thing a four-year-old would naturally sip. But why aren't we using those old antibiotics such as Ampycilin and Tetracycline? Well, they don't always work any more, for some of the bacteria have developed a resistance to them. We are always asked to finish the antibiotic course as prescribed, and told we shouldn't use antibiotics from an old bottle when we're coming down with something. Continued low doses of antibiotics create the ideal conditions for the rapid growth of the very bacteria that have developed the ability to resist the antibiotic.

Bacteria develop resistance in several ways. Firstly, by the normal process of genetic mutation. If a particular variety mutates and becomes resistant to a single or more antibiotic or antimicrobial agent, then it will thrive when all the other bacteria die. The broader the range of the antibiotic, then the broader the resistance will be. And of course it will be difficult to control any outbreak of disease from the resistant bacteria. Hence the alarming hospital superbug stories you may have come across (see page 33).

Disease prevention is not, however, the only reason why antibiotics are used in farming. Very low, or subtherapeutic, doses are routinely added to animal

feed, and are known to improve the growth rates of livestock. Quite why is not entirely clear, but it is probably because the body doesn't have to spend so much energy fighting off infection. But for whatever reason, antibiotics have become a standard tool of conventional livestock farming, where continual pressure to improve yields and growth rates, and to cut costs, has fathered many an ill-thought-out technique.

The continual overuse of antibiotics will become even more problematic as the world becomes increasingly urbanised, and follows the path of cheap chicken, hamburgers, intensive agriculture and routine antibiotic use. Bacteria do not respect borders. While controlling bacterial disease has to be a priority, we seriously need to change our ways if we are to win the battle. And going organic will most certainly help in this particular battle, which we are losing hands down at the moment.

Organic Chickens and Eggs

Two breeds, Ross and Cobb, an indolent pair, have provided the backbone of the poultry industry for many years, and dominated the British chicken world. These birds became the industry's benchmark and gave nice fat juicy breasts, grew quickly and were relatively hardy. It all sounds very serene, but behind the scenes are some ghastly Breughel-esque practices that may put you off eating chicken altogether: de-beaking, leg disorders, heart failure, breast blisters, chronic dermatitis, all basically the result of industrial levels of production. Conventionally farmed chickens will have been routinely treated with antibiotics, crammed into sheds, subjected to near permanent artificial daylight, stuffed with a high protein diet – can we really justify this sort of farming any more?

More privileged chickens roam free range, and this includes all organically reared birds which have to have access to the outside. Nibbling at worms and insects, and using their legs in a way that poor battery hens never can, these birds can bring the chick back into chicken, for diet and exercise are really the key to good quality. (However, giving them the opportunity to roam around doesn't always mean they take it. One farmer told me that he had to actually chivvy his flock to go outside every morning.) To keep the land free of disease, many organic farmers will use movable chicken coops that can be manoeuvred around the farm, and this has the added benefit of helping soil fertility with the little doses of chicken manure that chickens so lovingly leave. Good management is crucial.

Organic birds will take longer to get to market size – because their diet is lower in protein – and are usually culled at eighty-one days. A conventionally farmed chicken may be pumped and primed to a sort of marketability in as little as thirty-eight days. No antibiotics are used on organic chicken farms, except if welfare or illness makes it absolutely necessary, there are no GMOs in the feed, and organic birds must have at least 80 per cent of their feed from certified organic feed. This is the essence of organic chicken and egg production with, of course, the emphasis on the birds' welfare as you would expect.

Recently, the evil Ross/Cobb hegemony has been usurped by some excellent French birds that thrive under organic conditions. A growing number of hatcheries are now specialising in these French breeds, that are always at home on the free range, very happy to wander around outside, and give a good-sized – not vast, flabby and goose-like – carcass. When you buy organic birds you can tell an awful lot just by looking at the colour of the flesh and skin of the bird. The yellower and less pasty the bird looks, the better. I have to say that the word on the range is that there is a lot of poor-quality organic chicken about, and I particularly recommend that you try and seek out the growing band of small-scale producers that sell from farm shops and farmers' markets, and really try to find out how your chicken has been reared.

Although the Soil Association advises that the size of the flocks is limited to 500 birds, believing that anything more creates poor living conditions, there are exceptions allowed. Egg-layers must have access to the outside, and the organic units I have seen provide nesting boxes, with apparently happy and content chickens going about egg-laying in a relaxed and natural way. However, Organic Farmers and Growers (OF&G) take a different approach, and will certify units of up to 7,000 birds. There is an organic controversy here, a classic case where an agreed global standard would strengthen the organic cause. OF&G say that if UKROFS agreed to implement the Soil Association criteria, 90 per cent of the free-range units would close. This sort of attempt at compromise does not give the organic movement a good name, and is not what organics should be all about. So tread warily when it comes to organic eggs, which by the way will very likely be slightly paler due to the lack of colouring in the feed. Although some farmers produce enough feed for the birds on their farm, many don't and will buy in feed grown in accordance with *The Standards*. So the main difference between organically and conventionally produced eggs is down to feed, housing and welfare.

Given the real concern over the living conditions of the chickens that lay the eggs that we eat, how sure can we be that the organic eggs we buy have been produced from 'happy' birds? *The Standards* has been carefully worked out with the birds' welfare in mind, and this governs the living conditions, much of which relates to the density of birds per metre, and the flock size. Given that these are so closely controlled, and that access to the outside is compulsory, I think it's fair to say that an organic bird is very likely to be a happier bird. There are degrees of being organic though. Some

of the smaller units, selling only to local clients or maybe in farmers' markets, can give excellent product, where you can almost know by name the chicken that has produced the egg.

Some of the larger units, i.e. flocks of more than 3,000 birds, will have to be prepared for some fairly radical changes as to how the birds are managed and fed by the year 2005 – a big year for organics. It will then be obligatory to break up the size of these larger units, generally redesign the layout of the chicken unit and also feed them with 100 per cent organic feed. Some organic egg producers are wondering how on earth they are ever going to be able to afford these changes, given the meagre profits in farming. Concerned organic consumers will I think remain of the opinion that decent living conditions for the chicken are crucial and should not be compromised.

Organic Beef and Dairy

Sturdy, healthy calves, often from breeds that have grown and evolved in the area, can provide a sound start for an organic beef herd, but what makes it even easier is to use the suckler system where the calves actually stay with their mothers, feeding off milk, grass and whatever else is on offer. They are often even weaned naturally, again by their mothers, avoiding the problems of stress that may occur if mother and calf are separated or handled insensitively.

Organic beef production can be simplicity itself if you use the right breed, or cross. Overblown, over-muscled beasts, primarily Continental breeds, bred to grow as quickly as possible on high protein diets, are not likely to do well under organic production, but letting the mother be mother for once often means that organic beef herds are quite easy to manage. Tougher breeds may even stay outside all year round, although the farmer will know what's best in each particular case – there are no hard and fast rules here. Where cattle do go inside, the shelter has to conform to another set of rules to ensure that the animal's welfare is catered for. Allowing the herd to function as a herd helps them all stay happy and healthy. Keeping the grass in good condition depends on low stock levels, and good rotation helps keep the fertility up. But although grass is in some cases pretty much all that organically reared cattle are fed on, in other cases it is simply impossible to go the whole year without some sort of supplementary feed, and beef cattle may require 'finishing' to bring them up to the right condition for the market. Silage, grown and stored on the farm, is often available, and I was pleasantly surprised by just how sweet-smelling and appetising silage can be.

In both beef and dairy production there are close controls over the amount of the feed which is made up of what is called dry matter. In a conventional system, bought-in cattle cake and high-protein feeds are used to bring the animals either up to size in the case of beef, or up to a certain level of milk production in the case of dairy herds. There are problems on many levels here. Firstly, buying in is against fundamental organic principles and this type of high-protein feed is often essentially unnatural for a herbivore. And this brings us back to the sorry tale of BSE. An as yet unquantified amount of these high protein feeds contained recycled animal carcasses, including brains and spinal columns, and as we now know, this is how BSE has entered into our food chain (see pages 34-35).

Conventional cattle feed may also contain soya and maize which are produced on a massive scale in many countries all over the world, often using genetically modified seed. You could quite legitimately say that this intensive system of producing milk and beef has essentially locked vast tracts of land into another form of chemically dependent, intensive crop production. It is a vicious circle. Keeping cattle fed on this diet has implications on the health front as well, for these stressed, inappropriately fed, densely stocked animals are prone to all sorts of diseases, so are regularly treated with antibiotics and drugs as the farmer – and vet – see fit.

For these fundamental reasons, *The Standards* will control the use level of high-protein feeds. Some of that feed can still technically come from non-organic sources for the simple reason that there isn't enough organic feed being produced. If the animals are ruminants – essentially grass eaters – a maximum of 10 per cent non-organic feed is permitted and with non-ruminants – pigs, chickens – the level is 20 per cent but it is important to note that this derogation will be phased out by the Soil Association by 2005.

A lot of the problems for organic beef come when the animals are sent to slaughter. With some of the smaller abattoirs going bust, there aren't too many of the larger ones that will look after and co-operate with the organic farmers who are often concerned that their animals will suffer if they have to travel to a slaughterhouse that's too far away. Welfare has to be taken into account both on the journey as well as at the abattoir. And then as we have seen, the issue of costs has to be met, making organic meat either uncompetitive or unprofitable. (See 'Abattoirs' on page 79)

Some organic meat could in theory come from dairy bull calves, raised on a multiple suckling system, and it is one of the more troubling aspects of running a farm that a dairy farmer, organic or not, cannot always use these calves, and many are sadly shot shortly after birth. To avoid this, there is a move afoot to try and develop demand for a 'natural' organic veal, no crates or cruelty, to enable the farmer to make better use of their resources, and for the calf to have some sort of life.

Sadly for the dairy cows' calves, they won't have such a blissfully long time with their mother as a suckler beef calf, but will spend maybe two to four days suckling and guzzling their mothers' milk. Particularly important here is the colostrum, that thick rich milk that flows just after birth and gives the new-born animal its first dose of disease resistance, as well as sustenance. An organic farmer will then move the calves away from their mothers and place them with nurse cows, usually older animals who need a gentler lifestyle. While the organic calf will hopefully be happily bonding with its nurse mother, and learning to socialise with the other calves in the group, a conventionally reared cow will more than likely only be fed on artificial dried milk, strictly forbidden under organic regulations.

Throughout its life, the welfare of the animal is paramount, so if the farmer feels that a cow really needs some help from a vet, he/she won't stand idly by as a matter of principle. Organic solutions to mastitis when it does occur are usually homeopathic, but if that doesn't work regular massage on the infected udder will also be carried out. But there are times when conventional medicine may well be called for. If an animal then has to be taken out of the organic equation, then so be it. Conventional farms tend to use antibiotics to cure mastitis, but these are not always effective, and of course their routine use is not permitted in organic farming.

The welfare of the animal will also influence where the animals live: the cubicle or open yard where they may be housed in winter are subject to rigorous dos and don'ts, with a specific amount of space for each cow being allowed for.

The service doesn't end there. Do cows get enough sex? Dairy farmers, organic and conventional, are increasingly offering the use of a vasectomised bull to keep the cows' spirits up, and to help them through the boredom of everyday life on the farm and the interminable milking.

Getting the diet just right for milk production isn't easy. Cattle cake, an important source of protein, is brought in under both systems, although as you would expect, organic feed will be primarily made from organically grown crops. The amount allowed per cow is carefully controlled and monitored as well. Here the essential difference between conventional and organic cattle cake is the nature of the protein. Organic product will not contain fishmeal, and will replace this with protein from beans or peas, for example. Grass of course is what cows like best, but obviously during the winter it is in short supply so an organic farm will have stored supplies of silage to help the cow through the winter. Cows also like munching away at root crops such as swedes and mangolds – someone has to – which can help in the task of trying to provide a balanced diet all year round in order to keep the milk levels viable.

One of the biggest problems for all farm animals is internal parasites, which are given the chemical one-two on conventional farms. The organic solution is to practise what is called clean grazing, where young animals are kept away from land that has been recently grazed. Encouraging the development of gradual resistance, by using nurse cows, is also very useful, as the calves come into contact with the problems at a low and manageable level and their bodies react accordingly by developing resistance.

When it comes to organic cream cheese, and all the other by-products of milk, such as cheese and butter, the situation is blissfully simple. Cheese-makers may well produce their own milk but most will buy it in from certified organic sources, and will then be inspected as processors. Keeping the immensely detailed records required for organic status is absolutely *de rigueur,* which means that each organic cheese and organic pat of butter should be fully traceable back to the farm from where the milk was originally bought.

Organic Pork

I got to know Wiltshire a little better when I first met Sophie, and visited it again recently. The reason for this was a trip to Eastbrook Farm, a pioneering and highly successful organic farm sitting in the hills above Swindon. Virtually anything written about organics in the UK mentions the farm, and it's hardly surprising. Eastbrook (great name for an organic television soap) has been run by the Browning family on leased land

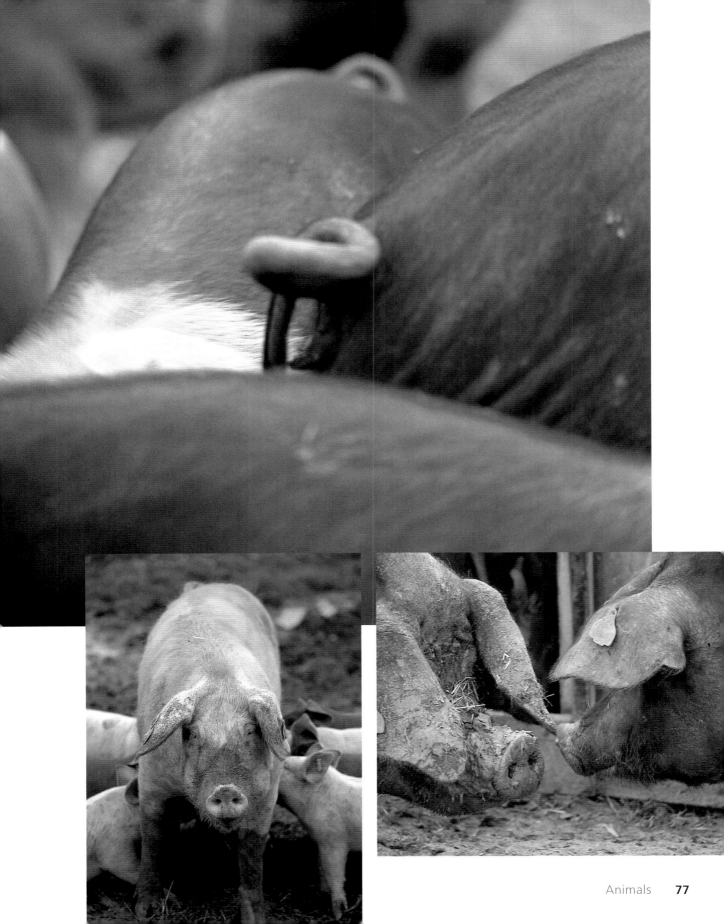

since 1950. Browning *père* has been succeeded by Browning *fille*, Helen, who took a dramatic plunge and went organic in 1986, when doing such things was agriculturally and commercially radical.

It wasn't easy, and in the early days she was the mad weirdo doing strange things on a well established farm. The local (male) farmers were intrigued but devotedly sceptical, although there was some local support. Jane Grigson, Sophie's late mother, would visit and pen notes of encouragement. Henrietta Green, Madam British Produce, and many others praised her bacon, for Helen's abiding passion was, and remains I suspect, pigs. In fact, our conversation became quite bizarre. Whatever we talked about, Helen would steer the conversation towards pigs. Like a game of tennis, I equally firmly lobbed back my answer, peppered with references to fish. But it is always invigorating to meet people with energy, passion and enthusiasm, and Helen has it bad for pigs and organics. In fact she has been the chair of Britain's Soil Association for four years, so she is very well aware of all that is going on.

The farm has its pigs, of course. Pigs are the 'farmyard intellectuals', and are happiest in groups, so a good pig farmer will go with the flow, and let a group establish its own dynamics. There's leader pig – usually a bit of a bully, possibly a reincarnated lager-and-pork-scratching soul here; quiet pig; and the everyday happy-go-lucky pig, the porcine proletarian. Respecting the group goes right through their short but happy lives, right through to their final destination – sad, I know – the abattoir.

The fundamental logic of conventional pig farming has always been this: keep the animals free of disease through the routine use of antibiotics. Thus armed, a farmer can stock the animals densely, and farm them intensively. Pigs in narrow pens and on concrete were once the norm, although it must be said that British pig-farming standards have now improved. Although British pork is getting better, many of the pigs – and pig farmers – are far from being deliriously happy. Take the antibiotic crutch away, as organic farming does, and it becomes unworkable to farm the pigs intensively, for the animals get stressed. And stress is not good for the health. *De facto*, an organic pig is definitely a happier pig.

With decent housing, and low stock levels, pigs can thrive under organic status. Attention to the animals' welfare starts from the word go, so piglets are allowed to spend as much as two months with their mother before weaning, which in pig-farming terms is a long time. Many organic farmers have revived some of the more esoteric breeds of pig, which not only can taste quite delicious, but are often hardier, and better suited to local conditions. The British Saddleback, the long-faced Tamworth, even the Gloucester Old Spot, despite its tendency to be a fat pig, can all do well under organic farming, and these breeds can of course be cross-bred to refine the animal if necessary.

On any pig farm, even the five-star porcine luxury hotel, Eastbrook Farm, where the pigs spend most of their lives outside, adequate shelter must be provided, the size and design of which must conform to the specifics laid out in *The Standards*. Here, the pigs are moved from field to field and their rooting becomes part of the whole scheme of rotation, but not all organic pig farms are managed along these lines.

Although organic pig farming under cover is permitted, *The Standards* expressly states that the pigs must have access to the outside wherever possible. Here the fundamental focus on welfare dictates that the animals must be allowed to establish a social group, and express their natural behaviour. This means that there must be a 'dunging' area for example; for pigs, despite what you may think, are naturally quite clean animals and in the wild would go off and pass a porcine motion well away from their group. And when it's time to go and give birth, Madame Pig must be allowed to wander off and do what comes naturally, so nesting boxes must also be part of the overall design. The floor is an important part of any covered pig unit, for given the pigs' love of a good rootle, imagine how unpleasant it must be for them to come across concrete. Straw helps here.

If there isn't enough natural roughage in the diet, i.e. where access to grass is restricted in the winter, it must be given. Although pigs are notoriously omnivorous, organic pigs are not fed off swill from unknown sources, but may be fed, for example, organic waste or second-grade vegetables. By the way, since this is a cookbook, organic pork really does tend to taste better than the conventionally farmed alternative.

Organic Lamb

Well, I have to say that I thought that raising lambs organically would be a doddle, but they can actually prove to be a wee bit tricky, mainly because of the need to keep them under a fairly high level of surveillance. This avoids the incidence of some particularly nasty complaints for which there are no effective organic cures – particularly something called fly strike, which is really unpleasant. Let me just say that it involves a wound, flies, and maggots, and if it isn't checked it can cause the animal great suffering. The conventional solution is preventative, and involves the routine dipping of sheep in a toxic pesticide, mostly organophosphates. These are some of the most toxic of all chemicals and are thought to be responsible for the increasing rates of illness among farm workers who have routinely been exposed to them, particularly by using them as sheep dips. Given the fact that lamb prices are so catastrophically low at the moment, there is not a lot of money to be made in lamb, whether reared organically or not. Sheep, however, are useful members of the brigade of animals that can contribute towards the successful, well balanced organic farm.

Abattoirs

Visits to slaughterhouses are not joyous affairs as a rule, but they reveal much about the way our animals are treated, for they range – just about – between the huge and efficient, and the small and often more considerate. In the UK abattoirs have become a contentious issue.

Much of the problem lies in the interpretation of EU law, particularly a French phrase, *vétérinaire ordinaire*, an expert who the EU says should always be present at the slaughter of animals. It is all a little involved and rather tedious but the UK Government insists that he/she should be more highly qualified than the French interpretation of the phrase, and charge the abattoirs at an hourly rate, including travelling time, for their services. But because of different interpretations of the law, these charges are actually levied at different rates throughout the Community. For the bigger abattoirs, supplying most of the supermarkets and the really big users, that's OK, but for the smaller ones, costs have increased exponentially. A smaller abattoir may be paying up to 6000 per cent more per unit than the larger plants and this is putting them out of business. Rapidly. Within the past ten years the number of abattoirs in the UK has fallen from 1400 to less than 400. It is estimated that within two years only 75 will remain. If these charges remain – and it is hoped that a per tonne rate will be used as elsewhere in the EU – then it will be very difficult for organic and rare breed meat to be viable.

All this affects organic farmers in a very pertinent way. Many have small numbers of animals that need to be dispatched, preferably locally, so that the meat can be sold on the farm, or to approved end users. This is becoming difficult. Another concern is that if they are obliged to use a bigger outfit the carcasses are often mixed among meat from conventional farms.

Actually, the emphasis on minute physical inspection by the *vétérinaire ordinaire* is really a little crazy. It has even been suggested that the process itself can be responsible for some microbiological infection. But given recent history it is understandable. Post BSE, consumers like to buy meat directly from producers wherever possible. We don't want to have to rely on the anonymity of supermarket shelves. We want to know about the breeds, about how the meat has been hung, about what's good next week. All this should come from informed, small-scale farmers, be they organic or not.

I hope this discussion will be a historical footnote by the time you read the book, but its relevance will remain.

Part 2

The Recipes

William's Crostini of Broad Beans
with Sun-dried Tomatoes (V)

My mother used to make a fantastic creamy broad bean purée which she piled into globe artichokes, but recently William discovered another version, this time in Anna del Conte's book *Gli Antipasti* (Pavilion, 1993). He has now made it his own, with a few small variations on the original, including the use of raw garlic, rather than cooked, and a final crowning glory in the form of a sun-dried tomato (or halved fresh cherry tomatoes, if we're clean out of sun-dried). Like Anna, he serves it on crostini, pieces of griddled bread drizzled with olive oil.

SERVES 4

900g (2 lb) fresh broad beans in their pods, or 300g (10½ oz) podded broad beans or frozen broad beans
1 small slice of good-quality white bread, crusts removed
a little milk
2 garlic cloves, roughly chopped

60ml (2 fl oz) extra virgin olive oil
salt and pepper

TO SERVE
slices of good-quality bread
extra virgin olive oil
sun-dried tomatoes

Pod the broad beans if fresh. Bring a large pan of salted water to the boil and add the fresh or frozen broad beans. Cook until tender. Drain, reserving a mugful of the cooking water. Refresh the beans under cold water, and then settle down to skinning them. A lengthy job, but necessary and it pays dividends. Slit the tough outer skin of each bean with your fingernail or a small knife, then squeeze out the bright green inner bean. When you have skinned them all, place the beans in the processor.

Soak the bread in a little milk for 5 minutes, drain, then add to the processor with the garlic and some salt and pepper. Process to a purée, gradually trickling in the olive oil. If the purée is still very thick, beat in a little of the cooking liquid. Taste and adjust the seasoning.

To make the crostini, heat a griddle pan until very hot, and griddle the bread on it until nicely toasted. Cut larger pieces in half or quarters. Drizzle a little olive oil over each piece, then smear thickly with the broad bean purée. Top each one with a piece of sun-dried tomato and serve before the bread turns soggy.

Baba Ganoush Ⓥ

This is the delightful name for a delightful Middle Eastern purée of aubergines, tahina and olive oil. Like hummus, it is usually served as a first course, or part of a mezze, or selection of little first courses. For the very best results, barbecue the aubergine to give the purée a smoky flavour. Failing that, the grill or oven do the job pretty well, and the resulting purée will still be very moreish. Serve it with warm *Pitta Bread* (see page 223), or crudités to scoop it up.

SERVES 4-6

1 large aubergine
1 garlic clove, chopped
4 tablespoons light tahina
30g (1 oz) shelled walnuts, chopped
juice of ½ lemon
generous ½ teaspoon ground cumin

5 tablespoons extra virgin olive oil
8 mint leaves, shredded
seeds of ½ pomegranate*
salt

Grill or barbecue the aubergine close to the heat, turning frequently until the skin is blackened and charred, and the flesh is soft. Alternatively, bake it in the oven, preheated to its highest setting, until blackened and soft. Peel the aubergine, chop the flesh roughly and drain in a colander until cool enough to handle.

Squeeze the aubergine to get rid of the remaining bitter juices, and process or liquidise with the garlic, tahina, walnuts, lemon juice, cumin, 4 tablespoons of the olive oil and a little salt, until smooth and creamy. Taste and add more salt or lemon juice, if needed. Stir in two-thirds of the mint. Spoon into a bowl, cover and chill until needed.

To serve, bring back to room temperature. Make a well in the centre and fill with the pomegranate seeds. Drizzle the last of the olive oil over the purée and sprinkle with the remaining mint. Serve at room temperature.

Avocado Hummus Ⓥ

The children and I fell hook, line and sinker for the contents of
a tub of this that William brought back with him from London.
It was gone in no time at all so, given that we live out in the sticks,
at least as far as the handy Greek corner shop goes, I decided that
I'd better try making some myself. It turns out to be no more
tricksy than making ordinary hummus.

   This tastes far better when it is made from home-cooked
chickpeas; but if you are really pushed for time, substitute tinned
chickpeas. You'll need about 280g (10 oz) drained weight.

SERVES 8-10

150g (5 oz) chickpeas,
    soaked overnight
juice of 2 lemons
2 garlic cloves, roughly
    chopped
3 tablespoons light tahina
2 tablespoons extra virgin
    olive oil

2 ripe avocados
salt

TO SERVE
a little olive oil
paprika or cayenne pepper
ground cumin

Drain the chickpeas and put into a pan with enough water to cover
by about 7.5cm (3 in). Do not season. Bring up to the boil and boil
hard for 10 minutes, then reduce the heat and leave to burble
away quietly until the chickpeas are very tender, adding extra hot
water if the level drops perilously low. This can take anything from
40 minutes for small, new-season chickpeas, to several hours for
larger, older codgers. When they are done, drain thoroughly,
saving a cupful of the cooking water.

Place the chickpeas in a processor with the lemon juice, garlic,
tahina, olive oil, salt to taste and about 3 tablespoons of their
cooking water. Peel and stone the avocados and cut into chunks.
Add to the contents of the processor. Process the whole lot
together to form a smooth cream, gradually adding more of the
cooking water as needed (another 3-5 tablespoons should do it).
Make sure that it is smooth and unctuous and luscious, not like
semi-dried clay. Taste and adjust the seasoning. Scrape into a bowl
and cover with clingfilm.

Shortly before serving, garnish with a swirl of olive oil and a light
dusting of paprika or cayenne, and ground cumin. Serve with
warm *Pitta Bread* (see page 223), or crudités.

Sweetcorn and Brie Fritters Ⓥ

These are always popular except, of course, with those like William who don't like sweetcorn. Still, with that one proviso, you can't really go wrong. Serve them as a first course, perhaps with a light tomato and sun-dried tomato salsa, or as a side dish to a more substantial main course. The mixture can be made up to a couple of hours ahead, but leave the frying until the last possible moment. Frozen sweetcorn kernels are fine for this, but if you use the kernels from a fresh cob, then you can expect to cut about 110g (4 oz) from each cob. I've also made these with half and half sweetcorn and sprouted mung beans. Very good too.

SERVES 4-6

85g (3 oz) plain flour
1 level teaspoon baking
  powder
¼ teaspoon salt
1 egg
150ml (5 fl oz) milk
110g (4 oz) sweetcorn
  kernels, defrosted if frozen

75-85g (2½-3 oz) not-too-
  ripe Camembert, Brie or
  Reblochon, de-rinded and
  roughly diced
freshly ground pepper
extra virgin olive oil for
  frying

Sift the flour with the baking powder and salt into a bowl. Make a well in the centre and break in the egg. Start whisking the flour into the egg, gradually adding the milk, to make a smooth batter. Stir in the sweetcorn, cheese and pepper.

Heat a little oil in a frying pan over a moderately high heat. Spoon tablespoonfuls of the batter mixture into the hot oil, allowing a fair bit of room between them. Fry until golden brown underneath, then turn over and fry on the other side until browned. Drain briefly on kitchen paper before serving.

Parsnip Crisps Ⓥ

A big bowl, piled high with these curving and twisting golden brown crisps is a beautiful sight. As long as you have a mandolin of one sort or another and can slice the parsnips paper thin from stem to root end, there is no great mystery to making them. The crucial thing is to get the temperature of the oil about right, and to keep an eye on them as they cook. If you want to make them in advance, that's fine, but if anything err on the side of undercooking. They'll flop a little, so to crisp them up again before serving spread out on a baking tray and pop them into the oven for a few brief minutes. Keep a close eye on them, as they burn swiftly if forgotten. I know, because I've had to consign one large batch to the bin, all because I was nattering when I should have been paying attention. Don't say I didn't warn you!

SERVES 8

500-600g (18-21 oz) large parsnips
sunflower oil for deep-frying
salt

Scrub the parsnips but don't bother to peel them. Using a mandolin, or the slicing blade on a grater, slice lengthways into paper-thin slices. If you have the time, drop them into a bowl of cold water with some ice cubes and leave for half an hour to encourage them to curl.

Heat the oil to 185°C/365°F. (To test, drop a cube of bread into the oil; if it fizzes energetically, and the bread browns within 30-45 seconds, then the oil is hot enough. If the bread browns too quickly, then the oil is too hot, so turn the heat down, but if it browns too slowly, the heat needs to be raised.) Drain and dry the slices of parsnip assiduously, then drop them into the hot oil, a handful at a time. Separate them in the oil (wooden chopsticks are rather handy for this), then lift them out as soon as they turn pale brown. Drain on kitchen paper, then season with salt. Repeat with the remaining parsnips. Serve immediately, or leave to cool and then...

...a few minutes before serving, spread them out on a baking sheet and pop into a moderate oven, about 180°C/350°F/Gas Mark 4, for about 1-3 minutes to reheat and re-crisp (they will wilt in the oven, then crisp up as they begin to cool again).

Pistounade Ⓥ

This is a new sauce from Provence, which brings together the inky black olives of the region with *pistou*, the local equivalent of Italy's pesto. Serve it as a dip, with crudités (sticks of celery, chicory leaves, radishes, strips of red pepper, cucumber, cauliflower florets, etc.) and good bread, or try it with grilled chicken or tuna.

SERVES 8

310g (11 oz) black olives, pitted
3 garlic cloves, roughly chopped
about 30g (1 oz) basil leaves

30g (1 oz) Parmesan, either in small chunks or freshly grated
150ml (5 fl oz) extra virgin olive oil

Put the olives, garlic, basil and Parmesan in the processor. Process to a roughed-up mush. Leave the blades running and gradually trickle in enough olive oil to give a creamy sauce, scraping down the sides once or twice so that it is evenly mixed. Taste and add a little more basil if you think it needs it, then scrape into a bowl and cover until needed.

Tzatziki Ⓥ

This makes a summery, restorative first course, on its own or with other small dishes, served with warm *Pitta Bread* (see page 223), but I love it as a sauce with meat, fish or vegetable kebabs, grilled or seared fish and chicken, or with fritters and even fish cakes.

SERVES 4

½ cucumber, peeled and finely diced
1 tablespoon white or red wine vinegar
150g (5 oz) thick Greek yoghurt

1 garlic clove, crushed
1 tablespoon finely chopped mint
salt and pepper

Spread the cucumber dice out in a colander or sieve, and sprinkle over the vinegar and a little salt. Leave to drain for 1 hour, then pat dry with kitchen paper or a clean tea-towel. Mix with the rest of the ingredients, then taste and adjust seasoning. Serve either lightly chilled or at room temperature.

Niçoise Aubergine Fritters with Aïoli Ⓥ

In many restaurants in and around the Provençal town of Nice they serve exceptional aubergine fritters, or rather *'beignets'*, which can also mean doughnuts. The reason I mention this is that the batter encasing the discs of aubergine is not thin and crisp, but thick and almost cakey with a modicum of crispness, though not of the brittle sort. There's nothing so very exceptional about the batter – it's just the proportions of flour to egg to liquid that have changed.

These fritters are easy to make at home, and are excellent served with a bowlful of garlicky *Aïoli* (see page 107), and/or the *Pistounade* (an olive, garlic and basil purée) shown opposite. Of course, you don't have to stick with aubergines. Try dipping slices of courgette, fennel or pepper into the batter instead.

SERVES 6-8

2 medium aubergines
salt
sunflower and/or olive oil
   for deep-frying
Aïoli (see page 107)
   and/or *Pistounade*
   (see opposite page)
   or lemon wedges

BATTER
250g (9 oz) plain flour
a big pinch of salt
2 eggs, separated
2 teaspoons extra virgin
   olive oil
1 teaspoon anchovy Ⓦ
   paste (optional)

Slice the aubergines into discs about 5mm (¼in) thick. Spread out on a tray, and sprinkle lightly with salt. Leave for half an hour, then wipe them dry. If you are pushed for time you can skip this salting process, but even with modern aubergines it does improve the flavour.

Meanwhile, make the batter. Sift the flour with the salt. Make a well in the centre and add the egg yolks, oil and anchovy paste (if using). Gradually pour in 200ml (7 fl oz) water, whisking constantly and drawing in the flour from the sides to give a thick batter. Set aside until ready to use.

Put the oil on to heat. Whisk the egg whites until they form stiff peaks, then fold into the batter. When the oil has reached a temperature of 190°C/375°F, or when a cube of bread dropped into the oil browns in 45 seconds, dip the aubergine slices one by one into the batter, coating thoroughly on both sides (since it is on the thick side, you may need to spoon it over the aubergine slices). Deep-fry a few slices at a time until golden brown and puffed. Drain briefly on kitchen paper, season with a little extra salt if needed, and serve with *Aïoli*, *Pistounade* or lemon wedges.

Sautéed Tomatoes and Red Onions with Parmesan and Cheddar Crisps ⓥ

You know how the best bit of practically any dish topped with cheese is the crisp bits that cling to the edges? Well, that's exactly what these crisps are like, except that you don't have to fight over them, because there are enough to give everyone their fair share. They can be served with all kinds of things, or just nibbled at on their own, but I like them with lightly sautéed cherry tomatoes, to add a touch of freshness.

SERVES 4-6

3 tablespoons extra virgin olive oil
1 red onion, cut into 12 thin wedges
2 garlic cloves, chopped
500g (18 oz) cherry tomatoes
a small handful of basil leaves, roughly torn up
salt and pepper

PARMESAN AND CHEDDAR CRISPS
85g (3 oz) Parmesan, freshly grated
85g (3 oz) Cheddar, freshly grated

Preheat the oven to 180°C/350°F/Gas Mark 4. Line a baking sheet with non-stick baking parchment.

Mix the two cheeses together. Take tablespoons of the cheese mixture and place on the baking sheet, flattening them out gently, and leaving plenty of space between each one. Bake for 8-10 minutes until the cheese has melted and is beginning to colour a touch around the edges. Take out of the oven and cool until tepid and crisp.

Heat the oil in a wide frying pan over a high heat. Add the red onion and sauté until soft and beginning to catch at the edges. Toss in the garlic and the cherry tomatoes and fry for about 2 minutes, until the skins of the tomatoes are beginning to burst. Draw off the heat, scatter over the basil, and season with a little salt and plenty of black pepper. And there you are, done already, so spoon them straight on to the plates, add the cheese crisps, and serve immediately.

Herb Scones with Beetroot Marmalade and Soured Cream ⓥ

These savoury scones are quite unusual with their topping of sweet-sour marmalade and soured cream, but the combination works really well. I serve them as canapés, or even as part of a first course, with a flurry of salad leaves around them.

MAKES ABOUT 20

SCONES
225g (8 oz) self-raising flour
½ teaspoon salt
45g (1½ oz) butter
2 tablespoons finely
  chopped parsley
½ tablespoon finely
  chopped sage
1 teaspoon chopped
  thyme leaves
½ teaspoon finely chopped
  tarragon leaves
around 150ml (5 fl oz) milk,
  plus a little extra to glaze

BEETROOT MARMALADE
110g (4 oz) thinly sliced
  onions
150g (5 oz) peeled and
  grated, raw beetroot
2 dried red chillies
15g (½ oz) butter
1 tablespoon extra virgin
  olive oil
1 heaped tablespoon
  caster sugar
2 tablespoons sherry
  vinegar
salt and pepper

TO SERVE
300ml (10 fl oz) soured cream or crème fraîche
small mint leaves to garnish

To make the beetroot marmalade, put the onion, grated beetroot and whole chillies in a pan with the butter and oil. Stir over a moderate heat until the butter has melted. Turn the heat down low, cover the pan and sweat the vegetables gently for 45-50 minutes, until very tender. Now add the sugar, vinegar, salt and a good grinding of pepper. Stir and leave to cook, uncovered, over a moderate heat for another 10-15 minutes. Stir frequently, and keep going until the mixture is thick and jammy, with virtually no liquid left. Taste and adjust seasoning. Remove and discard the chillies. This can be made several days in advance and stored, covered, in the fridge. Warm through gently before using.

To make the scones, begin by preheating the oven to 220°C/425°F/Gas Mark 7. Sift the flour with the salt. Rub in the butter then stir in the herbs. Add enough milk to make a soft unsticky dough. Roll out to a thickness of about 1cm (scant ½ in) and then stamp out 5cm (2 in) rounds with a biscuit cutter. Lay on a tray and brush the tops with milk. Bake for 10-12 minutes until well risen and lightly browned.

To serve, split the warm scones in half (they should not be cut with a knife, but use the knife just to start the cut, then pull apart with fingers). Spoon a little beetroot marmalade on to each half, top with a small dollop of soured cream and finish with a mint leaf.

Beetroot and Vodka (or Gin) Soup
with Soured Cream Ⓥ

Serendipity can be a happy thing. Big, beautiful bunches of organic beetroot, complete with leaves (which have an earthy, spinachy taste – check out the recipe on page 125), had insisted on being bought one shopping trip. Later on that day I came across an article on the latest organic gin and vodka. I guess it was the Russian connection that made me think of putting the two together. This is not actually a bona-fide borscht, the famous Russian beetroot soup, but what with the beetroot, caraway, soured cream and vodka (or gin...) it has strong Slav overtones. Definitely for grown-ups, but be careful not to overheat the soup once the vodka is stirred in, or all the heart-warming alcohol will be lost to the ether!

Grating beetroot is a messy business so this is one time when it is definitely worth hunting down the grating attachment for the processor, even if it does mean more washing up.

SERVES 4-6

1 onion, chopped
½ tablespoon caraway seeds
1 bouquet garni, consisting of 2 parsley stalks, 1 bay leaf, 2 large sprigs of dill or fennel
2 tablespoons sunflower oil
3 tablespoons risotto rice (e.g. arborio)
675g (1½ lb) raw beetroot, peeled and grated
1 tablespoon lemon juice

1 litre (1¾ pints) beef stock, *Chicken Stock* (see page 242) or classy *Vegetable Stock* (see page 243)
2 tablespoons vodka or gin
salt and pepper

TO SERVE
soured cream or crème fraiche
chopped chives or dill sprigs

Sweat the onion, caraway seeds and bouquet garni in the oil in a covered pan over a low heat for 10 minutes. Add the rice and stir for about 1 minute to coat it in the juices. Now add the beetroot and lemon juice (don't forget this as it sets the colour), and continue cooking, stirring constantly for a further 2-3 minutes.

Next tip in the stock, season with salt and pepper, and bring up to the boil. Simmer for 25-30 minutes until both the beetroot and rice are tender. Remove and discard the bouquet garni. Liquidise until smooth. Return to the pan, adjust the seasoning, and stir in the vodka (or gin). Heat through thoroughly, without letting it boil. Serve steaming hot, with a generous swirl of soured cream in each bowl (it balances the sweetness of the beetroot and the mild bitterness of the alcohol), and a garnish of dill or chives.

Spring Chowder Ⓥ

This is a delicious, comforting soup for early spring, when Jersey Royals are arriving in the shops, and warmer weather is well on the way, even if it hasn't quite yet hit home. It is based on a recipe of Lindsey Bareham's, from her inspiring book, *A Celebration of Soup* (Michael Joseph, 1993).

SERVES 4

1 large leek, thinly sliced
45g (1½ oz) butter
450g (1 lb) new-season Jersey Royal potatoes
45g (1½ oz) plain flour
1.2 litres (2 pints) *Chicken Stock*, *Vegetable Stock* (see pages 242-3) or water
6 generous sprigs of mint, finely chopped

125g (4½ oz) shelled peas, preferably fresh, but frozen will do
salt and pepper

TO SERVE
soured cream or crème fraiche
grated Cheddar

Put the leek and butter in a pan, set over a low heat, cover and sweat until the leek has softened. Scrape and rinse the potatoes, then slice thinly. Add to the pan, stir to coat in butter, then cover and continue cooking for 5 minutes.

Next, stirring all the time, sift in the flour to take up the fat. Add the stock and half the mint, and bring back to the boil. Add the peas, reduce the heat and simmer for about 10 minutes, until the potatoes are cooked but not collapsed. Season and sprinkle with the remaining chopped mint. Ladle into big bowls and top with a spoonful of cream, and a scattering of cheese. Serve immediately.

Carrot and Cumin Soup Ⓥ

This is a soup that I like to keep on the thick side, comforting and soothing with a dash of liveliness given by the lingering taste (and delightful smell) of the cumin seeds. There's so much flavour in the carrots, herbs and spices, that you really don't need to use a stock at all. Water is just fine. Don't worry if the milk curdles when you stir it into the pan – once everything is liquidised together, no-one will be any the wiser.

SERVES 4-6

1 onion, chopped
2 garlic cloves, chopped
1 leek, trimmed and sliced
2 tablespoons extra virgin
  olive oil
1 tablespoon cumin seeds
1kg (2¼ lb) carrots, sliced

1 bouquet garni, consisting
  of 2 sprigs of parsley,
  1 large sprig of thyme
  and 1 bay leaf
750ml (1¼ pints) water
600ml (1 pint) milk
salt and pepper

Put the onion, garlic, leek, oil, cumin seeds and carrots into a capacious pan. Throw in the bouquet garni as well. Give them all a quick stir, then cover and place over a low heat. Leave to sweat very gently for 10 minutes, stirring once or twice.

Now add the water, and season with salt and pepper. Bring up to the boil and simmer for 20-30 minutes until all the vegetables are very tender. Draw off the heat and discard the bouquet garni. Add the milk and liquidise the soup in batches. Taste and adjust seasoning, reheat and serve.

Roast Squash and Tomato Soup
with Rouille Croutons ⓥ

This soup is so easy to make – no need for frying or sweating this or that, and adding one thing now and another thing 10 minutes later. No, for this one you just chuck everything into a roasting tin, whip it into the oven and leave it to sort itself out. All you need to do is blend it in the liquidiser once the vegetables are tender.

And what are you going to do with all that liberated time? Knock up a quick rouille of course, that vibrant Provençal chilli- and garlic-flavoured mayo.

SERVES 4-6

1 chunk of winter squash (e.g. onion, red kuri, crown prince or pumpkin), 650-900g (1½-2 lb) de-rinded and deseeded, roughly diced
450g (1 lb) good tomatoes
6 garlic cloves
1 sprig of rosemary
2 sprigs of thyme
1 red onion, cut into 8 wedges
4 tablespoons extra virgin olive oil
1.2 litres (2 pints) *Vegetable Stock* or *Chicken Stock* (see pages 242-3)
salt and pepper

TO SERVE
freshly grated Comté or Gruyère* cheese

ROUILLE
1 small pinch of saffron strands
1 garlic clove, chopped
1 red chilli, seeded and roughly chopped
salt
1 egg yolk
1 tablespoon red wine vinegar
85ml (3 fl oz) sunflower oil
60ml (2 fl oz) extra virgin olive oil

CROUTONS
12 thin slices baguette, or pieces of good-quality bread cut to size
extra virgin olive oil

Preheat the oven to 220°C/425°F/Gas Mark 7. Put all the ingredients for the soup, except the stock, into a roasting tin. Turn with your hands, so that everything is coated in oil. Roast, uncovered, for about 45 minutes, turning occasionally, until everything is very tender. Discard the herb stalks. Scrape the rest into the liquidiser (in two batches if necessary) and liquidise with the stock. Pour into a large pan and adjust the seasoning.

While the vegetables are cooking, make the rouille. Soak the saffron in a tablespoon of warm water to release the colour. Pound the garlic, chilli and a good pinch of salt to a paste in a mortar. Work in the egg yolk and vinegar. Mix the two oils together, then start dripping them into the egg yolk mixture, whisking it constantly. When about one-third of the oil is incorporated, you can increase the flow to a slow but steady trickle. Once the oil is all used up, stir in the saffron. Taste and adjust seasonings, which should be on the punchy side.

To make the croutons, brush the slices of bread with a little oil, and bake until golden, at the same temperature as the vegetables, turning them once – around 5 minutes. Once they are done, pile into a bowl and keep warm.

To serve, reheat the soup and adjust the seasoning. Ladle it into bowls and pass the croûtons, the rouille, and the grated cheese around separately. Everyone helps themselves, floating croûtons smeared liberally with rouille in their bowls of steaming soup, and finishing with a flurry of grated cheese.

Aubergine and Red Pepper Soup Ⓥ

This is a two-in-one soup, a strawberry and slate ripple of a soup, a two-tone soup. The base soup is a mild and gentle aubergine cream, yanked into high gear by the sweeter, hotter red pepper soup swirled into it.

Naturally, if the thought of making two different soups is too much, you can just make one of them all on its own.

SERVES 6

AUBERGINE SOUP
2 tablespoons extra virgin olive oil
1 onion, chopped
2 tablespoons chopped parsley
1 level tablespoon crushed coriander seeds
2 large aubergines, diced
1 carrot, roughly sliced
1 tablespoon risotto or pudding rice
750ml (1¼ pints) *Chicken Stock* or *Vegetable Stock* (see pages 242-3)
salt and pepper

RED PEPPER SOUP
2 tablespoons extra virgin olive oil
2 garlic cloves, chopped
1-2 fresh red chillies, seeded and chopped
2 red peppers, seeded and cut into strips
250g (9 oz) tomatoes, skinned, seeded and roughly chopped
1 tablespoon tomato purée
1 tablespoon caster sugar
salt and pepper
600ml (1 pint) *Chicken Stock* or *Vegetable Stock* (see pages 242-3)

TO SERVE
a handful of basil leaves, shredded

To make the aubergine soup, place the olive oil, onion, parsley, coriander seeds, aubergine, carrot and rice in a saucepan, cover and sweat over a low heat for 15 minutes. Now add the stock and salt and pepper. Bring up to the boil and simmer for 15 minutes until the carrots and rice are tender. Cool slightly and liquidise.

To make the red pepper soup, place the olive oil, garlic, chilli and red pepper in a pan, and sauté until the pepper is very tender. Add the tomatoes, tomato purée, sugar, salt and pepper and cook down for a further 5-10 minutes until very thick. Stir in the stock, bring to the boil, then cool slightly and liquidise.

Reheat both soups in separate pans, then taste and adjust seasonings, remembering that the acidity of the pepper soup will be offset by the mildness of the aubergine. Draw both off the heat. Now divide the aubergine soup between six soup bowls, then add a ladleful of the pepper soup to each one, swirling it in lightly. Sprinkle with basil and serve at once.

Italian Cabbage and Bean Soup ⓥ

On a chilly day, when the sky is grey and the light fading by lunchtime, or so it seems, there is little more restorative than one of the brethren of Mediterranean bean and vegetable soups. This one is so gorged with bits of this and that, that it is enough to stand as a meal in itself, served hot with ciabatta or slices of toast rubbed with garlic and drizzled with olive oil.

These kind of soups invariably improve with keeping. If you have the time, cook the soup up to the point where the cabbage is added the day before eating. Then next day, reheat, adding a little extra water, and when it is boiling tip in the cabbage and finish cooking.

SERVES 4-6

175g (6 oz) dried borlotti or pinto beans, soaked overnight
4 tablespoons extra virgin olive oil
1 onion, chopped
3 garlic cloves, chopped
1 large carrot, diced
1 celery stalk, diced
2 sprigs of thyme
1 sprig of rosemary
1.5 litres (2½ pints) water, *Chicken* or *Vegetable Stock* (see pages 242-3)

350g (12 oz) potatoes, peeled and cut into 2cm (¾ in) cubes
1 x 400g (14 oz) tin chopped tomatoes
2 tablespoons chopped parsley
salt and pepper
about ½ Savoy cabbage, shredded

TO SERVE
freshly grated Parmesan
best extra virgin olive oil

Drain the beans and rinse. Heat the oil in a large, heavy pan and add the onion, garlic, carrot and celery. Sauté until soft and lightly browned. Add the beans, thyme, rosemary and the water or stock. Bring up to the boil, boil hard for 5 minutes, and then simmer until the beans are just cooked and tender, around 40 minutes.

Now add the potatoes, tomatoes, half the parsley and some salt and pepper, and simmer until the potatoes are nearly cooked. Add the shredded cabbage and finish cooking, about 3-5 more minutes. Taste and adjust seasoning, and serve. Pass around the Parmesan and olive oil, so that everyone can flavour their own bowl of soup to their stomach's content.

Double Cheese Omelette with Chives Ⓥ

When you can lay your hands on truly sumptuous eggs, really free-range, really organic, with yolks of a rich, flaunting yellow, then you are lucky indeed. And with good eggs, there is nothing nicer than a well-made omelette. Though I like a plain one well enough, the added touch of cheese is, for me, what turns it into a feast. Serve it with a green salad and home-made bread, or some lightly cooked spinach and new potatoes on the side.

SERVES 2

4 eggs
either 30g (1 oz) top-notch British Cheddar, or 15g (½ oz) Parmesan, freshly grated
2 tablespoons chopped chives

salt and pepper
85g (3 oz) cream cheese
a knob of butter

Beat the eggs with the Cheddar or Parmesan, half the chives, and some salt and pepper. Beat the cream cheese with the remaining chives.

Place a heavy frying pan over a fairly high heat and add the butter. Let it melt and heat through thoroughly. Give the egg mixture one last stir and pour into the pan.

Swirl around to coat the base evenly. Then stand and watch. Don't be tempted to quickly do something else, or your omelette will go to rack and ruin. When the edges have set, run the corner of a fish slice or a palette knife around the edge, loosening it slightly. Lift it up here and there, nudging the set mixture towards the centre, and let the runny egg flow down to fill the gap. Repeat, working your way around, and bursting any bubbles, so that the egg can slip underneath, until the omelette is cooked to the point where just a film of moist egg remains on the surface.

Draw off the heat, spoon the cream cheese down the centre, and fold one side over. Tip and roll out on to a plate, all plump, browned and luscious, then cut in half and eat immediately.

Mayonnaise Ⓥ

I've tried several different brands of organic mayonnaise and so far I've been disappointed. The ingredients lists may read well, but something dire happens by the time it gets into the jar and on to the shop shelf. No two ways about it, home-made organic mayonnaise is infinitely superior, and it's not really that much of a bother to make, either. A bit of patience, a bit of heavy whisking, and suddenly there it will be – a big, resplendent, glinting mound of pale yellow with a magic flavour, ready to go with all kinds of other foods.

MAKES 300ML (10 FL OZ)

2 egg yolks
2 teaspoons Dijon mustard
1-2 tablespoons lemon juice
200ml (7 fl oz) sunflower or
  groundnut oil*

100ml (3 fl oz) extra virgin
  olive oil
coarse salt

Mix the egg yolks, mustard and 1 tablespoon of the lemon juice together well. Mix the two oils in a jug. Now, start whisking the egg yolk mixture, adding the oils in a very, very slow trickle. Keep going, whisking constantly, until about a third of the oil has been incorporated.

At this point you can increase the trickle to a slow, steady stream, still whisking all the time. When all the oil has gone, you can finally rest that wrist, and contemplate the beautiful mass of unctuous, golden mayonnaise in the bowl. Then taste it, and adjust the seasoning, adding more salt or lemon juice as needed. Store, covered, in the fridge if not using immediately.

Aïoli Ⓥ

This is a garlic mayonnaise, but you can't get away with merely stirring some crushed garlic into a bowl of mayonnaise. It's never quite the same as starting from scratch, with the crushed garlic right in there from the very beginning. Try it and see.

Provençal aïoli is one of the Mediterranean's most perfect cold sauces, working its own kind of magic on hot or cold fish and shellfish, as well as grilled foods of all kinds.

MAKES 300ML (10 FL OZ)

2 garlic cloves
coarse salt
2 egg yolks
1 tablespoon Dijon mustard
1-2 tablespoons lemon juice

200ml (7 fl oz) sunflower
  or groundnut oil*
100ml (3 fl oz)
  extra virgin olive oil

Put the garlic into a mortar or sturdy bowl with a pinch of coarse salt, and crush to a paste with a pestle or the end of a rolling pin. You can use a garlic crusher instead, but this gives a slightly bitter edge to the flavour. Add the egg yolks, mustard and 1 tablespoon of the lemon juice and mix them all together well. Mix the two oils in a jug. Now, continue just as for ordinary *Mayonnaise* (see opposite), adding the oils very slowly and whisking constantly. When all the oil is incorporated, taste and adjust flavourings, and then serve.

Twice-baked Cheese Soufflés ⓥ

These have had a bit of a comeback of late and with good reason. They are perfect dinner-party fare, with all the pleasure of a soufflé and none of the angst. They are also extremely rich, launching them a bit beyond the pale of everyday eating. Serve them either as a first course, as long as both the main course and the pudding are light and cream-free, or make them the main element of a meal, as long as you accompany them with plenty of freshly cooked vegetables.

SERVES 6

1 clove
1 slice of onion
1 bay leaf
300ml (10 fl oz) milk
45g (1½ oz) butter, plus extra for greasing
45g (1½ oz) plain flour
150g (5 oz) best Cheddar, grated

1 teaspoon English or Dijon mustard
salt, pepper and freshly grated nutmeg
3 eggs, separated
200ml (7 fl oz) double cream

Preheat the oven to 200°C/400°F/Gas Mark 6. Push the clove into the onion, and place in a pan with the bay leaf and milk. Bring gently up to the boil, then draw off the heat.

Melt the butter and stir in the flour. Keep stirring for about 1 minute without letting it colour. Draw off the heat. Now remove the onion and bay leaf from the milk, then start to add the milk gradually, stirring it in thoroughly between each addition. Return to the heat, stirring constantly, until it is very thick and virtually boiling – just a matter of a few minutes. Draw off the heat and stir in three-quarters of the cheese (reserving the remainder to sprinkle over the soufflés for the final cooking), the mustard, salt, pepper and nutmeg, being generous with the seasonings. Beat in the egg yolks too.

Put the kettle on to boil. Grease six ramekins or teacups very generously, particularly on the base. Whisk the egg whites until stiff, then fold into the cheese sauce. Spoon into the greased ramekins, filling almost to the brim. Stand in a roasting tin and pour in enough boiling water to come about halfway up their sides. Bake in the preheated oven for 15-20 minutes until the mixture is set, springy to the touch, and patched lightly with brown. Leave to cool. When cold run a knife around the edge of each ramekin to loosen the soufflés. Turn them out one by one and place in a greased ovenproof serving dish, lightly browned side up. Cover until ready to finish.

To finish, preheat the oven to 220°C/425°F/Gas Mark 7. Season the cream with salt and pepper, and spoon over the soufflés. Scatter over the reserved cheese. Bake for about 15 minutes, until the cream is bubbling and the tops have browned lightly. Serve immediately.

Glamorgan Sausages
with Plum and Tomato Relish Ⓥ

These sausages contain not a shred of meat. It's cheese and breadcrumbs that form the substance of them, flavoured with a little greenery.

To add an invigorating element to the dish, I like to partner my Glamorgans with a tart, mildly hot, zesty relish made of tomatoes and plums. It's a bright appealing sauce that goes well with cheese dishes, as well as with barbecued meats and oily fish such as herring or mackerel.

I wouldn't advise using all wholemeal breadcrumbs for they make the sausages too heavy and worthy, but if you want to instil a little more fibre et al, then use half white and half wholemeal.

SERVES 2

175-200g (6-7 oz) fresh
   white breadcrumbs
150g (5 oz) Caerphilly
   cheese or Lancashire
   cheese, crumbled or
   grated
½ leek, or 6 spring onions,
   very finely chopped
1 tablespoon chopped
   parsley
½ teaspoon thyme leaves
2 eggs, lightly beaten
1½ teaspoons English
   mustard or Dijon
   mustard
2-3 tablespoons milk
45g (1½ oz) butter
   or 3 tablespoons
   sunflower oil
salt and pepper

PLUM AND TOMATO RELISH
1 small onion, chopped
1 hot red chilli, seeded
   and chopped
½ tablespoon coriander
   seeds, coarsely crushed
1 tablespoon sunflower oil
400g (14 oz) ripe tomatoes,
   skinned, seeded and
   roughly chopped
450g (1 lb) ripe plums,
   quartered and stoned
1-2 tablespoons caster sugar
salt and pepper

Both sausages and relish can be made in advance, in whichever order takes your fancy. I'm going to start with the relish. Fry the onion, chilli and coriander seeds gently in the oil until tender, without browning. Now add the remaining ingredients and simmer for about 20-25 minutes until thick, stirring frequently to prevent browning. Taste – the sauce should be mildly tart and sweet, sort of like a fresh chutney. Leave to cool, and serve either hot or cold.

To make the sausages, put 150g (5 oz) of the breadcrumbs in a bowl with the cheese, leek or spring onion, parsley, thyme and plenty of salt and pepper. Mix well. Beat the eggs with the mustard. Set aside 2 tablespoons of this mixture, and stir the remainder into the crumbs and cheese. If the mixture is still a little dry, add a touch of milk, to help bind it together without making it sloppy.

Divide the mixture into eight and shape each one into a sausage about 2.5cm (1 in) thick. Put the reserved egg and mustard mixture into a shallow bowl, and spread the remaining breadcrumbs out on a plate. One by one, dip the sausages into the egg mixture and then coat in crumbs. If you have time, chill the sausages in the fridge for about half an hour (or more) to firm up.

To fry, just heat the butter or oil in a frying pan and fry the sausages briskly for about 5 minutes until brown, then reduce the heat and cook for a further 3-4 minutes. To grill, drizzle the sausages with a little melted butter or oil, line the grill rack with foil, and then grill the sausages under a preheated grill until well browned on all sides, turning frequently. Serve with the plum and tomato relish.

Griddled Courgette Salad ⓥ

Sometimes I come over all complicated and add lots of bits and bobs to courgette salads, but in the end I nearly always return to the elemental ones, where the true flavour of the vegetable is enhanced by nothing more than a mild smokiness, and lemon and olive oil. It's the best.

SERVES 4

450g (1 lb) small to medium courgettes
5 tablespoons extra virgin olive oil

2 tablespoons lemon juice
2-3 tablespoons roughly chopped parsley or mint
salt and pepper

Split the courgettes in four lengthways if small, or cut into long lengthways slices, about as thick as a £1 coin if larger. Put a lightly oiled griddle pan over a high heat and leave for about 4 minutes to heat through. Lay the courgettes on the mercilessly hot griddle, and turn only when the underneath has developed distinct brown lines from the ridges of the pan. Repeat on the other side.

While the courgettes are cooking, mix the remaining olive oil with the lemon juice and season with pepper and a little salt. Taste and adjust seasoning. As soon as the courgettes are cooked, lay them in a shallow dish and spoon over enough of the dressing to coat nicely. Leave for at least half an hour before serving. Sprinkle with chopped parsley or mint, and the salad is ready to eat.

Apple Slaw Ⓥ

This quick variation on a traditional slaw has been something of a hit within our small clan. It's one of the few ways I can get the children to ingest cabbage with enthusiasm, and we adults enjoy it almost as much. I've played about with the recipe, adding this and that (onion, carrot, nuts and raisins, etc.), but in the end, the simplest version is still the one we like best.

 Although it can hang around for a while, the dressing will become diluted by the juices of the cabbage and apple. Better, if at all possible, to mix it together less than half an hour before eating.

SERVES 6

½ white cabbage
2 apples, quartered and
 cored
2-3 tablespoons thick
 yoghurt

2-3 tablespoons *Mayonnaise*,
 preferably home-made
 (see page 106) but bought
 will do
salt and pepper

Halve the cabbage, discarding the outer layer of leaves, and slice out the thick stem (a delicious morsel, but not suitable for the slaw, so make it the cook's perk). Shred the cabbage finely. Grate the apple coarsely. Mix all the ingredients together, taste and adjust seasoning and serve.

Roast Carrot, Parsnip and Onion Salad
with Parsley and Cinnamon Dressing ⓥ

The natural sweetness of the vegetables, enhanced by the slow roasting in olive oil, meets its match in a lemony dressing touched with a hint of cinnamon and loads of parsley. A great salad served as a side dish, or as a starter, perhaps with a little goat's cheese or feta.

SERVES 4-6

450g (1 lb) small carrots
450g (1 lb) small parsnips
2 onions
3 tablespoons extra virgin olive oil
2 sprigs of thyme
salt and pepper

PARSLEY AND CINNAMON DRESSING
1 teaspoon ground cinnamon
juice of 1 lemon
salt and pepper
4 tablespoons extra virgin olive oil
5 tablespoons chopped parsley

Preheat the oven to 200°C/400°F/Gas Mark 6. Peel the carrots and parsnips and top and tail. If they are on the large side, cut them in two, then halve, or quarter lengthways, and remove the woody core of the parsnips. Cut each onion into eight wedges. Put all the vegetables into a roasting tin and pour over the olive oil. Season with salt and pepper, add the sprigs of thyme, then turn with your hands so that all the vegetables are well coated in oil. Spread out as evenly as you can and then roast, uncovered, for about 55-60 minutes, until very tender. Turn the vegetables a couple of times as they cook.

Meanwhile, make the dressing. Whisk the cinnamon with the lemon juice, a touch of salt and pepper, oil and parsley. As soon as the vegetables are done, discard the thyme stalks. Tip out into a bowl, scraping in all the cooking juices, and toss with the dressing. Leave to cool, then serve at room temperature.

Grilled Aubergine, Red Pepper and Red Onion Salad

There's no getting around it: grilled vegetable salads are fabulous. Well, they are as long as the vegetables have been grilled to ample tenderness, aubergine especially. This has become one of my very favourites, with its South-East-Asian-style cumin, coriander and chilli dressing.

The great advantage of serving a salad like this as a starter is that it benefits from being made a few hours in advance, or even the day before. The disadvantage is that it always takes more time than you imagine to prepare and cook all the vegetables. Still, it's absolutely worth it.

Some people may appreciate a hunk of warm crusty bread to eat with the salad, though personally I'd be quite happy without.

SERVES 8

2 large aubergines
salt
3 red peppers
3 red onions
extra virgin olive oil
30g (1 oz) sunflower seeds, toasted

CUMIN, CORIANDER
AND CHILLI DRESSING
1 tablespoon cumin seeds
2 red chillies, seeded and roughly chopped

1 garlic clove, crushed or very, very finely chopped
1 tablespoon light muscovado sugar or palm sugar*
juice of 2 limes
2 tablespoons fish sauce (nam pla)*
4 tablespoons roughly chopped coriander leaves

If you have the time, then it really is worth salting the aubergines to expel that slightly tinny taste that they sometimes have – just slice them into rounds, about 1cm (½ in) thick and lay them on trays. Sprinkle lightly with salt and leave for an hour. Rinse or wipe clean.

To make the dressing, dry-fry the cumin seeds over a moderate heat until they turn a shade darker and smell enticing and exotic. Tip into a bowl and leave to cool, then place in the mortar with the chilli, garlic and sugar. Pound until you have a knobbly paste. Gradually work in the lime juice and the fish sauce, then stir in 3 tablespoons water. Stir in the coriander and it's ready to use.

Preheat the grill thoroughly. While the aubergines are salting, grill the peppers and onions. Grill the peppers whole, close to the heat, turning frequently, until the skin is blackened and blistered all over. When they are done slip them into a plastic bag, knot loosely and leave until cool enough to handle. Then strip off the skins, and pull out the stem which will come away with most of the seeds attached. Tip any juice trapped inside (or left behind in the bag) into a bowl so that it is not wasted. Cut the peppers into eighths.

To grill the onions, peel and slice into discs just over 5mm (¼ in) thick. Push a wooden cocktail stick through each one, like the handle of a lollipop, to keep the rings more or less together and make turning easier. Brush the onions with oil and grill close to the grill until well browned on each side. Remove the cocktail sticks and add the onions to the peppers. Now brush the aubergine slices lightly with oil and grill on both sides until tender and mottled with brown. Add these to the other grilled vegetables and sprinkle with sunflower seeds.

Toss the vegetables in the dressing. Leave at room temperature for a couple of hours or more if time allows. Turn again and then serve with or without good bread.

Green Bean and Bacon Salad

This salad is a long-time favourite of mine; the natural sweetness of the beans is perfectly enhanced by the salty flavour of the bacon.

SERVES 4

450g (1 lb) green beans, topped and tailed
salt
4 rashers streaky bacon
2 tablespoons chopped parsley

DRESSING
1 garlic clove, crushed
½ tablespoon white wine vinegar
1 teaspoon Worcestershire sauce*
3 tablespoons extra virgin olive oil
salt and pepper

To make the dressing, whisk the crushed garlic with the vinegar and Worcestershire sauce. Gradually beat in the oil and season to taste.

Cut the beans in half. Drop into a pan of boiling salted water and simmer for about 3 minutes, or until just tender but retaining a slight crunch. Drain thoroughly and mix with enough of the dressing to coat well. Grill the rashers of bacon until browned then cut into small strips. Toss with the green beans and the parsley. Taste and adjust the seasoning, adding a little extra Worcestershire sauce if you fancy a touch more.

Lentil and Red Pepper Salad Ⓥ

This earthy slate-grey salad with streaks of red snaking through it is good enough to eat on its own (perhaps with the extra addition of a few slices of goat's cheese), but makes a happy component of a whole collection of salads, perhaps for a buffet lunch.

SERVES 6-8

225g (8 oz) Puy lentils, or other small, dark lentils
1 bouquet garni, consisting of 2 sprigs of parsley, 1 large sprig of thyme and 1 bay leaf
1 onion, quartered
1 garlic clove, peeled
2 red peppers, grilled, skinned and seeded (see page 116-7), cut into strips
2 tablespoons chopped parsley

DRESSING
1½ tablespoons red wine vinegar
½ teaspoon Dijon mustard
4 tablespoons extra virgin olive oil
salt and pepper

Put the lentils into a saucepan with the bouquet garni, the quartered onion and the garlic, but no salt. Add water to cover by about 5cm (2 in). Bring up to the boil, then reduce the heat and simmer gently for 15-30 minutes (depending on the age of the lentils) until they are tender, but not yet so soft that they are inclined to collapse. Drain thoroughly, and discard the bouquet garni, onion and garlic.

Meanwhile, make the dressing. Whisk the vinegar with the mustard and salt and pepper, then whisk in the oil a tablespoon at a time. Taste and adjust seasoning, which should be on the hefty side, to counteract the mealiness of the lentils. Toss the lentils and red peppers in all of the dressing then leave to cool. Stir in the parsley and serve.

Salad of Jersey Royals, Cherry Tomatoes and Fresh Peas or Broad Beans
with Mint Dressing Ⓥ

This salad celebrates all that is most joyful about spring food in this country: the exquisite taste of Jersey Royals, the first hint of fresh peas or broad beans, and the freshness of mint. Even if you have to use frozen peas or beans, it still tastes glorious. I first served it for William's forty-fifth birthday luncheon, to accompany a whole roast turbot. And that is about as good as it gets.

SERVES 8

1kg (2¼ lb) Jersey Royals, halved if large, scraped, then steamed or boiled
250g (9 oz) cherry tomatoes, halved
380g (13 oz) shelled fresh peas (or broad beans, but see below), or frozen peas, lightly cooked

MINT DRESSING
a generous handful of fresh mint leaves – about 30g (1 oz)
240ml (8 fl oz) extra virgin olive oil
3-4 tablespoons white wine vinegar or lemon juice
½ tablespoon caster sugar
salt and pepper

To make the dressing put the mint leaves into a liquidiser with all the remaining ingredients. Liquidise until smooth. Taste and adjust seasoning.

Toss the vegetables in the dressing while the potatoes and peas are still warm from cooking. Leave to cool and serve with good bread as a starter, or with barbecued chicken or seared salmon or other plainly cooked fish.

Note: If you use broad beans, blanch in boiling water for a minute, or thaw if frozen, then use a small knife to slit open the tough grey-green skin, and pop out the delicious bright green beanlet that's hiding inside. Finish cooking for a few minutes in boiling salted water.

Cianfotta
(Pepper, Aubergine and Potato Stew) ⓥ

This light vegetable stew comes from the Amalfi coast, where it is made with the gorgeous, twisting, irregular, wildly curvaceous peppers of mixed hues that have such a superb flavour. Here organic peppers tend to be closer in flavour to those southern ones than the dismayingly uniform box-shaped sweet peppers that are to be found in most supermarkets and greengrocers. Combined with aubergine, tomatoes (not too many – they should not predominate) and potatoes, they make a substantial vegetable stew that can be served as a side dish, or a main course, with a nice hunk of warm crusty olive oil bread and perhaps a few shavings of Parmesan if you fancy.

SERVES 3-4

3 tablespoons extra virgin olive oil
2 garlic cloves, chopped
1 large onion, chopped
150g (5 oz) ripe tomatoes, skinned and seeded
500g (18 oz) mixed yellow and red peppers (around 2-3 peppers), seeded and cut into strips
1 large aubergine, cut into 2.5cm (1 in) cubes
400g (14 oz) potatoes, peeled and cut into 2.5cm (1 in) cubes
¼ teaspoon caster sugar
salt and pepper
a handful of basil leaves
1 teaspoon dried oregano

Warm the olive oil and add the garlic and onion. Cook gently until the onion is tender, then add the tomatoes. Stir well, then add all the vegetables and the sugar. Season with salt and pepper, then stir. Cover and cook over a low heat for 30-40 minutes until all the vegetables are tender, but not totally collapsing, adding a little water if necessary, though the vegetables should produce enough all on their own. Taste and adjust seasoning, then stir in the basil and oregano. Serve hot or at room temperature.

William's Savoy Cabbage
with Yoghurt and Black Pepper ⓥ

William has a bit of a thing about Greek-style yoghurt. It's a necessity as far as he's concerned, and if there's none in the fridge, he feels bereft. As well as eating it with honey, sliced banana, and/or nuts for pudding, he throws it with gay abandon into pasta and, probably best of all, he makes this dish of tender-leaved Savoy cabbage, enriched with yoghurt and a little Parmesan. It can be made in an instant or two, and is marvellous with fish or meat. I rather like it just on its own, with a slice of bread.

SERVES 2-3

½ large Savoy cabbage
salt
6 tablespoons Greek-style
  yoghurt

lots and lots of freshly
  ground black pepper
15g (½ oz) Parmesan, freshly
  grated

Discard the outer leaves of the cabbage, or save to add to a vegetable stock. Halve the hunk of cabbage, and cut out the tough central stem. Cut the cabbage into strips about as wide as your middle finger. Put about 3cm (1¼ in) of water in a large pan, season with salt and bring up to the boil. Add the cabbage, cover and simmer, shaking the pan frequently, and turning the cabbage regularly, until it is just tender, a matter of some 3-5 minutes. Drain it thoroughly, pressing out excess water.

Return to the pan, and shake over a moderate heat for 30 seconds or so to dry out any lingering moisture, then stir in the yoghurt, oodles of freshly ground black pepper, Parmesan, and salt if needed. Let it heat through gently but briefly, without overheating, then taste and adjust seasonings. Serve hot or warm.

Stir-fried Beetroot Greens
with Plum Sauce

The organic beetroot I've been buying recently comes in gorgeous, healthy-looking come-hither bunches, complete with abundant glossy green leaves (a sign of freshness for they soon start to wilt) and roots, which is just how I like it best. The leaves are edible, so it seems a shame to waste them. They can be cooked like spinach, or the greens of Swiss chard, but have an earthier taste. William and I love it, though it may be too strong for some tastes (his mother is a case in point!). The salt of good dry-cured bacon and the fruity tartness of plums sets it off to great advantage.

If your beetroot come shorn of their leaves, bad luck, but you can try this with the green leafy part of Swiss chard, which has a similar consistency.

SERVES 3-4

200g (7 oz) fresh beetroot
   greens
1 tablespoon soy sauce
1 tablespoon caster sugar
1 tablespoon sunflower oil
2 garlic cloves, chopped
2cm (¾ in) piece of fresh
   root ginger, chopped

85g (3 oz) back or streaky
   bacon, rinded and cut
   into strips
250g (9 oz) plums, stoned
   and roughly chopped
plenty of freshly ground
   pepper

Pile the leaves up in bundles, roll up tightly and cut into ribbons about 2cm (¾ in) thick. Mix the soy sauce with the sugar, stirring until the sugar has more or less dissolved.

Arrange all the ingredients, fully prepared, around the hob. Place a wok over a high heat and leave until smoking. Now add the oil, swirl around for a few seconds to heat through, then throw in the garlic, ginger and bacon. Stir-fry for about 1 minute or so, until the bacon is beginning to colour. Now add the beetroot greens, and stir-fry for about 2 minutes until beginning to turn limp. Then in go the plums, the sugar and soy sauce mixture and plenty of pepper. Stir-fry for a final 2 minutes or so, until the plums have collapsed down to form a sauce clinging to the greens. Taste, adjust the seasoning and serve.

Beetroot with Potato Skordalia ⓥ

This is a dish that I came across recently in Crete, and then only a month or so later in Hoxton in East London, at The Real Greek, a restaurant which showcases the best of Greek products and dishes as they have never been seen before in this country. What fascinated me was that the skordalia, the garlic sauce, was made in both cases with potato, rather than bread and almonds. The result, when the cook is generous with the oil, is a rich sauce something akin to Provençal aïoli, but with the comforting grain and flavour of potato.

SERVES 6-8, AS A STARTER OR SIDE DISH

1kg (2¼ lb) raw beetroot
1½ tablespoons red wine
  vinegar
4 tablespoons extra virgin
  olive oil
salt and pepper
a little chopped parsley or
  dill

POTATO SKORDALIA
5 garlic cloves
salt
2 baking potatoes
1-2 teaspoons red or white
  wine vinegar
150ml (5 fl oz) extra virgin
  olive oil

Trim the leaves from the beetroot, leaving 2.5cm (1 in) of stem. Do not cut off any roots. Wash, then wrap each beetroot in foil. Bake at 160-170°C/325°F/Gas Mark 3 for about 2 hours, until the skin scrapes away easily. Bake the potatoes at the same time.

Meanwhile, beat the vinegar with the olive oil, salt and pepper to make a dressing. Skin the beetroot, then either quarter or cut into eight wedges, if on the large side. Toss in the dressing while still warm then leave to cool to room temperature.

To make the skordalia, pound the garlic to a paste with a good pinch or two of salt. Halve the baked potatoes while still warm and scoop out 150g (5 oz) potato flesh into a moderately large bowl. Add the garlic, together with the vinegar. Start beating with an electric beater, or if you don't have one, work the mixture first with a fork, and then start whisking with a strong balloon whisk. Start trickling in the oil, rather as if you were making mayonnaise, though you don't have to be quite as cautious, beating or whisking continuously. By the time it is all in, you should have a light, fluffy mayonnaise-like mixture.

To serve, either pile the skordalia and the beetroot into separate bowls, and let people help themselves, or make a thick bed of the skordalia on a serving dish and pile the beetroot on top. Either way, sprinkle with parsley or dill before serving.

Gratin Dauphinoise ⓥ

This lies somewhere up on high with the brethren of utterly divine potato dishes, the kind that you may not crave every day, but that knock you for six on those occasions when you do tug them down to your table. There is little to beat it, what with all those melting slices of potato baked slowly in a pool of cream to utter, unabashed tenderness.

SERVES 4-6

15g (½ oz) butter
1 tablespoon plain flour
600ml (1 pint) single cream
1kg (2¼ lb) main-crop
   potatoes, peeled and
   thinly sliced

1 large onion, halved and
   thinly sliced
2 garlic cloves, finely
   chopped
salt, pepper and
   freshly grated nutmeg

Preheat the oven to 170°C/325°F/Gas Mark 3. Grease an ovenproof gratin dish thickly with the butter. Mix the flour with a little of the cream to a smooth paste, then stir back into the cream. Now build up layers of potato, onion and garlic, finishing with a layer of potato and seasoning between layers with salt, pepper and nutmeg. About halfway through, pour over enough of the cream to come up to the level of the potatoes. When the potatoes are all in the dish, pour over the remaining cream (it should come up to the top layer of potatoes, but if necessary add a little extra), season again, and then bake uncovered for about 1½ hours, until the potatoes are tender all the way through, and the top is brown. Serve hot or warm.

New Potato and Mascarpone Mash Ⓥ

Rougher and chunkier than an ordinary mash, the combination of the waxy, earthy flavours of new potatoes and the smooth slightly sweet creaminess of mascarpone makes for a rich and irresistible sort of a mash, the kind of thing that shouldn't be eclipsed by an incredibly fancy main dish. Keep it simple, and let the side dish hog its fair share of the limelight.

SERVES 3-4

675g (1½ lb) new potatoes,
 or waxy salad potatoes
salt
30g (1 oz) butter

85g-110g (3-4 oz)
 mascarpone
salt, pepper and
 freshly grated nutmeg

Scrub the new potatoes if necessary. Boil the potatoes in salted water until tender, then drain and strip off as much of the skin as you can bear to (the odd bit left in is fine, if your patience is running out). Tip the potatoes into a heavy saucepan and add the butter. Mash with a potato masher over a low heat, stirring frequently, until you have a rough, chunky mash. Add the mascarpone (the lower quantity is enough, the larger superbly rich), and season with salt, pepper and nutmeg. Stir for a minute or two longer until piping hot, then serve at once.

Lemon and Grain Mustard Mash ⓥ

This dolled-up mash is quite different to the preceding one. The freshness of the lemon zest makes it particularly suited to serving with fish, while the mustard gives it a pleasing lift without making it noticeably ferocious.

SERVES 3-4

1kg (2¼ lb) potatoes
30g (1 oz) butter
salt
150-300ml (5-10 fl oz) hot
   milk

finely grated zest of
   1 lemon
2 tablespoons coarse-
   grained mustard

Either bake the potatoes until tender or microwave them. Don't boil them – they get soggy and produce a damp, watery mash that will need to be dried out, which is a tedious process. Scoop out the flesh into a saucepan and add the butter. Mash them together thoroughly, and season with salt.

Place the pan over a low heat and gradually beat in enough milk to give the kind of consistency that you like. Add the lemon zest and mustard and beat in well. Taste, adjust the seasoning and serve.

Rocket Mash ⓥ

This is, I suppose, what one might call a designer version of those Irish classics, colcannon and champ. Well, designer maybe, but it tastes darned good for all that. It works well with all kinds of main courses from vegetable burgers to juicy steaks, including dishes made largely with cheese, stews, and grilled fish or chicken.

Note: If you would rather stick to something more classic, replace the rocket with a bunch of spring onions, finely chopped and softened briefly in butter.

SERVES 4

1kg (2¼ lb) potatoes
30-45g (1-1½ oz) butter
salt and freshly grated
    nutmeg

150-300ml (5-10 fl oz) hot
    milk
30g (1 oz) rocket, roughly
    chopped

Either bake the potatoes until tender, or microwave them. Don't boil them – they get soggy and produce a damp, watery mash that will need to be dried out, which is a tedious process. Scoop the flesh out into a saucepan and add 30g (1 oz) of the butter. Mash them together thoroughly and season with salt and a touch of nutmeg.

Place the pan over a low heat and gradually beat in enough milk to give the kind of consistency that pleases you. When it is just right and piping hot, draw off the heat and stir in the rocket. Taste again and adjust the seasoning. Pile up in a mound in a warm bowl and make a dip in the top with the back of a spoon. Place the remaining butter in the dip and then serve with the molten butter oozing down the sides in a provocative fashion.

Chips Ⓥ

Chips are not something I make regularly, but when I do turn my hand to them, everyone seems to be delighted. Make them an occasional home-made pleasure and you'll enjoy them all the more.

SERVES 3-4

3 large floury potatoes
salt

sunflower oil or other fat
for deep-frying

Peel the potatoes and cut into slices about 1cm (½ in) thick. Cut lengthways into batons of the same thickness. Cover with cold water to prevent browning, until ready to start the cooking.

Set the oil to heat to 150°C/300°F. Drain the potato thoroughly and pat dry assiduously on kitchen paper or clean tea-towels. Deep-fry in several batches so that the temperature of the oil is not lowered too much, allowing them to cook for about 4 minutes, without browning, until tender. Drain thoroughly on kitchen paper and leave to cool. Just before eating, reheat the oil, this time to 180°C/350°F. Fry the chips again, in batches, until golden brown.

And now a great tip from my friend Annabel's mum. If you have any brown paper bags, tip the chips into them as soon as they are cooked, then add salt, fold over the top and shake – the bag absorbs excess fat and the salt gets evenly distributed. Brown paper bags are not so easily found these days, so the alternative is to drain the chips briefly on kitchen paper and then sprinkle with salt. Either way, serve piping hot.

Tomatoes to the Fore ⓥ
Three related but individual ways with tomatoes

Roasted tomatoes, sun-dried tomatoes and the so-called 'sun-blush' or semi-dried tomatoes all have one thing in common: by one means or another, they are dehydrated to a greater or lesser degree, so that their flavour is concentrated and semi-caramelised to a wonderful, rich, sweet-sharp intensity. Straightforward roasted tomatoes are amongst my all-time favourite accompaniments to a myriad of foods from fish to steak, couscous to chicken, lentils to lamb. And they are superb tossed into pasta with garlic and olive oil, fresh basil and plenty of Parmesan. A real treat.

Organic sun-dried tomatoes are relatively new and very welcome. So far, I've only seen them sold dry in packets, ready to be rehydrated gently to add their rich flavour to salads, sandwiches, breads, stews, sauces and wherever you might relish their savour (which, incidentally, makes them an interesting substitute for bacon in otherwise meatless dishes).

Sliding in somewhere between the two are 'sun-blush' tomatoes, more fleshy and juicy than fully dried, but fuller flavoured and a little chewier than roast. Again, fab for salads and sauces, stews or sandwiches, and as part of an antipasti with salamis, cured hams, cheeses and good bread.

1. Roast Tomatoes

Once hooked on the joys of roast tomatoes, this will become second nature, which is why I give only a method, rather than a precise recipe. Preheat the oven to 220°C/425°F/Gas Mark 7. Halve the tomatoes – lengthways for plum tomatoes, horizontally for round ones – and arrange cut side up in an ovenproof dish that has been generously anointed with extra virgin olive oil. Tuck a small handful of unpeeled garlic cloves in amongst them, and then slip in a couple of sprigs of thyme, and/or a sprig of rosemary. Season with coarse salt, plenty of freshly ground pepper and a light sprinkling of sugar (unless your tomatoes are brilliantly, perfectly sweet). Drizzle over a little more extra virgin olive oil, then roast, uncovered for 40-45 minutes, until sizzling and soft, and touched with brown here and there. Serve hot or warm.

2. Sun-dried Tomatoes in Oil

Organic sun-dried tomatoes are with us, and very good they can be too, but if the only supplies you can lay your hands on are totally dried and leathery with not a drop of mollifying oil in sight, this is how to transform them into ready-to-use, semi-soft aromatic sun-dried tomatoes in olive oil.

First spread your tomatoes out in a shallow dish. Pour over boiling water, and leave them for anything between 4-5 minutes and 20 minutes, testing them every now and then to see if they are sufficiently softened. Don't leave them too long – you want them to retain a slight chewiness and not to soften to a slimy mush.

Now drain the tomatoes and pat them dry on kitchen paper or in a clean tea-towel. Start packing them into a scrupulously clean glass jar, tucking peeled cloves of garlic, coriander seeds, sprigs of thyme and rosemary, and/or the odd dried chilli in amongst them, and covering each layer with extra virgin olive oil as you fill the jar. Make sure that the final layer is submerged in olive oil. If the tomatoes keep bobbing up, try cutting two wooden cocktail sticks, or a fine wooden skewer, so that they are marginally longer than the diameter of the opening. Push the first one down under the rim of the jar, and do the same to the second, at right angles, so that they form a cross which holds the sun-dried tomatoes down.

Put the jar away in a cool, dark place for a few days before sampling.

3. 'Sun-blush' or Oven-dried Tomatoes

Of course, if you have sufficient sun, this is something you can do gently outdoors, but let's assume that the sun is not in constant, strong supply. Instead, you must replace it with the more consistently reliable oven, set to a caressingly gentle 170°C/325°F/Gas Mark 3. Halve your tomatoes and seed them. Season the cut sides with salt and turn upside down on a rack to drain for half an hour.

Line a baking tray (or several if you are laying down copious stocks) with non-stick baking parchment. Arrange the tomatoes, cut sides up, on the trays and bake for about 1-2 hours until dehydrated to just the perfect degree for your taste. Check regularly towards the latter part of the cooking time, to ensure that they do not over-dehydrate.

If you are not intending to use them that very day, preserve them in olive oil in exactly the same way as rehydrated sun-dried tomatoes (see above).

Spiced Parsnip and Cashew Nut Gratin Ⓥ

Cumin, mustard and anise-scented fennel seeds bring a touch of the exotic to an otherwise straightforward parsnip gratin, with a light, crisp breadcrumb finish.

**SERVES 2-3 AS A MAIN COURSE,
4 AS AN ACCOMPANIMENT**

675g (1½ lb) parsnips
salt
45g (1½ oz) butter
1 tablespoon sunflower oil
1 onion, chopped
2 teaspoons cumin seeds
1 teaspoon mustard seeds

1 teaspoon fennel seeds
85g (3 oz) shelled cashew nuts
2 tablespoons fresh breadcrumbs
1 tablespoon finely grated Parmesan

Peel and core the parsnips and slice thickly. Cook in boiling salted water for about 7-10 minutes until just cooked through. Arrange in a snug, lightly greased ovenproof dish. Preheat the grill.

Set aside about a third of the butter. Heat the oil with the remaining butter over a moderate heat. Add the onion and cook until tender. Now add the cumin, mustard and fennel seeds and the cashew nuts. Sauté until the mustard seeds begin to pop and jump. Spoon over the parsnips. Mix the breadcrumbs and Parmesan and sprinkle lightly over the top. Dot with the remaining butter and whizz under the grill until lightly browned.

If you prefer, the gratin can be prepared in advance, without actually grilling. Then reheat and brown in the oven, set to about 200°C/400°F/Gas Mark 6, for around 30 minutes.

Petits Pois à la Française ⓥ

This old-fashioned way of cooking peas deserves a big comeback. The sweetness of the lettuce and herbs permeates the peas, which are semi-steamed in the juices. When you have fresh peas to hand, this is probably the best way of all to cook them.

SERVES 4

280g (10 oz) shelled fresh peas
1 small lettuce, shredded
8 spring onions, chopped
salt and pepper

2 parsley stalks
2 sprigs of mint
30g (1 oz) butter
100ml (4 fl oz) water

Mix the peas with the lettuce and onions in a saucepan, seasoning with salt and pepper. Tie the herbs together with a piece of string and bury them in the peas. Dot with butter, and pour in the water. Take a sheet of greaseproof paper, fold in half, then lay it over the top of the saucepan. Press the lid down firmly, to make a tight seal. Cook over a moderate heat for 15-20 minutes, until the peas are very tender. Discard the bouquet garni, then taste, adjust the seasoning and serve.

Stir-fried Mangetouts, Chinese Leaf and Radishes Ⓥ

Stir-frying is one of the ideal ways of cooking vegetables, preserving a freshness of flavour married with that particular tender-crisp texture. Here a combination of mangetouts, rosy radishes and Chinese leaf are flavoured with ginger and oyster sauce. Note that if there is a vegetarian or two lurking amongst the gathering, the addition of some stir-fried tofu to a generous portion of these vegetables will create a good main course, providing of course, that you either use one of the vegetarian versions of oyster sauce (yes, they really do exist though not, to my knowledge, in organic guise) or maybe substitute a few spoonfuls of ready-made black bean sauce.

SERVES 4

1½ tablespoons sunflower oil
2.5cm (1 in) piece of root ginger, finely chopped
2 garlic cloves, chopped
150g (5 oz) mangetouts
150g (5 oz) red radishes, halved lengthways
½ Chinese leaf, thickly shredded
1-2 tablespoons oyster sauce*
pepper

Place a wok over a high heat until smoking. Add the oil and allow to heat through for a few seconds. Now add the ginger and garlic, and stir-fry for about 20 seconds. Next pile in the mangetouts and radishes. Stir-fry for 1 minute then add the Chinese leaf. Stir-fry for 2 further minutes until all the vegetables are soft at the edges but retain a degree of crispness at heart. Stir in the oyster sauce and season with pepper. Taste and adjust the seasoning, adding a slurp more sauce if it needs it, then tip into a warm serving dish. Once done and in the bowl, don't keep them hanging around. Present to the table straightaway.

Baked Vegetable Rice ⓥ

I just love baked rice with lots and lots of vegetables in it. It's such a good, effortless way to cook up an all-in-one main course (or side dish if you prefer) that is very satisfying. Of course, you don't have to stick with the same selection of vegetables as I have listed here – once you've tried it, then you can start playing around with what goes into it. For a non-vegetarian version, try adding shreds of cooked chicken or turkey, or maybe sautéing some bacon or pancetta with the vegetables.

SERVES 4

3 tablespoons olive oil
4 shallots, cut into quarters or eighths, depending on size
1 carrot, diced
1 head of fennel, trimmed and diced
3 garlic cloves, sliced
150g (5 oz) shelled peas, fresh or frozen and thawed
2 tomatoes, seeded and diced

400g (14 oz) basmati rice, rinsed
1 litre (1¾ pints) *Vegetable Stock*, or *Chicken Stock* if not for vegetarians (see pages 242-3)
1 good pinch of saffron threads
salt and pepper

Preheat the oven to 200°C/400°F/Gas Mark 6. Heat the olive oil in a wide frying pan over a high heat. Add the shallots, carrot and fennel and sauté until they are beginning to catch at the edges. Add the garlic and sauté for another 1-2 minutes. Draw off the heat and mix with all the remaining ingredients in a shallow ovenproof dish. Use one that is about 30 cm x 20 cm (12 in x 8 in). Cover with foil and bake for 40-45 minutes until the rice is tender and has absorbed all the liquid. Taste, adjust seasoning and serve.

Fennel Pissaladière

Towards the end of a recent trip to Provence, we ate a last lunch in the courtyard of a small restaurant in Vence. The main course was a magnificent edifice of crisply fried sardine fillets, fennel, peppers and other vegetables, atop a pissaladière made not of onions, as is customary, but of thinly sliced fennel. The mild hint of aniseed against the dough was superb and easy to reproduce back at home. Here is my version of that fennel pissaladière.

SERVES 8 AS A MAIN COURSE, 16 AS A STARTER

DOUGH
310g (11 oz) strong white bread flour
1 sachet easy-blend yeast*
1 teaspoon salt
1 tablespoon extra virgin olive oil, plus a little extra for greasing

FILLING
2 large or 3 small heads of fennel, about 600g (1 lb 5oz) in all, trimmed and very thinly sliced
1 onion, halved and thinly sliced
1 sprig of thyme
2 tablespoons extra virgin olive oil
5 tinned anchovy fillets, chopped Ⓦ
16 black olives
salt and pepper

For the dough, mix the flour, yeast and salt in a large bowl, and make a well in the centre. Add the olive oil, then enough water to make a stiff, but very slightly sticky, dough. Knead vigorously, dusting lightly with flour at first, until you have a very elastic, smooth dough – some 5-10 minutes. Cover with a damp tea-towel and leave until doubled in bulk – about 1 hour, depending on the warmth of the room.

Meanwhile, make the filling. Put the sliced fennel and onion into a large saucepan with the thyme and olive oil. Cover and cook very gently for about 50-60 minutes, stirring occasionally, until both are meltingly tender. Uncover and continue to cook over a higher heat, until most of the liquid has evaporated off. Add the anchovies, stir and cook for a final couple of minutes, stirring frequently. Remove the thyme stalk, then taste and adjust the seasoning – the mixture should be sweet, savoury and mildly aniseedy all at once.

Preheat the oven to 200°C/400°F/Gas Mark 6. Roll the dough out to form a rectangle, then lay it on an oiled 23 x 32cm (9 x 13 in) baking sheet, and tease it out firmly to the edges. Don't despair – it will shrink back on you repeatedly, but if you persevere you will get there in the end. Spread the fennel and onion mixture over the dough, leaving a narrow border of bare dough around the edge. Dot with olives. Bake for 30-40 minutes until the edges of the fennel and onion mixture are browned here and there. Cut into wedges or squares and serve warm or cold.

Dry Cauliflower, Cashew Nut and Potato Curry Ⓥ

This 'dry' vegetable curry is actually rather moist, but comes with no sauce – all of the cooking liquid and the flavourings it carries are absorbed by the vegetables, or at least that is the theory. Serve it with naan bread, or home-made *Pitta Bread* (see page 223) and a simple raita, such as the one on page 239.

You will end up with more garam masala than you need for this recipe, but the remainder can be stored in an airtight jar for several weeks and used to spice up all kinds of things from baked potatoes and plainly cooked veg, to grilled fish or more complicated curries.

SERVES 4

1 large onion, roughly chopped
2.5cm (1 in) piece of fresh root ginger, finely chopped
3 garlic cloves, finely chopped
1-2 dried red chillies, seeded and chopped
1 teaspoon ground turmeric
1 tablespoon ground cumin
salt
3 tablespoons sunflower oil
450g (1 lb) potatoes, peeled and cut into 2.5cm (1 in) cubes
½ cauliflower, cut or broken into small florets

1 tablespoon lemon juice
100g (3½ oz) shelled cashew nuts
3 tablespoons roughly chopped coriander leaves

GARAM MASALA
1 tablespoon cumin seeds
1 tablespoon coriander seeds
1 teaspoon fennel seeds
1 teaspoon black peppercorns
4 green cardamom pods
2 dried bay leaves, crumbled
1 teaspoon ground cinnamon

Put the onion, ginger, garlic, chilli, turmeric, cumin and a level teaspoon salt into the processor with 2 tablespoons of water, and process to a paste. If you do not have a processor, or yours will not handle small quantities, grate the onion and chop the ginger, garlic, and chillies as finely as you can. Mix together with the ground spices and a level teaspoon salt. Don't worry about the water.

Heat 2 tablespoons of the oil in a wide heavy pan. When hot, add the paste and then fry, stirring constantly, for about 3 minutes. Next add the potato and cauliflower to the pan, and stir so that they are coated in the spice paste. Pour in 100ml (4 fl oz) water and the lemon juice, then bring up to the boil. Reduce the heat to low, cover and cook gently for about 10-15 minutes, until the vegetables are tender but not collapsing, stirring once or twice.

Meanwhile, sauté the cashew nuts until lightly browned in the remaining oil.

To make the garam masala, dry-fry all the whole spices together in a heavy pan over a moderate heat until they smell thrillingly aromatic. Cool slightly, mix with the bay leaf and the cinnamon, then grind to a powder. Reserve.

Check the water levels when the vegetables are nearly done. If there is still a noticeable amount left, take off the lid and let most of it boil away. Now stir in the cashew nuts, and cook for a further minute or so. Taste for seasoning. Sprinkle with a teaspoon of garam masala and the coriander, and serve at once.

Courgette and Comté Tart Ⓥ

You might be inclined to think that a combination of courgette and rice baked in a pastry case would be a trifle insipid, but you would be wrong. Sweating the courgettes brings out the best in them, while a taste of Parmesan in the crust, and Comté (a fine French cheese, the organic version is sold in good cheese shops and some of the better supermarkets) or perhaps Cacciocavallo (an excellent Italian cheese, now also available in organic form in good cheese shops) in with the courgettes adds more zip and zest. If you can't lay your hands on Comté or Cacciocavallo, use a sweetish, not too strong cheese instead, such as Gruyère. I haven't yet found an organic Gruyère, which is a great shame, but there is a fantastic unpasteurised version which is well worth searching out.

SERVES 6

PASTRY
225g (8 oz) plain flour
¼ teaspoon salt
60g (2 oz) butter
45g (1½ oz) Parmesan, freshly grated
2 tablespoons extra virgin olive oil
1 egg

FILLING
2 shallots, chopped
1 garlic clove, chopped
1 tablespoon extra virgin olive oil

400g (14 oz) courgettes, sliced
110g (4 oz) cooked long-grain white or brown rice
1 tablespoon chopped tarragon
2 eggs
5 tablespoons single cream
85g (3 oz) Comté, Cacciocavallo or Gruyère* cheese, finely diced
1½ tablespoons freshly grated Parmesan
salt and pepper

To make the pastry, begin by sifting the flour with the salt. Rub in the butter, stir in the Parmesan and then make a well in the centre. Add the oil and the egg. Mix to a soft dough, adding a splash of ice-cold water if absolutely necessary. Wrap in clingfilm and rest in the fridge for half an hour. Roll out and line a 23cm (9 in) deep tart tin. Prick the base all over with a fork then chill in the fridge for half an hour before baking.

Preheat the oven to 180°C/350°F/Gas Mark 4. Line the pastry case with foil or greaseproof paper, weight down with baking beans and bake blind for 20 minutes. Remove the beans and foil or paper and return to the oven for a further 5-10 minutes until dried out and just beginning to colour a tad. Leave to cool.

To make the filling, fry the shallot and garlic in the oil until tender without browning. Now add the courgette slices, stir, then cover and sweat over a low heat for about 10-15 minutes, stirring occasionally, until the courgettes are very tender. Cool slightly then mash the courgette and onion roughly with a large fork or a potato masher. Stir in the rice, tarragon, eggs, cream, and Comté, and season. Spoon into the pastry case and smooth down. Sprinkle the top with Parmesan. Bake at the same temperature for 30-40 minutes, until just barely set. Serve warm or cold.

Red Onion and Red Wine Risotto ⓥ

This is an unusual risotto, with an unusual colour given by the red wine. It does look a little muddy in the pan, but don't worry. Once each helping is topped with the red onion marmalade and a scattering of fresh chives, it is more than presentable. One mouthful and everyone will be happy.

  Choose a good, fruity red wine, as the flavour really does come through in the end. The red onion marmalade can be made up to a day ahead, but leave cooking the risotto until half an hour or so before serving.

SERVES 4-6

4 red onions, halved and
  thinly sliced
60g (2 oz) unsalted butter
1 tablespoon caster sugar
1 tablespoon balsamic
  vinegar
1.2 litres (2 pints) *Chicken
  Stock* or *Vegetable Stock*
  (see pages 242-3)
1 tablespoon extra virgin
  olive oil
2 garlic cloves, chopped
225g (8 oz) risotto rice

1 cinnamon stick
2 leeks, trimmed and sliced
1 celery stalk, thinly sliced
1 carrot, shredded
2 tablespoons chopped
  parsley
1 glass fruity red wine
3 tablespoons chopped
  chives
30g (1 oz) Parmesan,
  freshly grated
salt and pepper

Take one-third of the onion and place in a pan with 15g (½ oz) of the butter. Cover and place over a low heat. Leave to sweat gently for 20-30 minutes, stirring once or twice, until the onion is very tender. Uncover and add the sugar and vinegar. Cook very gently uncovered, stirring frequently, until the mixture is thick and jammy. Set aside and reheat just before serving. Bring the stock up to the boil, then reduce the heat to a thread to keep it hot.

For the main body of the risotto, begin by heating half the remaining butter with the olive oil over a moderate heat. Add the rest of the onion and the garlic, and fry until tender, without browning. Now add the rice and the cinnamon stick, and stir-fry for a minute or so. Add the remaining vegetables and the parsley, stir once or twice, then pour in the wine and season with salt and pepper. Let the wine bubble through gently, stirring, until virtually all has evaporated.

Now add a good ladleful of the hot stock, and carry on stirring until it has cooked away. Repeat, until the rice is all but tender, but still with a slight hint of resistance to the bite. If you run short of stock, finish off with hot water instead. When the rice is done, and bathed in a little sauce but not swimming in liquid, draw off the heat and stir in 2 tablespoons of the chives, the Parmesan and the last of the butter. Taste and adjust seasoning, then serve and top each serving with a little of the gently reheated red onion marmalade and a sprinkling of the remaining chives.

Spinach, Chickpea and Rice Tagine ⓥ

A tagine is anything cooked in a particular Moroccan vessel with a shallow base and a tall conical lid. According to Moroccan friends, if you scrambled eggs in it, you would have scrambled egg tagine. However, you are far more likely to unearth a spiced stew of some sort under the witch's hat lid of your average Moroccan tagine. And that is precisely what you are getting here: a mildly spiced stew, an all-in-one dish best eaten with warmed Arab or *Pitta Bread*s (see page 223).

SERVES 2-3

2 tablespoons extra virgin olive oil
1 onion, grated
2 garlic cloves, finely chopped
1 teaspoon ground cumin
1 teaspoon sweet paprika
½ teaspoon coarsely ground black pepper
3 tomatoes, skinned, seeded and chopped

450g (1 lb) fresh spinach
salt
45g (1½ oz) long-grain rice (e.g. basmati)
1 x 400g (14 oz) tin chickpeas, drained and rinsed
1½ tablespoons chopped coriander leaves

Spoon the oil into a wide, shallow saucepan or roomy skillet (or the base of a heatproof tagine, if you have one). Add the onion, garlic and spices. Place over a low heat and cook gently for 3 minutes. Now add the tomatoes, spinach, salt and 5 tablespoons water. Cover and cook for 10 minutes. Stir in the rice, then cover again and cook very gently for a further 10-15 minutes, until the rice is tender. Stir once in a while and, if necessary, add a spoonful or two more water to prevent catching. Now add the chickpeas and cook for a minute or two more to heat through. Taste and adjust seasoning, scatter with coriander, and serve.

Goat's Cheese, Tomato and Asparagus Calzone Ⓥ

I love wholemeal bread (as long as it's not like a lead weight), but I draw the line at wholemeal pasta and wholemeal pizzas. Healthy they may be, but they don't half annihilate the fun. To ring the changes, however, I do sometimes use a quarter wholemeal flour to white flour in the dough for home-made pizzas, which gives a good nutty taste without overwhelming worthiness. Here the dough is used to make calzone, pizza turnovers, filled with a big helping of tomato, goat's cheese and asparagus. If you make these calzone part of a larger meal, then one could be stretched between two people. If you are really hungry and want to keep things simple, on the other hand, serve one per person.

SERVES 2-4

DOUGH
310g (11 oz) strong white bread flour
110g (4 oz) wholemeal bread flour
1 sachet easy-blend yeast*
½ tablespoon salt
2 tablespoons extra virgin olive oil

TOMATO SAUCE
2 garlic cloves, chopped
1 tablespoon extra virgin olive oil
1 x 400g (14 oz) tin chopped tomatoes

1 tablespoon tomato purée
½ teaspoon caster sugar
1 bouquet garni, consisting of 2 sprigs of parsley, 1 sprig of thyme, and 1 bay leaf
salt and pepper

REST OF FILLING
400g (14 oz) asparagus, trimmed
200g (7 oz) goat's cheese, de-rinded and crumbled
a handful of mint leaves, shredded
a little extra virgin olive oil

To make the dough, mix the flours, yeast and salt in a mixing bowl. Add the oil and then enough water to make a soft but not too sticky dough. Knead vigorously for 5-10 minutes until silky smooth and elastic. Drizzle a touch more oil into the bowl, then gather the dough up into a ball, turn in the oil in the bowl until coated and leave it there, covered with a damp cloth. Place in a warm spot and forget about it for an hour or so until doubled in bulk.

Meanwhile, prepare the tomato sauce. Fry the garlic gently in the oil until lightly coloured. Add the tomato, tomato purée, sugar, and bouquet garni. Season with salt and pepper. Simmer gently for about 20 minutes until thick and pulpy. Taste and adjust seasoning and discard the bundle of herbs. For the rest of the filling, trim the asparagus, discarding the lower more fibrous part of the stem (or save for soups or stocks). Cut into 5cm (2 in) lengths and blanch in boiling salted water for about 3-4 minutes until just tender. Drain thoroughly.

Place a baking tray or pizza stone or some earthenware tiles in the oven. Preheat the oven to 220°C/425°F/Gas Mark 7. Punch down the dough, knead again briefly, and then divide into two. Knead each piece a little and shape into a ball. Roll out as thin as you can get it with a rolling pin (it will keep shrinking back in an irritating fashion, but don't hold that against it), then pick up and stretch with your hands to form a circle about 20cm (10 in) in diameter.

Lay it on a well-floured board or baking tray. Spread half the tomato sauce over each one, leaving a bare 2cm (¾ in) border around the edge. Then load up one side of each circle with asparagus and goat's cheese. Scatter with mint, and drizzle each with about a teaspoon of olive oil. Grind over loads of black pepper. Fold the dough in half, lifting the unladen side over the pile of filling on the other.

Fold the edges over together firmly, sealing in the filling. Brush the top with a little olive oil. Slide and shake the calzone gently on to the baking sheet (or stone or tiles) in the oven. Finish the second one and slide that in too. Bake for about 20 minutes until puffed up and browned. Serve immediately.

Thai Fried Noodles

One of the things that characterises these noodles is the addition of raw egg, the other is the balance of the sweet, salt, sharp and hot. In Thailand, bowls of sugar and flaked or powdered chilli will be on the table as well as rice vinegar and fish sauce, both spiked with fresh chilli, so that each diner can adjust the seasonings to his or her taste.

Sen-lek noodles are flat, medium-wide noodles made from rice flour. Chinese egg noodles are no equivalent, but they still taste good fried the Thai way.

SERVES 3

175-225g (6-8 oz) Thai sen-lek noodles* or Chinese egg noodles
3 tablespoons sunflower oil
3 garlic cloves, chopped
2.5cm (1 in) piece of fresh root ginger, finely chopped
1 small red chilli, seeded and thinly sliced
225g (8 oz) minced pork
3 tomatoes, seeded and cut into strips
2 eggs, lightly beaten
juice of ½ lime
1½ tablespoons fish sauce (nam pla)*
½ tablespoon caster sugar
3 tablespoons chopped roasted peanuts
4 spring onions, sliced
60g (2 oz) beansprouts
2 tablespoons chopped coriander leaves

Soak and drain the noodles, or cook according to packet instructions. Assemble and prepare all the ingredients before you start cooking – this is what takes the time, and once the heat is turned on, there won't be time to run off and fetch something you've forgotten.

Heat a large wok until it begins to smoke. Add the oil, warm through for a few seconds then add the garlic, ginger and chilli. Give them a couple of stirs, then add the pork. Stir-fry for about 2 minutes, breaking up lumps, then add the tomatoes and eggs. Fry for a couple of seconds, then add the noodles and toss and stir, scraping up egg and bits from the sides of the wok.

Now in goes the lime juice, fish sauce and sugar. Mix well, then in with the peanuts. Another quick stir, and add the spring onions and beansprouts. Toss once more. Draw off the heat, taste and adjust seasonings and serve sprinkled with chopped coriander.

Pancit Luglug
(Filipino Lobster and Pork Noodles)

Noodles are enormously popular in the Philippines, and this version is amongst the best. Normally, this dish is made with prawns, but since prawn farming is deeply problematic I prefer to use lobster. You'll find that a little goes a long way when used like this.

SERVES 4

1 large lobster, cooked Ⓦ
1 teaspoon ground turmeric
225g (8 oz) belly of pork
2 tablespoons sunflower oil
4 garlic cloves, finely chopped
1 large onion, finely chopped
5 tablespoons finely chopped parsley
3 tablespoons cornflour

250g (9 oz) rice noodles* or Chinese egg thread noodles
salt and pepper

TO GARNISH
1 fillet smoked mackerel Ⓦ or smoked trout, flaked
6 spring onions, chopped
2 hard-boiled eggs, shelled and quartered
1 lime, cut into wedges
fish sauce (nam pla)*

Extract the meat from the lobster and slice. Break up the shell with a meat mallet, then put into a saucepan with the turmeric and 300ml (10 fl oz) water. Bring up to the boil and simmer for 15 minutes. Tip shells and liquid into the processor and process until the shells are well chopped up. Strain and reserve the liquid.

Put the pork into another pan and add enough water to cover. Bring up to the boil, then simmer gently for about 30 minutes until tender. Drain, reserving 300ml (10 fl oz) of the cooking water. Slice the pork thinly, discarding any small bones.

Heat the oil and fry the garlic and onion until lightly coloured. Next add the pork, the lobster stock and pork stock, 4 tablespoons of the parsley, salt and pepper. Bring up to the boil. Mix a few tablespoonfuls of the hot stock with the cornflour to form a runny paste, then stir in a few more tablespoonfuls of the stock. Now pour into the pan, stirring, and let it simmer together for a few minutes until the sauce has thickened. Add the lobster and let it just heat through for a few seconds.

Meanwhile, cook the noodles according to packet instructions. Drain and divide between four bowls. Pour the lobster sauce over the noodles. Top each bowl with mackerel, spring onion and eggs, and sprinkle with the reserved parsley. Serve immediately with a wedge of lime, and fish sauce for those who want it.

Tagliatelle with Broad Beans, Goat's Cheese and Sun-dried Tomatoes Ⓥ

Pasta and broad beans is one of my favourite combinations, best of all made with fresh broad beans, but almost as good with frozen. Add soft goat's cheese, the sort that has no rind and the consistency of cream cheese, and sun-dried tomatoes, and you have as good a pasta dish as you can hope for.

SERVES 4

450g (1 lb) shelled broad beans, fresh or frozen
400-450g (14-16 oz) tagliatelle
5 tablespoons extra virgin olive oil
2 garlic cloves, chopped
110g (4 oz) sun-dried tomatoes in olive oil, or 'sun-blush' tomatoes (see page 136), chopped

150g (5 oz) soft young goat's cheese or cream cheese
30g (1 oz) Parmesan, freshly grated
2 tablespoons chopped parsley
salt and pepper

Tackle the broad beans first. If they are frozen, let them thaw. If they are fresh, blanch for 3 minutes in salted water then drain. Now continue in the same way for either sort. With your fingernail or the tip of a small knife, slit open the tough skin around each bean and pop out the pretty little bright green bean inside. Slow work, but it pays in the end.

Put a large pan of well-salted water on to boil, and when boiling, add the tagliatelle. Cook until al dente. Meanwhile, heat the oil and add the beans and the garlic. Cook gently, stirring occasionally, until the beans are tender. Stir in the dried tomatoes, and draw off the heat if the pasta is not yet ready. Reheat when needed.

As soon as the pasta is cooked, drain thoroughly, reserving a cup of the cooking water. Return to the pan. Add the cheeses and parsley, and pour over the hot, sizzling broad beans and their oil. Season with salt and pepper, then pour in a slurp of cooking water to lighten the texture of the soft cheese. Toss to mix evenly and serve straightaway.

Fusilli alla Genovese

Not, as you might imagine, pasta with pesto, but actually a dish of pasta in a meat and onion sauce that is extremely popular around Naples right in the south of Italy! It's hardly an instant dish, but the long slow hours of simmering produce a rich, sweet yet savoury sauce. I first tasted it in one of the best pasta restaurants in Italy, Cumpá Cosimo, in Ravello on the Amalfi coast. There, Signora Netta throws the meat out when the sauce is ready – 'it's done all its work' – but in other, more thrifty versions the meat is shredded into the sauce or eaten separately as a main course. The choice is yours.

SERVES 4-6

500g (18 oz) piece of braising beef
1kg (2¼ lb) onions, thinly sliced
2 celery stalks, chopped
2 carrots, chopped
6 slices raw prosciutto* (e.g. Parma ham), chopped
4 tablespoons chopped parsley
2 sprigs of marjoram or thyme
150ml (5 fl oz) tomato passata
3 tablespoons extra virgin olive oil
1 glass of dry white wine
400-450g (14-16 oz) fusilli, or other pasta shapes
freshly grated Parmesan
salt and pepper

Put all the ingredients except the wine, pasta, cheese and seasonings into a large saucepan, together with 150ml (5 fl oz) water. Cover and cook very gently for 2½-3 hours, until the meat and vegetables are so soft and tender that they are collapsing. Now add the wine, stir around and cook uncovered for another 5 minutes. Take out the meat and shred roughly with a couple of forks if you want to stir it back into the sauce. Using a potato masher, mash all the vegetables together to form a thick sauce. Stir the meat back in, if using. Taste and adjust seasoning, and reheat when needed.

When the sauce is nearly cooked, put a large pan of salted water on to boil. Add the pasta, and boil until al dente. Drain, and mix with the sauce. Serve immediately with lots of freshly grated Parmesan.

Conchiglie with Peppered Cherry Tomatoes and Basil Ⓥ

Tossing roast tomatoes into pasta has become very popular (and very good it is too), but this method of slowly braising little sweet cherry tomatoes in olive oil with loads of coarsely crushed pepper tastes even better mixed into a bowl of steaming hot pasta shells with a handful of aromatic basil and plenty of fresh Parmesan.

If young children are sharing the pasta with the grown-ups, you don't have to forego the flavour of the peppercorns altogether. Just lift the tomatoes out of the oil and then strain out the pepper – the oil will retain flavour but not fire.

SERVES 4

400-450g (14-16 oz) conchiglie (pasta shells), or other pasta shapes
a big, generous handful of fresh basil leaves
freshly grated Parmesan
salt

SAUCE
550g (1¾ lb) cherry tomatoes
2 sprigs of thyme or lemon thyme
1 sprig of rosemary
1 teaspoon coarse salt
½ tablespoon black peppercorns, coarsely crushed
6 garlic cloves, halved
150ml (5 fl oz) extra virgin olive oil

The tomatoes can be cooked well in advance then reheated gently in the oven when needed. Preheat the oven to 150°C/300°F/Gas Mark 2. Begin by nicking a small cross in the base of each tomato with a sharp knife. Scatter the thyme, rosemary, salt and pepper over the base of an ovenproof dish, just large enough to take the tomatoes in a closely packed single layer. Spread the tomatoes over the seasonings, tuck in the garlic, then pour in the oil. Cook in the preheated oven, uncovered, for about 50 minutes, shaking them gently about halfway through the cooking time. Remove the thyme and rosemary twigs. Keep warm or reheat gently when the pasta is just cooked.

Meanwhile, put a large pan of well-salted water on to boil. Add the pasta, and boil until al dente. Drain thoroughly and return to the pan. Quickly spoon over the tomatoes and about two-thirds of their hot oil. Throw in the basil leaves, toss together quickly and serve immediately with freshly grated Parmesan.

Gnocchi with Mushroom and Sage Ragout Ⓥ

Home-made gnocchi, small potato dumplings, are some of the most comforting and restorative foods in the world. They demand a little patience and time to make, but it is worth acquiring the knack. Of course, if time is at a premium you can cheat by using ready-made gnocchi, though they will never be as light and delicious. Alternatively, you could just spoon this tomato-ey mushroom sauce straight over pasta, which is almost as good as having it with gnocchi.

SERVES 4-6

GNOCCHI
1.5kg (3½ lb) floury
  potatoes, boiled in their
  skins
1 egg, beaten
250g (9 oz) plain flour,
  sifted, plus extra for trays
salt, pepper and freshly
  grated nutmeg

RAGOUT
15g (½ oz) dried porcini
  mushrooms Ⓦ
1 onion, chopped
3 tablespoons olive oil
2 garlic cloves, chopped

6 large sage leaves,
  shredded
225g (8 oz) button or
  chestnut mushrooms,
  cleaned and quartered
1 x 400g (14 oz) tin
  chopped tomatoes
1 tablespoon tomato purée
1 tablespoon caster sugar
1 tablespoon chopped
  parsley
salt and pepper

TO FINISH
freshly grated Parmesan

To make the gnocchi, peel the potatoes while they are still hot, then rub through a ricer, a mouli-légumes or a sieve. Weigh out exactly 1kg (2¼ lb) of the potato purée. Make a well in the centre and add all the remaining gnocchi ingredients. Work all of them together thoroughly to make a soft, warm dough. Cover with a tea-towel.

Flour three baking trays generously. Break off tennis-ball-sized knobs of the dough and roll out to form long sausages about the thickness of your thumb. Cut into pieces 2.5cm (1 in) long. Now they have to be shaped, and this is what helps to make them light and luscious, so ignore these instructions at your peril! Take a fork and hold it with the tip of the tines down on the work surface, their outer curve facing upwards. With the tip of the finger, lightly press a piece of the dough against the tines, right at the bottom. Now in one swift movement, roll and flip the dough up and off the fork, so that one side is ridged from the tines, while the other

has an indentation from the tip of your finger. You don't need to take the piece of dough far up the tines – we're talking just enough to imprint the ridges on one side only. It gets easier as you get the hang of it, and soon you'll be flipping away merrily and snappily. As you make them, spread the gnocchi out on the floured trays. Once made, cover with a clean tea-towel until needed.

Now for the ragout, which can be made in advance if you prefer. Begin by soaking the porcini in warm water for half an hour until softened. Pick them out of the water and chop roughly. Leave the soaking liquid to settle until needed.

Fry the onion gently in the olive oil until tender, then add the garlic and sage. Fry for a further minute or two. Now add the chopped mushrooms and the porcini. Fry together over a high heat until the mushrooms are tender. Pour in the tomatoes and add the tomato purée, sugar, parsley, salt and pepper. Carefully pour in the mushroom soaking liquid, leaving the grit behind at the bottom of the bowl. Now simmer everything together gently for half an hour, adding a dash more water if the sauce threatens to catch. Taste and adjust seasoning.

Preheat the oven to 200°C/400°F/Gas Mark 6. Put a large pan of salted water on to boil. When it is at a rolling boil, carefully drop the gnocchi into the water, not too many at a time (a quarter to a third of the entire batch will be quite enough). When they bob back to the surface, check one to make sure it is cooked, then quickly lift the rest out with a perforated spoon. Arrange the gnocchi in an oiled, shallow, close-fitting dish, and spoon the hot ragout over them. Scatter with a handful of grated Parmesan, and then bake for 15-20 minutes until sizzling hot. Serve with extra Parmesan for those who want it.

Courgette Lasagne

This is one of our son, Sidney's, favourite dishes. Pasta, courgettes and both meat sauce and béchamel all caught up in one perfect load. Of course, you could add other vegetables instead of the courgettes, though I do like the freshness they bring to what is otherwise a rich, sturdy dish.

SERVES 6

150-175g (5-6 oz) lasagne
   sheets
salt
450g (1 lb) courgettes, cut
   into 1cm (½ in) thick slices
olive oil
30g (1 oz) Parmesan, freshly
   grated
30g (1 oz) Cacciocavallo
   or Gruyère cheese,
   freshly grated

MEAT SAUCE
1 onion, chopped
1 carrot, finely diced
1 celery stalk, finely diced
2 tablespoons extra virgin
   olive oil
3 garlic cloves, chopped
500g (18 oz) lean minced
   beef
1 glass red wine (optional)

1 x 400g (14 oz) tin
   chopped tomatoes
1 tablespoon Worcestershire
   sauce*
1 tablespoon tomato purée
1 teaspoon caster sugar
   (optional)
salt and pepper

CHEESE BECHAMEL
2 cloves
½ onion
1 bay leaf
600ml (1 pint) milk
3 tablespoons extra virgin
   olive oil
3 tablespoons plain flour
30g (1 oz) Parmesan or
   Pecorino cheese, freshly
   grated
salt, pepper and
   freshly grated nutmeg

Both the sauces can be made well in advance. To make the meat sauce, sauté the onion, carrot and celery in the olive oil until they begin to colour. Add the garlic, cook for about 1 minute longer, then raise the heat and add the beef. Fry over a high heat, breaking up the lumps with the edge of a spoon or fish slice, until the mince is beginning to brown (and I do mean brown, not just changing from raw red to semi-cooked grey). Now add the wine (if using) and bring up to the boil, stirring. Tip in the chopped tomatoes and add the Worcestershire sauce, tomato purée, sugar (if using), salt and pepper. Bring up to the boil again, then reduce the heat and simmer gently for at least an hour (1½-2 is even better), adding more water when it threatens to catch, and stirring every now and then. Taste and adjust seasoning.

To make the béchamel, push the cloves into the onion half and place in a pan with the bay leaf and the milk. Bring gently up to the boil, draw off the heat, cover and leave to infuse for 5-10 minutes, before discarding the onion with its cloves and the bay leaf. Heat the olive oil in a heavy-based pan, and stir in the flour. Stir over a low heat for about 1 minute, then draw off the heat and gradually stir in the hot milk. Return to the heat, bring up to the boil, stirring frequently, and then simmer gently for 5-10 minutes, until the taste of raw flour has completely gone.

Draw off the heat, and if not using immediately, spear a small knob of butter on the tines of a fork and rub quickly over the surface while it is still hot, to prevent a skin forming. Reheat before using. Then, stir in the cheese and season generously with salt, pepper and freshly grated nutmeg.

Check the lasagne packet. If there is no need to pre-cook, then skip this paragraph. Otherwise, three-quarters fill a frying pan with salted water and bring up to the boil. Two or three at a time, lay sheets of lasagne in the water, and cook for about 3-4 minutes, until softened and pliable. Drain on a clean tea-towel.

Preheat the oven to 200°C/400°F/Gas Mark 6. Bring a pan of lightly salted water to the boil and tip in the courgettes. Simmer for 2 minutes, until barely tender, then drain.

Everything is ready for the final assembly job now. Take a 24 x 22cm (9 x 8 in) shallow ovenproof dish (or one that is somewhere close in size) and grease with a little olive oil. Ladle about a quarter of the meat sauce into it and spread out thinly to cover the base. Lay enough sheets of lasagne over the sauce to cover, without overlapping. Ladle half of the remaining meat sauce over the lasagne and smooth down. Dot with half the courgettes and then spoon over one-third of the bèchamel, smoothing it down as best you can. Repeat this layer of lasagne, meat sauce, courgettes and bèchamel once more. Now lay the final layer of lasagne on top and spoon the last of the bèchamel over that, covering everything completely. Sprinkle with the grated cheeses. (The dish can be prepared to this stage up to a day in advance.)

Bake the lasagne for about 30-40 minutes until patched with brown on top, and singing and sizzling with heat. Serve and enjoy.

Fusilli or Conchiglie with Courgettes and Yellow Peppers Ⓥ

This is a very simple pasta dish, and all the better for that. Once the pasta is in the pot, there's just enough time to cook the vegetables (assuming it is dried pasta, of course). If you want to make it for four, you will have to cook the courgettes and peppers in two frying pans.

SERVES 2

200-225g (7-8 oz) pasta shapes or spaghetti
3 tablespoons extra virgin olive oil
250g (9 oz) courgettes, sliced
1 yellow pepper, seeded and cut into strips

1 garlic clove, chopped
a handful of fresh basil leaves, roughly torn up
15g (½ oz) Parmesan, freshly grated, plus extra to serve
salt and pepper

Bring a large pan of well-salted water to the boil. Add the pasta and leave to cook.

Heat the oil in a wide frying pan. Sauté the courgettes and pepper until browned and tender. Add the garlic to the pan when the vegetables are nearly cooked.

Drain the pasta and toss with the vegetables and their cooking oil (reheated if necessary), the basil and the cheese. Season with a little salt and lots of pepper and then serve with extra cheese.

Newspaper-roast Trout
with Ginger, Lime and Fennel Butter

There's more than one way to recycle a newspaper! Some time ago, back in the 1970s, I think, there was a fashion for baking trout wrapped in damp newspaper. Quite why it came to my mind again, a horrifying quarter of a century or so on, I don't know, but I thought I'd give it a try. The news is that it works remarkably well. The dampness of the newspaper protects the fish from the heat, semi-steaming it to a perfect state of done-ness. And what's more the newsprint doesn't transfer itself to the fish, though it does do quite a good job of pulling some of the skin away to reveal the moist flesh.

Note: By a sheet, I mean one double-page spread.

SERVES 4

4 trout, cleaned
1 newspaper
salt and pepper

BUTTER
125g (4½ oz) lightly salted
  butter
1 teaspoon grated fresh
  root ginger
juice of ½ lime
2 tablespoons chopped
  fresh fennel or dill
salt and pepper

To make the butter, process all the ingredients together or let the butter soften, and then beat the ginger, lime juice and finely chopped fennel or dill into it. Mould into a sausage shape, then wrap in foil or clingfilm and chill until firm. Slice before serving.

Preheat the oven to 200°C/400°F/Gas Mark 6. For each trout, take a sheet of a broadsheet newspaper, or two of a tabloid, and wet them thoroughly. Wrap each fish up neatly in the damp paper, and place on a baking tray. Bake for 20 minutes. Let each diner unwrap his parcel at the table (make sure there's a handy waste-paper bin), and quickly pass around a small dish with slices of the flavoured butter while the fish are still hot enough to melt it into the flesh.

Fish 'n' Chips

Here, at William's specific request, is a recipe for our most famous dish after roast beef and Yorkshire pudding. Making your own fish and chips takes a little bit of organisation but it is very satisfying. (Do I cook the chips or the fish first? Answer: the chips, and then keep them warm in the oven.)

SERVES 4

4 x 175g (6 oz) pieces of
  skinned cod fillet
sunflower oil or dripping
  for deep-frying

BATTER
225g (8 oz) plain flour,
  sifted
salt and pepper
300ml (10 fl oz) lager
1 egg
1 tablespoon sunflower oil

TO SERVE
Chips (see page 133)
lemon wedges
malt vinegar*
tartare sauce
tomato ketchup

To make the batter, season the flour with salt and pepper. Make a well in the centre and add the lager, egg and oil. Gradually whisk these into the flour to make a smooth batter. Leave to rest for at least half an hour.

Heat the oil to 180°C/350°F, or until a cube of bread dropped into it sizzles fairly vigorously. One by one, dry the cod pieces, then dip into the batter, making sure that they are completely coated. Slide into the oil and fry for about 5-6 minutes, depending on the thickness of the fish, until golden brown. Drain briefly on kitchen paper and sprinkle with salt. Eat immediately with chips of course, plus lemon wedges, vinegar, tartare sauce or ketchup, as the fancy takes you.

Fish Pie with Smoked Trout

This is really just a fairly straightforward fish pie, with a bit of organic smoked trout thrown in and an idea pinched from clever Jamie Oliver. Most recipes for fish pie begin with cooking the fish, but he just puts it in the dish raw. Since the pie is to be baked, there will be quite enough heat to cook it in situ. This, though, isn't quite as rich as his version, and owes far more to more traditional recipes.

SERVES 6

2 fillets of cold smoked trout or 2 slices of smoked salmon (optional)
900g (2 lb) skinned cod fillet, or other firm-fleshed white fish fillet
4 hard-boiled eggs, shelled and quartered
150g (5 oz) lightly cooked peas (if frozen, just thaw)
2 tablespoons chopped dill

1 clove
1 onion slice
1 bay leaf
450ml (15 fl oz) milk, plus a little extra for the potatoes
45g (1½ oz) butter
30g (1 oz) plain flour
700g (1 lb 9 oz) cooked potatoes, skinned
salt and pepper

Cut the trout or salmon into strips. Cut the cod into bite-sized dice. Mix the two in the bottom of a pie dish. Scatter over the eggs, peas and dill.

Push the clove into the slice of onion, and place in a pan with the bay leaf and milk. Bring slowly up to the boil, remove from the heat and leave to infuse for 10 minutes. Melt 30g (1 oz) of the butter in a saucepan large enough to take the milk comfortably. Add the flour, and stir for 1 minute. Draw off the heat, and then gradually stir in the hot drained milk, a small splash at a time, until you have a creamy sauce. Now you can add the remainder of the milk in big slurps. Return to the heat and bring up to the boil, stirring to beat out any lumps. Simmer gently for 5-10 minutes, stirring occasionally to prevent catching, until the sauce is good and thick (juices from the fish will seep out to thin it down as the pie cooks). Season generously with salt and pepper. Pour the finished sauce over the fish mixture.

Preheat the oven to 190°C/375°F/Gas Mark 5. Mash the potatoes with the remaining butter and a little milk. Dollop over the fish and sauce, then smooth down lightly. With a fork make wavy patterns in the surface. Dot with just a little extra butter. Bake for 30 minutes until the top is browned. Serve while still piping hot.

Gravad Lax

The Scandinavian dish of gravad lax, dill-marinated salmon, always seems frightfully glamorous and yet it is so easy to make. You do need a little patience – it needs at least two days in the fridge, but tastes even better after chilling for four to seven days – but otherwise there is very little to it. Choose the best, freshest-looking organic salmon and you are away. Serve it as a first course, pile it on to open sandwiches for lunch, or use for canapés.

SERVES 8-10 AS A FIRST COURSE

1-1.5kg (2-3½ lb) very fresh salmon fillet, scaled and with skin on
1 tablespoon coarse sea salt
2 tablespoons caster sugar
1 tablespoon dried dill weed, or 2 tablespoons chopped fresh dill
½ tablespoon black peppercorns, coarsely crushed

SAUCE
2 tablespoons Dijon mustard
1 egg yolk (optional)
1 level tablespoon caster sugar
150ml (5 fl oz) sunflower oil
1 tablespoon white wine vinegar
3 tablespoons chopped fresh dill, or 1½ tablespoons dried dill weed
salt and pepper

Start on the salmon two to seven days before you want to eat it, but leave the sauce until the day you serve. Ideally, you will have two pieces of salmon fillet of about the same size and shape, which can be neatly sandwiched together. If not, cut the fillet into large pieces which do fit more or less together.

Mix the salt, sugar, dill and peppercorns. Sprinkle an even, thin layer of this curing mix over the base of a shallow dish that will take the sandwiched pair of salmon fillets snugly. Lay half the salmon, skin-side down, on top. Now sprinkle over a generous helping of the curing mix and cover with the rest of the salmon, skin side up. Sprinkle over more of the curing mix, but don't feel that you have to use it all up. Cover with clingfilm or foil, weigh the fish down with a board or plate, perch a few tins or weights on top and leave in the fridge for at least two days, turning the sandwiched fillets over once or twice during that time. As the salt draws out the water in the salmon, the curing mix will dissolve to a liquid.

The egg yolk for the sauce is not entirely necessary, though it does make for a nicer, more velvety texture. To make the sauce, mix the mustard, egg yolk (if using) and sugar. Gradually whisk in the oil as if you were making a mayonnaise (though it is by no means such a

temperamental business). Stir in the vinegar, dill, salt and pepper. Taste and adjust the seasoning.

To serve the gravad lax, wipe the pieces of salmon clean and slice a little thicker than you would smoked salmon, cutting on the diagonal, down towards the skin, in the direction of the thinner tail end. Serve straightaway, with the sauce.

Seared Salmon Fillet
with Olive, Parsley and New Potato Salsa

I think it was probably the year's first haul of potatoes from the garden, so perfect and sweet and smooth, that set me on the tracks to this unexpectedly good salsa. The texture and flavour of the potatoes is an excellent foil for piquant olives and capers, which, together with the lemon, go so well with salmon.

If you stick with the cooking method and times below, your salmon will end up cooked 'à la rosé', or in other words, still a little translucent in the centre. Some may think this underdone, but try it anyway – you'll find that the salmon tastes fresher and moister and altogether superior.

SERVES 4

4 pieces of salmon fillet,
  weighing around
  175-200g (6-7 oz) each
a little extra virgin olive oil
salt and pepper

SALSA
310g (11 oz) new potatoes
110g (4 oz) black olives,
  pitted and chopped
finely grated zest of 1
  lemon

1 tablespoon lemon juice
3 tablespoons chopped
  parsley
1 garlic clove, crushed
1 heaped tablespoon
  capers, chopped
2 tablespoons extra virgin
  olive oil
salt and pepper

Cook the potatoes for the salsa in advance. Skin them and dice finely, then mix with all the other salsa ingredients. Taste and adjust flavourings, keeping them on the strong side – this is a salsa, not a vegetable dish. Leave to cool.

Season the salmon with salt and pepper. Shortly before serving, put a heavy frying pan to heat over a high flame. Leave for about 2-3 minutes so that it is truly, utterly, outrageously hot. Brush the skin side of the salmon fillets with oil and lay them skin-side down in the pan. Leave for 3 minutes, without any experimental prodding or nudging or lifting of corners to check on progress. Once the 3 minutes is up, brush the upper sides lightly with oil, then turn the salmon over. Cook for a further 2-3 minutes until almost cooked through but still with a line of bright pink, undercooked flesh at the heart. Now whip them out, and serve immediately with the salsa.

Grilled Trout
with Cucumber and Tarragon Sauce

Cucumber, yoghurt and tarragon all have a pleasing affinity with the flavour of trout. Here they combine with a touch of cream to make a quick sauce to partner grilled trout. As always, when grilling fish, don't be scared of heat. Make sure the grill is thoroughly hot, and get the fish as close as is reasonably possible – say about 5cm (2 in) from the heat. That way you should end up with trout that is nicely, lightly browned on the exterior, but still moist inside. Oh, and don't overdo it – far better to take the fish away from the grill when it is still a tad underdone (it will go on cooking a little in its own heat), than mercilessly overcooked and dry as a bone.

SERVES 4

4 trout, cleaned
juice of 1 lemon
a little melted butter
salt and pepper

SAUCE
½ cucumber, coarsely grated
salt
100ml (4 fl oz) double
  cream
150g (5 oz) yoghurt
1 tablespoon tarragon
  vinegar
1 tablespoon chopped
  tarragon

Make a couple of deep diagonal slashes across the fattest part of each fish on each side. Rub lemon juice, salt and pepper all over each fish and set aside until ready to cook.

To make the sauce, spread the cucumber out in a colander and sprinkle lightly with salt. Leave for 30-60 minutes to drain. Pat dry on kitchen paper, or a clean tea-towel. Whip the cream lightly so that it is thick but still a little floppy. Fold into the yoghurt, together with the cucumber, vinegar and tarragon. Chill until needed. Stir just before serving.

Preheat the grill. Pat the fish dry then brush with melted butter. Grill close to the heat, turning once, until just cooked through. Serve immediately with the cucumber and tarragon sauce.

Polenta-fried Herring Fillets

For many people, the thing that puts them off the humble but ever-so-healthy herring is the bones. I sympathise. I hate them too. So, two solutions. One is to bone them, and secondly, for the really iffy, to bone them and marinate them in an acidic mixture that will soften the few remaining offending whiskery bones.

For the latter, head straight for the recipes for pickled herrings. But if you can take the possibility of just one or two lingering on, then try this one straightaway. This is an updated version of the classic Scottish dish of oatmeal-coated herring, given a splash of colour by the polenta and green herbs. Once the little silver darlings have been boned, it takes only a few minutes to cook them and place them on the table, all crisp and crunchy on the outside, then tender and soft on the inside. Superb.

SERVES 4

4 herrings, cleaned
   and scaled
1 egg
125g (4½ oz) polenta,
   or fine oatmeal
2 tablespoons very finely
   chopped parsley

2 tablespoons finely
   chopped dill or fennel
extra virgin olive oil for
   frying
lemon wedges to serve
salt and pepper

Bone the herrings (see the next recipe, for *Sweet Spiced Pickled Herrings*). Beat the egg in a shallow dish, and mix the polenta with the parsley, dill or fennel, and plenty of salt and pepper in another shallow dish or plate.

Heat a thin layer of oil in a large frying pan over a moderately high heat. One by one, coat the herring in egg, shaking off the excess, then coat thoroughly in the polenta mixture. Fry each boned herring briskly for about 1-1½ minutes on each side, until golden brown. Drain briefly on kitchen paper and serve at once with wedges of lemon to squeeze over them.

Sweet Spiced Pickled Herrings

Don't you just love all those Scandinavian pickled herrings in sweet spicy, mustard or dill or red wine marinades? Well, you'll be delighted to hear that it is relatively easy to make your own. It takes six days, but you need only be actively involved for about half an hour or so. All the rest is just herring-hanging-around time. Since the herring are never actually cooked (it is the salt in the brine and the vinegar and sugar in the second stage which both transform the texture and preserve the fish, not heat), it is imperative that you choose very fresh herrings with a gleam in their eye.

Once they've finished marinading, serve them as a first course or a light lunch with good bread and something saladly, or make them part of a more substantial salad with boiled new potatoes and lots of chopped shallot or chives.

SERVES 4

6 herrings, cleaned and scaled
60g (2 oz) Maldon salt or other sea salt

MARINADE
10 black peppercorns
4 cloves

1 teaspoon coriander seeds
1 dried red chilli
225g (8 oz) granulated or demerara sugar
150ml (5 fl oz) red wine vinegar
1 large onion, sliced
3 bay leaves

First of all, you are going to have to salt the herrings. Make the brine by dissolving the salt in 600ml (1 pint) hot water. Leave to cool.

Now you will need to bone the herrings. Cut off their heads and discard. Trim off fins and dorsal fins. Elongate the slit made to empty the innards, right down to the tail end. One by one, take each herring and sit it cut downwards, with the side flaps splayed out, and the back upward. Press firmly all down the length of the back bone with the heel of your hand, effectively squashing the herring down flat. Now turn it over, and you will find that the backbone pulls away easily, leaving you with a neatly boned herring. Trim off the narrow band of bones down the edges.

When they are all done, place in a shallow dish and pour over the brine. Cover loosely and leave for some 6 hours or so before draining. Now you have in your possession six boned salted herrings, (which will be excellent for salads – try them mixed with potato, shallot, crème fraiche and lemon juice with lots of pepper, or alternatively with cubes of apple and beetroot in a light vinaigrette with plenty of chives).

To make the marinade, begin by crushing the spices roughly in a mortar. Tip into a pan with the sugar and vinegar. Bring up to the boil, simmer for 3 minutes, then draw off the heat and leave to cool. Have a quick nibble of a corner of one of the herrings. If it is too salty for comfort, soak for 10-20 minutes in a mixture of equal quantities milk and water, then drain and pat dry. Now layer the herring fillets in a shallow container, with the onion and bay leaves. Pour the marinade over them, cover and stash away for at least five days in the fridge, turning occasionally, before eating.

Lamb and Dried Apricot Pilau

This is just my kind of dish – a pile of golden rice, flavoured with a little meat, but not too much, plenty of spices and a hint of sweetness in the form of dried apricots. I like to eat it topped with a generous spoonful of yoghurt, and my daughter likes to add a puddle of mango chutney on the side.

SERVES 4

250g (9 oz) basmati rice
2 tablespoons extra virgin olive oil or sunflower oil
30g (1 oz) butter
1 onion, chopped
2 garlic cloves, chopped
250g (9 oz) minced lamb
1 teaspoon ground cinnamon
1 teaspoon ground coriander
1 teaspoon ground turmeric
600ml (1 pint) *Chicken Stock* (see page 242), lamb stock or water
110g (4 oz) dried apricots, diced
a handful of fresh coriander leaves
salt and pepper

Tip the basmati rice into a sieve and rinse thoroughly under the cold tap. Leave to drip dry. Heat the oil with half the butter in a large pan. Add the onion and garlic and cook until just about tender, and translucent. Now raise the heat and add the lamb mince. Fry, breaking up the lumps, until browned. Now add the spices and cook for a further minute or two. Add 150ml (5 fl oz) of the stock or water, then simmer very gently until virtually all the liquid has evaporated off.

Now add the apricots, rice and remaining stock or water. Season with salt and pepper, then bring up to the boil. Turn the heat down very low, cover tightly and leave to cook for 10-15 minutes, until the liquid has all been absorbed and the rice is tender. Check occasionally towards the end of cooking time to make sure that it is not catching, but don't stir it unless you feel it is 100 per cent necessary. Draw off the heat, stir in the coriander and the last little bit of butter, then taste and adjust seasoning.

The pilau is best served immediately, but if you have to hold it, tip into a shallow dish, cover with foil and place in a low oven. Fluff up the grains with a fork just before serving.

Picadillo

The list of ingredients for this Cuban dish of minced beef reads in a decidedly eccentric way, but they do all harmonise together in the end to produce a fine blend of savoury, sweet and piquant. Serve with rice and sliced avocado.

SERVES 4

2 tablespoons sunflower oil
1 onion, chopped
1 green pepper, seeded and finely chopped
4 garlic cloves, chopped
450g (1 lb) lean minced beef
150ml (5 fl oz) tomato passata
12 green olives, pitted and roughly chopped
60g (2 oz) raisins
1 tablespoon capers
150ml (5 fl oz) dry white wine
1 teaspoon caster sugar
salt and pepper

Heat the oil in a frying pan and cook the onion and green pepper until tender without browning. Add the garlic and cook for about 5 minutes. Now add all the remaining ingredients, reduce the heat, cover and simmer for a further 25-30 minutes, stirring occasionally. By the time it is cooked, the sauce should be reduced and thick, but not quite wet. Taste and adjust seasoning, and serve.

Sloppy Joes

The American answer to plain mince or more fancy bolognaise, these are simply a down-home mess of mince eaten in hamburger buns. I love them, though admittedly I prefer to replace the pap of a soft hamburger bun with the chewy texture of a baker's or home-made roll. If you don't have time to bake your own, your choice of organic bread rolls is likely to be limited anyway, so you'll just have to make do with what you can get hold of.

This recipe, accompanied by a baked sweet potato topped with yoghurt, and some lightly cooked broccoli on the side, has become something of a family favourite in our household, a quick and unsophisticated supper that is wolfed down by children and parents alike.

SERVES 4

15g (½ oz) butter
450g (1 lb) lean minced beef
1 medium onion, chopped
2 celery stalks, chopped
60g (2 oz) green pepper, seeded and chopped
1 generous tablespoon Worcestershire sauce*
½ teaspoon chilli sauce

3 tablespoons tomato ketchup
85ml (3 fl oz) water
4 toasted split rolls (see above)
salt and pepper

Take a large, heavy-based frying pan and melt the butter in it. Add the mince, onion, celery and pepper all together. Fry briskly over a good heat, breaking up the mince with a fork. When the mince is lightly browned and the vegetables are tender, add the Worcestershire sauce, chilli sauce, ketchup, salt and pepper and the water. Stir, then cover and simmer over a gentle heat for a further 10-15 minutes, until the mixture is moist and tender but not oozing liquid. Taste and adjust seasonings, then spoon into the toasted rolls and serve.

Braised Sausages in Red Wine

A warming and comforting way to doll up sausages, the slow braising works particularly well with lean meaty sausages, which can sometimes be a little chewy. Whatever else is to be part of the meal, don't fail to serve the braised sausages with lots of mashed potato to soak up the juice and plenty of mustard.

SERVES 4

8-12 good quality pork sausages (about 750g/ 1¾ lb)
30g (1 oz) butter
1 large onion, red or white, sliced
2 garlic cloves, sliced
300ml (10 fl oz) fruity red wine

1½ tablespoons redcurrant jelly
1 bouquet garni, consisting of 1 bay leaf, 2 sprigs of thyme and 2 sprigs of parsley
salt and pepper

Preheat the oven to 190°C/375°F/Gas Mark 5. Prick the sausages all over and brown them quickly in half the butter. Transfer to an ovenproof dish that is just large enough to take them in a single snug layer. Reduce the heat under the pan, add the remaining butter, and fry the onion and garlic gently until tender and translucent. Add to the sausages. Drain any fat from the pan then return to the heat. Pour in the red wine and bring up to the boil. Stir in the redcurrant jelly then pour over the sausages. Tuck in the bouquet garni and season with salt and pepper. Cover with foil and bake for about 30 minutes.

Rillons

These are one of the staples of any French *charcuterie*. Golden brown, tender cubes of slowly cooked pork belly, they are eaten cold, sliced, with bread and salads, or nicer still hot (reheated in the oven), on a bed of mashed potato with slices of fried apple, or a tart apple sauce and dollops of mustard.

SERVES 4

1kg (2 lb) belly of pork
60g (2 oz) lard
1 bay leaf
3 cloves
1 cinnamon stick

a grating of fresh nutmeg
1 blade of mace
1 big sprig of thyme
salt and pepper

Preheat the oven to 150°C/300°F/Gas Mark 2. Cut the belly of pork into pieces about 10cm (4 in) long by 7cm (2½ in) wide. Smear the lard over an ovenproof dish large enough to take all the pork in a single layer. Place the pork in the dish and season lightly with a little salt and pepper. Tuck the bay leaf, all the spices and the thyme in among the pork. Add water to a depth of about 5mm (¼ in) and cover with foil.

Bake in the preheated oven for about 3 hours, basting occasionally, until the meat is tender. Uncover and drain off the fat and liquid. Strain and leave to set, then lift off the fat (use it for frying potatoes, or bread – it has an excellent flavour).

Return the cubes of meat to the oven uncovered, this time at a higher heat, 200°C/400°F/Gas Mark 6, to brown. Once they are lightly browned, remove. Serve hot or cold.

Lancashire Hot-pot

It's old-fashioned and homely, but a slowly cooked Lancashire hot-pot, with its crust of browned potatoes on top, is a very welcome sight. There are plenty of variations on the basic theme, but this is how I make it, browning the meat first for colour, and adding flat-cap mushrooms for their particular flavour.

SERVES 6

6 meaty lamb loin chops, or 12 lamb cutlets
6 lamb's kidneys, halved
60g (2 oz) dripping or butter, melted
1kg (2¼ lb) potatoes, thinly sliced
3 large onions, sliced

225g (8 oz) flat-cap mushrooms, thickly sliced (optional)
300ml (10 fl oz) lamb stock, *Chicken Stock* (see page 242) or water
salt and pepper

Preheat the oven to 220°C/425°F/Gas Mark 7. Brown the chops and the kidneys in half the dripping or butter over a high heat, to give them a little colour. Layer the potatoes, chops, kidneys, onions and mushrooms (if using) in a deep casserole, seasoning well between each layer. End with a layer of potatoes, neatly overlapping and covering the contents of the dish. Pour over the stock or water. There should be enough to come about halfway up the ingredients. If you seem to be running short, add a little more water. Brush the remaining dripping or butter over the top layer of the potatoes, then season well.

Cover the casserole and place it in the oven. Give it 20-25 minutes to heat through, then reduce the oven temperature to 150°C/300°F/Gas Mark 2 and leave to cook for a further 2 hours. Finally remove the lid, raise the oven temperature back to 220°C/425°F/Gas Mark 7, and cook for a final 20-30 minutes until the top layer of the potatoes is browned.

Yoghurt-marinaded Lamb Kebabs

Serve on a mound of the *Baked Vegetable Rice* on page 141, or just plain rice, together with the *Tzatziki* on page 90, or slip the meat into warmed pitta pockets, along with diced tomato, cucumber and pieces of lettuce, and perhaps a spoonful or two of tzatziki or hummus.

The longer you marinade the lamb the tenderer it will be. A full 24 hours is what you should be aiming for.

SERVES 4

900g (2 lb) boned shoulder or leg of lamb, trimmed and cut into 2cm (¾ in) chunks
lemon wedges
Pitta Bread (see page 223)

MARINADE
6 tablespoons plain whole milk yoghurt
1 small tomato, roughly diced, skin and all
3 garlic cloves, roughly chopped
1 teaspoon thyme leaves
1 tablespoon dark or light muscovado sugar
salt and pepper

To make the marinade, put all the ingredients in a processor and process to a paste. Smear all over the cubes of lamb and leave to marinade for at the very least 2 hours, and for best results, a full 24 hours.

Preheat the grill or barbecue. Use metal skewers or well-soaked wooden skewers. Thread up the lamb on to the skewers, taking care not to push the bits of meat too tight against each other, just gently nestling shoulder to shoulder, so that the heat can curl and work its way round and through the lamb. Cook close to the heat, turning occasionally, until crusty and brown on the outside. Eat immediately with a squeeze of lemon and some tzatziki.

Beef, Carrot and Shallot Stew
with Thyme and Lemon Dumplings

What a wonderful thing a sturdy beef stew can be when it is properly made with a classy cut of stewing beef. And there's no better cut, to my mind, than the shin, with its gelatinous folds that melt down to give a particularly savoury, lip-smacking velvety quality to the sauce. You'll have to go to a proper butcher to get it (it may be worth ordering in advance) as I don't think I've ever seen it, organic or not, for sale in a supermarket. It is well worth the bother.

   This stew is eked out with plentiful carrots and browned shallots for sweetness. A surface studded with dumplings is the final crowning joy. If you want to make the stew in advance (a good idea as the flavour definitely improves with reheating), cook it up to the point of adding the dumplings, stopping just before. Reheat thoroughly on the hob, then dot the dumplings over the surface and return to the oven for the final stage.

SERVES 4

400g (14 oz) small shallots
4 tablespoons extra virgin
   olive oil
1 onion, chopped
2 garlic cloves, sliced
1.5kg (3½ lb) boned shin of
   beef, trimmed and cut
   into 2.5cm (1 in) thick
   slices
seasoned plain flour
1 bouquet garni, consisting
   of 1 sprig of rosemary,
   1 large sprig of thyme,
   2 parsley stalks and
   1 bay leaf
1kg (2¼ lb) carrots, cut into
   4cm (1½ in) lengths

500ml (18 fl oz) bitter
600ml (1 pint) beef stock,
   Chicken Stock (see page
    242) or water
salt and pepper

DUMPLINGS
60g (2 oz) shredded suet, or
   frozen butter
110g (4 oz) self-raising flour
½ teaspoon baking powder
¼ teaspoon salt
2 teaspoons fresh thyme
   leaves
finely grated zest of ½
   lemon
1 tablespoon lemon juice

Preheat the oven to 170°C/325°F/Gas Mark 3.

Top and tail the shallots and place in a bowl. Cover with boiling water, leave to stand for about 30 seconds then drain. This loosens their skins, which will now slip off easily. Dry the shallots. Heat half the olive oil in a frying pan and fry the shallots until browned. Set aside. Now fry the chopped onion and the garlic in the same pan, adding a little extra oil if needed. Once they are tender and translucent, scrape into an ovenproof casserole.

Add the remaining olive oil to the frying pan. Dust the pieces of beef in the seasoned flour and brown thoroughly over a high heat in several batches – don't overcrowd the pan, or else they will simply sweat and swelter in their own juices. Once the meat is done, transfer to the casserole. Season generously, tuck in the bouquet garni and the carrots, and sprinkle over about 1 tablespoon of the leftover seasoned flour. Pour the bitter and the stock or water into the frying pan and bring up to the boil, scraping in all the residues from frying. Pour the boiling liquid over the meat in the casserole. Cover and place in the oven. Cook for about 2 hours until the meat is very tender, then add the shallots and continue cooking for a further 30 minutes.

Meanwhile make the dumplings. If using butter, put it in the freezer for half an hour or more. Sift the flour with the baking powder and salt. Grate in the frozen butter, or add the suet, then add the thyme and lemon zest. Mix in the lemon juice and just enough water to make a very slightly sticky dough. Flour your hands, and roll into small balls about as big as a quail's egg.

When the meat is done, check to make sure that there is ample sauce to poach the dumplings in. If it is a bit on the dry side, stir in a little more water or stock. Now dot the dumplings over the surface of the stew and return it to the oven, covered, for a further 40 minutes until the dumplings have swelled up in size and are cooked through. Baste them once or twice with the stew's sauce as they cook – they won't look quite so pretty but they'll taste all the better for it. Serve steaming hot with mashed potatoes and some kind of greens.

Poached Chicken
with Basil and Mint Mayonnaise

For really moist cold chicken, with oodles of flavour, try poaching. No, not traipsing out after dark with snares and a large grubby overcoat, but cooking the bird gently in water with a few vegetables and herbs tucked alongside. Not only do you end up with delicious chicken, but you also have a good chicken stock (boil it down and freeze if you can't use it immediately). Serve with this mayonnaise, boiled new potatoes, a big salad and good bread, and the meal is made.

SERVES 4, GENEROUSLY

1 large free-range chicken
1 leek, halved
1 onion, quartered
1 carrot, quartered
1 bay leaf
2 sprigs of parsley
1 lemon, halved
a few fresh basil and mint
   leaves to serve
salt and pepper

MAYONNAISE
a big handful of mint leaves
a big handful of basil leaves
1 level teaspoon coarse salt
½ teaspoon caster sugar
2 egg yolks
2-4 tablespoons lemon juice
1 teaspoon Dijon mustard
100ml (3 fl oz) extra virgin
   olive oil
200ml (7 fl oz) sunflower oil

Place the chicken, the vegetables, bay leaf, parsley, lemon halves and some salt and pepper in a large saucepan. Pour in enough water to just cover the chicken. Bring up to the boil, then reduce the heat and let the chicken cook gently, at a very lazy simmer or even just below, turning it once in a while, until cooked through – about 1-1½ hours. Leave to cool in its own stock.

To make the mayonnaise, put the mint and basil leaves in a mortar with the salt and sugar. Pound to a paste, then work in the egg yolks, 2 tablespoons of the lemon juice and the mustard. Mix the two oils together in a jug. Start whisking the egg yolk and herb mixture, adding the oil continuously, but very slowly, verging on drop by drop. When you have incorporated about half the oil, increase the flow to a slow steady trickle, still whisking all the while. By the time all the oil is used up, you will have before you a bowl of thick, slippery mayonnaise, flecked with green. Taste, adding more salt or lemon juice as required.

When the chicken has cooled, take out of the stock, discard the skin, then carve it up and arrange the carved flesh on a serving plate. Drizzle over a little of the cooking liquid to keep it moist and strew with a few basil and mint leaves. Serve with the mayonnaise.

Tunisian Chicken, Olive and Bean Stew

A delicious stew from north Africa, flavoured liberally with coriander seeds. Use thigh meat in preference to breast as it will impart more flavour. Serve with couscous or rice.

SERVES 4

500g (18 oz) boned and skinned chicken
¼ teaspoon cayenne pepper
¼ teaspoon freshly ground black pepper
1 heaped tablespoon coriander seeds, crushed
3 tablespoons extra virgin olive oil
1 onion, chopped

250g (9 oz) black-eyed beans, soaked for at least 4 hours
2 sprigs of thyme
2 tablespoons tomato purée
85g (3 oz) black olives
1½ tablespoons red wine vinegar
salt

Cut the chicken into cubes about 2-2.5cm (¾-1 in) across. Mix with the cayenne, black pepper and coriander. Stir to coat evenly. Fry in half the oil over a medium heat for about 3 minutes. Add the onion and continue to fry until the onion is tender.

Drain and rinse the beans, then add to the pan with the thyme and enough water to cover by about 3cm (but no salt yet). Bring up to the boil and simmer until the beans are tender (about 40 minutes) and most of the liquid has evaporated. Stir in the tomato purée, olives, vinegar and salt. Simmer for another 3-4 minutes, then taste and adjust seasoning. Serve hot.

Chicken Provençal

This is a southern French way of cooking chicken, which benefits enormously from really full-flavoured tomatoes and peppers. Although ten cloves of garlic go into the pot, you will not be blasted away by their reek. The cloves are left whole, and soften and mellow as they cook.

SERVES 4

1 medium to large free-range chicken, cut into 8 pieces
2 tablespoons extra virgin olive oil
1 large glass of dry white wine
1 tablespoon tomato purée
½ teaspoon caster sugar
10 garlic cloves, peeled

a small bunch of thyme
1 kg (2¼ lb) ripe tomatoes, skinned, seeded and roughly chopped
60g (2 oz) black olives
2 red peppers, grilled and skinned (see pages 116-7), cut into eighths
salt and pepper

Preheat the oven to 170°C/325°F/Gas Mark 3. Brown the chicken pieces in the olive oil over a fierce heat. Transfer to an ovenproof casserole. Pour the wine into the frying pan and bring up to the boil, scraping in any residues from frying the chicken. Boil until reduced by two-thirds. Stir in the tomato purée and the sugar. Draw off the heat.

Tuck the cloves of garlic and the bunch of thyme in amongst the chicken pieces. Cover with the tomatoes, season with salt and pepper and pour over the hot wine. Cover and cook in the oven for about 40 minutes until the chicken is tender.

Meanwhile, blanch the olives in boiling water for 1 minute and drain thoroughly. Add to the chicken stew, with the peppers, after it has been cooking for 45 minutes. Stir, then return to the oven, uncovered, for a final 15 minutes. Taste and adjust seasoning, then serve with noodles, or mashed potatoes.

Griddled Chicken Escalopes
with Blackcurrant and Mint Salsa

The great thing about flattening out chicken breasts to make escalopes is that they then cook in a jiffy, whilst remaining moist and tender. Partnering them with a fruity yet earthy salsa sets them off at their best.

SERVES 4

4 boned and skinned
   chicken breasts
extra virgin olive oil
salt and pepper

SALSA
200g (7 oz) blackcurrants,
   topped and tailed
4 teaspoons caster sugar

1 tablespoon white wine
   vinegar
a small handful of mint
   leaves, finely shredded
400g (14 oz) tomatoes,
   skinned, seeded and
   finely diced
4 spring onions, thinly sliced
salt and pepper

To make the salsa, put the blackcurrants into a pan with the sugar and vinegar. Stir over a low to moderate heat until the blackcurrant juices begin to run. Cook for a further 3 minutes or so, until the blackcurrants are bathed in a dark purple bath of sweet-sour juice.

Draw off the heat and cool until tepid. Reserve a pinch of the mint, then mix the rest of the mint with the blackcurrant mixture and all the remaining salsa ingredients. Set aside for at least half an hour before using. Stir once more just before serving, then taste and adjust the seasonings.

To prepare the chicken breasts, take a sharp knife and one by one, place them flat on the work surface and slice them in half horizontally without cutting right through, so that you can open them out flat. Let the fillet, the loose flap of flesh underneath, cling on to the edge of the opened chicken, but don't worry if it comes astray. Sandwich each chicken breast, opened out, between two sheets of greaseproof paper or clingfilm. Slap the chicken with a meat mallet or a rolling pin until it has flattened out to about 1½ times its original size. Brush on each side with olive oil and season well.

Place a griddle pan over a high heat, and leave to heat through for 3-4 minutes. Lay the chicken escalopes in the pan (you will probably have to do them in several batches, unless you have an enormous pan), and cook for 1½-2 minutes on each side, until just cooked through. Keep the cooked ones warm, and loosely covered with foil while you griddle the rest.

Serve the griddled chicken escalopes with the blackcurrant salsa, sprinkled with the reserved mint.

Spatchcocked Chicken
with Lemon and Fennel

I've just realised that there's been a spatchcocked chicken recipe in two out of three of my most recent books, and here I am at it again. Can this possibly be justified? Yes, yes, yes! This is one of the easiest and most delicious ways of cooking a chicken, and it is just that big bit sexier than a whole roast bird, much as I love chicken cooked that way. So, for version number three, here is a splendidly crisp, lemony, fennely bird that can be prepared in a jiffy, and will be devoured with notable enthusiasm.

SERVES 4

1 gorgeous, medium to large free-range chicken
1 lemon, halved
2 garlic cloves, crushed
coarse salt and pepper

4 tablespoons olive oil
2 heads of fennel
4 garlic cloves, whole and unpeeled

Preheat the oven to 220°C/425°F/Gas Mark 7. To spatchcock your chicken, take a pair of poultry shears, a sturdy pair of scissors or a sharp knife, and cut along the backbone (i.e. the underneath, opposite the breast) from neck to tail end, trimming off extraneous flaps of fat as you go. Now, press down firmly along the breast bone with the flat of your hand, flattening out the chicken like a squashed toad. Lay the bird in an oiled roasting tin, large enough to take it flat with a little room to spare.

Squeeze the lemon over the chicken, and tuck the spent lemon halves alongside the bird. Rub the crushed garlic over the chicken and season generously with salt and pepper. Finally spoon a couple of tablespoons of oil over the bird.

Turn to your fennel. Cut off the green feathery leaves and chop roughly. Scatter over the chicken. Quarter the fennel bulbs and toss in the remaining oil with the whole garlic cloves. Tuck them all, with every last dribble of oil, around the chicken and season lightly. Cover the tin with foil.

Bake for about 30 minutes, then remove the foil, baste the chicken and turn the fennel. Return to the oven, uncovered, for a further 20-30 minutes, basting once, until both chicken and vegetables are cooked through. Serve immediately, cutting the chicken up into large chunks with the poultry shears, scissors or knife (all immaculately cleaned, of course).

Fruit Fools

Fruit fools are amongst the simplest and most elegant of summer puddings. One mouthful of a gooseberry fool and I am transported by nostalgia back to my childhood, and the eternally warm and sunny June days of memory, when we ate lunch in the garden beside the medlar tree. They combine elemental purity and luxuriousness in one almost effortless swoop.

There are no end of possible fruit fools to be made throughout the summer months, starting with rhubarb just as the weather begins to warm, on to strawberry or raspberry, gooseberry (and elderflower if they are still in bloom), blackcurrant, tayberry and loganberry, blackberry and so on. The coterie of fools divides broadly, first, into those made with soft fruit, or firmer, often tarter fruit that needs to be cooked, and secondly into those made simply with whipped cream, mascarpone or clotted cream, and then those based on a thick custard. I give here two approximate recipes (when it comes to making fools, you have to judge the balance of fruit, sugar and enriching cream or custard by taste which encompass all the basic possibilities, leaving you free to improvise and swap and play with whatever summer bounty comes your way). The rough rule of thumb, by the way, is equal quantities of fruit and base.

Raspberry and Mascarpone Fool ⓥ

Any soft fruit that can be eaten raw, e.g. strawberries, loganberries, tayberries and blackberries, can be used instead of the raspberries. If you don't like clotted cream, or cannot get an organic clotted cream, then substitute lightly whipped cream or mascarpone instead.

SERVES 6

around 400g (14 oz) ripe, juicy, sweet raspberries
sugar

roughly 250g (9 oz) clotted*cream
or mascarpone,
or 300ml (10 fl oz) double cream, whipped

Mash the raspberries with a fork and stir in sugar to taste (I reckon about 2-3 tablespoons should do it). Beat the clotted cream, or mascarpone if using, lightly to loosen. Fold the fruit into the cream or mascarpone. Taste and add a little more sugar if needed, though the best fools retain a touch of sharpness to balance the richness. Serve with thin biscuits such as langues de chat.

Gooseberry Fool Ⓥ

This method is also suitable for rhubarb or blackcurrants, both of which require cooking before consuming. Of course, you can simply mix the cooked fruit with cream, as in the preceding recipe, though they go particularly well with custard.

SERVES 6-8

500g (18 oz) green
 gooseberries, topped
 and tailed ⓦ
4 elderflower heads
 (optional)

a splash or two of water
caster sugar to taste
300ml (10 fl oz) thick
 Custard (see page 217)

Put the gooseberries into a pan. Tie the elderflowers together (if using) and pop them into a pan along with a splash or two of water. Place over a low heat, stirring occasionally, until the juices begin to run. Then raise the heat to moderate, and bring to the boil, stirring occasionally. Simmer for 5 minutes or so until tender. Draw off the heat, stir in sugar to taste and leave to cool. Remove the elderflowers. Mash the larger pieces of gooseberry, then stir into the custard. Serve with little thin biscuits.

Compote of Dried Fruit Ⓥ

In winter, this pudding of dried fruit simmered in a sweet dessert wine is very welcome. Sometimes I make it just with a brace of dried fruits – apricots and prunes perhaps – but at other times I throw in every kind of dried fruit I can lay my hands on, just for the fun of it.

   Serve the compote for pudding, and eat leftovers with cereal for breakfast next day.

SERVES 4

250g (9 oz) mixed dried
 fruit (apricots, pears,
 prunes, peaches, raisins)
1 cinnamon stick

300ml (10 fl oz) sweet
 dessert wine
30g (1 oz) toasted flaked
 almonds

Cut the larger pieces of fruit into strips. Place all the fruit in a saucepan with the cinnamon and wine. Bring gently to the boil. Simmer for 20-30 minutes until the fruit is tender and the liquid is thick and syrupy. Serve hot or cold, scattered with almonds, and with lashings of thick yoghurt or cream.

Blackcurrant Kissel
with Crème Chantilly Ⓥ

A kissel is a Russian fruit pudding, a purée really, thickened traditionally with a little potato starch, though I usually use cornflour. When it is made with tart blackcurrants and topped with a swirl of vanilla-sweet whipped cream, it is just divine.

SERVES 6

900g (2 lb) blackcurrants, or a mixture of blackcurrants, redcurrants and raspberries
1 large or 2 small cinnamon sticks

300g (10½ oz) caster sugar
2 tablespoons cornflour
Crème Chantilly (see below)

Put the currants (don't bother to strip them), cinnamon, sugar and 300ml (10 fl oz) water into a saucepan and bring up to the boil. Simmer until the blackcurrants are very tender and have mostly popped – a mere 2-3 minutes. Rub through a sieve and return to the pan. Mix the cornflour to a paste with a tablespoon or so of cold water, then stir into the warm fruit purée. Bring up to the boil, stirring constantly. Let it simmer for about 3 minutes, then draw off the heat. Tip into a serving bowl and leave to cool. Serve with a bowl of Crème Chantilly.

Crème Chantilly Ⓥ

Such a pretty name for something that is almost elemental. It is nothing more than sweetened whipped cream flavoured with vanilla. It takes only a few minutes to whip up, and is a great accompaniment to all sorts of puddings made with slightly tart fruit.

SERVES 4

300ml (10 fl oz) whipping cream or double cream

2-3 tablespoons caster sugar
1 teaspoon vanilla extract

Put all the ingredients into a bowl and whip together until the cream just about holds its shape in a gentle, floppy fashion. Spoon into a serving bowl and chill lightly until ready to serve.

Poached Plums in Cider ⓥ

The smell that wafts through the house as these plums poach gently in the oven is a real joy, with its fruit and cinnamon tones. So too are the poached plums themselves, tender and semi-sweet in their scented syrup. Serve them cold, with a bowl of extra sugar or some honey on the table for those with a sweet tooth, and plenty of cream.

SERVES 6

1kg (2¼ lb) plums, halved and stoned

1 litre (1¾ pints) dry cider
1 cinnamon stick
175g (6 oz) caster sugar

Preheat the oven to 150°C/300°F/Gas Mark 2. Arrange the halved plums in a snug, single layer in a roasting tin. Put the cider, cinnamon stick and sugar into a saucepan, and stir over a moderate heat until the sugar has dissolved. Bring up to the boil and simmer for 10 minutes to make a light syrup. Pour over the plums and place in the oven while still hot. Bake for 20-35 minutes, depending on the ripeness of the plums, basting once or twice as they cook, until very tender. Lift the plums out with a slotted spoon and pile into a shallow serving dish. Put the roasting tin on the hob and boil the juices hard until reduced by about half. Pour over the plums and leave to cool. Serve cold with cream.

St Clements Syllabub Ⓥ

This pudding is dastardly rich and creamy with a shaft of concentrated orange and lemon juice piercing through it. Divine. Unutterably unhealthy with all that cream, but then this is definitely a special-occasion, once-in-a-while sort of affair.

SERVES 4

4 oranges
1 lemon
3 tablespoons vanilla sugar
   or caster sugar

300ml (10 fl oz) double
   cream
1 tablespoon brandy or
   Grand Marnier* (optional)

Use a zester to take fine shreds of orange zest from half of one of the oranges and half of the lemon. If you don't have a zester, use a potato peeler, then cut the strips of zest into very fine needles. Blanch in boiling water for 2 minutes, then drain, run under the cold tap and leave to drain completely.

Squeeze the juice from the oranges and lemon and place in a small pan. Bring up to the boil and boil hard until reduced to about 3 or 4 tablespoonfuls of concentrated juice. Pour into a large bowl and leave to cool.

Now add the sugar and cream (and Grand Marnier/brandy if using). Whisk the whole lot together until it holds its shape in a floppy, soft fashion. Divide between four glasses or small pretty bowls, and decorate with the blanched shreds of orange and lemon zest. If not eating immediately, chill in the fridge for up to 3 hours, before eating.

Lemon Curd Ice-cream Ⓥ

This is an ice-cream to die for. It is, quite simply, a mixture of lemon curd and cream, frozen to a gloriously rich, lemony-sweet concoction that melts on the tongue in the most delightful way. However, don't think you can get away with chucking a jar of commercial lemon curd in with a tub of cream. The lemon curd has to be home-made, since only home-made has the right flavour, strong and perfect enough to carry the ice-cream. There's no great mystery to making your own lemon curd – it just takes a little patient stirring – and the results are so good that you will never buy it again.

SERVES 4-6

300ml (10 fl oz) whipping cream

LEMON CURD
finely grated zest and juice of 3 lemons

225g (8 oz) caster sugar
150g (5 oz) unsalted butter
2 large eggs
2 egg yolks

First make the lemon curd. Put the zest, juice, sugar and butter into a bowl set over a pan of lazily simmering water, making sure that the base of the bowl does not touch the water. Stir until the butter and sugar have dissolved. Now beat the eggs together lightly, and sieve into the lemon mixture. Stir continuously, until the mixture has thickened without letting it come anywhere near boiling point. Remember that it doesn't have to be phenomenally thick, as it will thicken up a great deal as it cools. Just make sure that it coats the back of a spoon thickly. Scrape into a cool, clean bowl and leave to cool.

Whip the cream lightly, so that it is still floppy, but has some substance to it. Fold into the cold lemon curd. Either freeze in an ice-cream machine or, if you don't have one, pour the mixture into a shallow container and place in the freezer, set to its lowest setting. Leave until the sides are beginning to set, then break them up and push into the centre. Leave for another half hour or so and repeat. Now leave until the ice-cream has just about set but is not yet rock-hard. Process briefly until smooth, or beat hard with a wooden spoon to break up all the ice crystals. Return to the freezer and leave to finish freezing.

Transfer the ice-cream from the freezer to the fridge about 45 minutes before serving so that it has time to soften.

Brown Bread Ice-cream ⓥ

I think it is fair to say that this is a quintessentially British ice-cream with its note of thrift (using up leftover stale bread and all that) coupled with its high tenor of indulgence. When it comes to puddings, we are not inclined to stint, however thrifty we are hoping to be. Recently I made this for large events, both in the Philippines and Vietnam. The worldly-wise dessert chefs who, with their teams, were the ones who actually did all the work, thought I was barking mad. They had never come across it before. Now, they both include it occasionally on their hotel menus. A triumph!

SERVES 6-8

110g (4 oz) wholemeal breadcrumbs
175g (6 oz) light muscovado sugar
300ml (10 fl oz) single cream, or single cream mixed with milk, or just milk

1 vanilla pod, slit in half lengthways
1 egg
1 egg yolk
1 tablespoon dark rum
300ml (10 fl oz) double cream

Preheat the oven to 200°C/400°F/Gas Mark 6. Mix the breadcrumbs with 100g (3½ oz) of the sugar, and spread out on a baking tray. Roast for about 8-12 minutes, stirring at least twice so that the ones on top and at the edges don't get burnt, until the breadcrumbs have turned a shade or two darker and have melded with the sugar. Don't let it burn! As soon as they are done, and while still very hot, stir again, scraping up any pieces that have stuck to the bottom of the pan. Keep stirring for a few minutes, until the crumbs have cooled slightly and are crisp rather than sticky. Leave to cool.

Put the single cream into a pan with the vanilla pod and bring up to the boil. Draw off the heat, cover and leave to infuse for 15 minutes, then bring back almost to the boil. Meanwhile, whisk the egg and egg yolk with the remaining sugar until pale and fluffy. Whisk in the hot infused cream then pour the mixture back into the pan. Stir over a low heat for a few minutes until the custard thickens slightly. Draw off the heat, stir in the rum and then pour into a clean bowl. Leave to cool, stirring occasionally.

Whisk the double cream until it just about holds its shape but is still a little sloppy, then fold into the custard with the breadcrumbs.

Freeze in an ice-cream machine or, if you don't have one, pour the mixture into a shallow container and place in the freezer, set to its lowest setting. Leave until the sides are beginning to set, then break them up and push into the centre. Leave for another half hour or so and repeat. Now leave until the ice-cream has just about set but is not yet rock-hard. Beat hard with a wooden spoon to break up all the ice crystals. Return to the freezer and leave to finish freezing.

Transfer the ice-cream from the freezer to the fridge a good 30-40 minutes before serving, to soften.

Summer Pudding Ⓥ

This has to be one of the great puddings of the world, and it is all ours. There is little better in early July, on a sunny day, than the first mouthful of this pudding, made with first-class bread and the freshest soft fruits. Though you can use whatever selection is at its finest when you pick or shop for the fruit, it is essential, I think to include currants of at least one sort, if not two – in other words, both redcurrants and blackcurrants.

SERVES 6-8

750g (1¾ lb) mixed summer fruit (raspberries, red, white and black currants, tayberries, loganberries, blackberries, cherries, blueberries, etc.)

185g (6½ oz) caster sugar
2 tablespoons Crème de Cassis* or Crème de Mûre*
1 medium loaf of good-quality white bread, thinly sliced, crusts removed

If you have time, mix the fruit with the sugar in a saucepan, cover with a tea-towel or clingfilm and leave for a few hours to get the juices running. Place the pan over the heat and bring gently up to the boil, then simmer for about 3 minutes. Draw off the heat and stir in the Cassis. Carefully spoon out about 2 tablespoons of juice and set aside in a small bowl.

Rinse a 1 litre (2 pint) bowl out with cold water, then shake out the excess. Cut a round out of one piece of bread to fit the bottom of the bowl, then cut the remaining slices into more or less triangular wedges. Line the sides of the bowl with wedges of bread, nudging them together tightly so that there are no gaps at all. Spoon in all the fruit and their juices (apart from the reserved juice). Cover the surface with more wedges of bread. Find a saucer that fits neatly inside the bowl, to cover the upper layer of bread, then weight it down with weights (bags of rice, tins of baked beans or whatever comes to hand). Leave in the fridge overnight.

Remove the weights and saucer, and run a thin blade around the edges, then invert on to a shallow serving plate. Brush the reserved juices over any blotchy, whitish patches, and then just pour the last few drops over the pudding to burnish. Serve with cream.

Peaches and Cream Tart ⓥ

This is a sensational tart with its stunningly crisp, buttery cornmeal pastry – a recipe borrowed from food writer Brian Glover – and a rich, vanilla-scented filling blanketing the peach halves.

SERVES 8

CORNMEAL PASTRY
75g (2½ oz) plain flour
75g (2½ oz) fine yellow
  cornmeal
a pinch of salt
45g (1½ oz) icing sugar
85g (3 oz) unsalted butter,
  softened
1 large egg yolk

FILLING
120ml (4½ fl oz) double
  cream
1 vanilla pod
3 strips of lemon zest
2 eggs
60g (2 oz) caster sugar
1 tablespoon plain flour,
  sifted
½ tablespoon lemon juice
2 tablespoons fine yellow
  cornmeal
4-6 ripe peaches, skinned,
  halved and stoned

For the pastry, sift the flour with the cornmeal, salt and icing sugar. Process with the butter, egg yolk and 2 tablespoons iced water to form a soft dough (you may need a splash more water). Scrape out and knead lightly to smooth out, then form a ball, wrap in clingfilm and chill for at least 1 hour.

Preheat the oven to 170°C/325°F/Gas Mark 3. Roll out the pastry to line a 25cm (10 in) diameter tart tin. Chill for half an hour. Line this in turn with non-stick baking parchment and weight down with baking beans. Bake blind for 20 minutes, then remove the beans and paper and return the tart shell to the oven for 10 minutes to dry out. Cool.

Now for the filling. Preheat the oven to 180°C/350°F/Gas Mark 4. Put the cream into a pan with the vanilla pod and lemon zest. Bring gently up to the boil, then turn the heat down extremely low and leave to infuse for half an hour, covered.

Whisk the eggs with the sugar until very pale and light and foamy. Whisk in the sifted flour, then the lemon juice, followed by the warm cream. Sprinkle the cornmeal over the base of the tart. Slice the peach halves, cutting them almost, but not quite, through at one end, then lay them, curved side up in the tart tin, pressing them down slightly to fan out. Spoon over the custardy mixture. Bake for 40-45 minutes until lightly browned and just about set. Serve warm or cold.

Rice Pudding
with Blueberry and Lime Compote ⓥ

The slowly baked rice pudding is a thing of great, great joy. And the skin, oh, that brown and gold, condensed milk caramel layer of skin... there's nothing else quite like it. Despite the virtually infinite versions of rice pudding to be found wherever rice has made its mark in the world, I still think our old-fashioned baked pud, lightly sweetened with a dollop of red jam in the centre, is one of the very best. To give it a gentle twist towards the twenty-first century, I've made one teensy change. Not to the pudding itself, of course (heaven forfend), but to the jam. No longer a splodge of anonymous scarlet, I have transformed it into a darkest purple puddle of blueberries simmered with zesty lime. And if you can't get organic blueberries, then make it with blackcurrants, using only half the lime juice.

SERVES 4-6

75g (2½ oz) pudding rice
1 litre (1¾ pints)
  creamy milk
30g (1 oz) unsalted butter
45g (1½ oz) sugar
pinch of salt
150ml (¼ pint) double
  cream

BLUEBERRY AND LIME
COMPOTE
340g (12 oz) blueberries
170g (6 oz) sugar
finely grated zest of 1 lime
juice of 2 limes

Preheat the oven to 140°C/275°F/Gas Mark 1. To make the rice pudding, put the rice and 600ml (1 pint) of the milk into a pie dish with the butter, sugar and salt. Stir, then place in the oven and leave for 1 hour. Stir in the remaining milk and cook for another 1 hour. Finally, stir in the cream and return to the oven for a final hour, until the mixture has thickened and a bubbling, golden brown skin has formed on the surface.

To make the compote, put all the ingredients into a pan and stir over a moderate heat until the juices begin to run. Bring up to the boil and simmer for 4 minutes. Draw off the heat and leave to cool.

Serve the pudding hot or cold, each helping topped with a spoonful of the blueberry compote.

Brown-sugar Meringues
with Chocolate Crème Fraiche ⓥ

I'm a keen meringue-maker – well, I just can't stand the idea of more whites lingering on in the back of my fridge until they are well beyond redemption. I know I could freeze them, but somehow they never quite make it as far as the freezer! It only takes a few minutes to knock up a meringue, anyway, and they always go down well. This butterscotch variation on the basic whiter-than-white meringue makes a welcome change and, for special occasions, the addition of a dark, dark chocolate cream dresses them up very nicely. My husband and I prefer the sharper, darker version made with nothing more than chocolate and crème fraiche, especially against the sweetness of the meringues, but the children prefer a slightly sweeter version, softened with icing sugar.

Whichever you choose, don't bring the meringues and cream together until at most an hour before eating, as the cream will soften the meringue.

SERVES 5-6

2 egg whites
60g (2 oz) light muscovado
  sugar
60g (2 oz) caster sugar

CHOCOLATE CREME FRAICHE
100g (3½ oz) dark plain
  chocolate
150g (5 oz) crème fraiche
icing sugar (optional)

Preheat the oven to very low, about 110°C/225°F/Gas Mark ½, and line two baking trays or sheets with non-stick baking parchment.

To make the meringues, whisk the egg whites until they form stiff peaks. Add the muscovado sugar and whisk until the mixture is an almost irresistible glossy, thick, butterscotch meringue. Now fold in the caster sugar. Either pipe or spoon mounds of meringue (around a tablespoonful each, unless you want to make particularly petite mouthfuls), on to the parchment-lined trays. Place either in the very low oven, or in the plate-warming oven of an Aga, or even in the airing cupboard if it is on the warm side. Leave for at least 2 hours in the oven, or longer, perhaps even overnight, in the Aga or airing cupboard, until the meringues have completely dried out. At this stage, they will lift easily from the tray without sticking, and the bottoms will be firm to the touch. Cool on a wire rack and store in an airtight container if not using immediately.

To make the chocolate cream, break the chocolate into pieces and place into a bowl over a pan of lazily simmering water, making sure that the base of the bowl does not come into contact with the water. Leave until the chocolate has melted, but don't let it overheat, or it will seize up like cement. Lift the bowl off the pan of water and leave to cool until tepid, but still runny. Stir in the crème fraiche and a little icing sugar (if using) then sandwich the meringues together in pairs with a thick layer of the chocolate cream. Wait for the adulation and love of those around you as they tuck in.

Shrikand Ⓥ

This is a scented, rich Indian pudding made from nothing grander than strained yoghurt. Serve it in small bowlfuls as a little goes a long way.

SERVES 4

600ml (1 pint) Greek-style
  yoghurt
a generous pinch of saffron
  threads
2 teaspoons rosewater*

3 cardamom pods
icing sugar
1 tablespoon toasted
  slivered almonds or
  pistachio nuts

Line a large sieve with a double layer of butter muslin. Pour the yoghurt into the lined sieve and gather up the edges of the muslin. Tie a knot to form a bag and hang it up to drip over the sink or a bowl. Leave for about 4 hours, until it is good and thick.

Scrape all the strained yoghurt into a bowl. Dry-fry the saffron threads for a few seconds to crisp up, then cool and pound to a powder. Mix with the rosewater and let it stand for 10 minutes to dissolve. Split the cardamom pods and crush the seeds inside as finely as possible. Stir the rosewater and cardamom into the yoghurt and add sugar to taste. Divide between four small bowls and scatter the almonds or pistachio nuts over the top.

Strawberry Cheesecake Ⓥ

Every summer there comes a point when you've stashed away more than enough bowls of plain strawberries and cream, and it is time to move on. And this is a pretty good place to head for: a handsome-looking and handsome-tasting cheesecake topped with oodles of strawberries.

SERVES 8

BASE
225g (8 oz) digestive
   biscuits, crushed
85g (3 oz) butter, melted

FILLING
425g (15 oz) cream cheese
1 teaspoon vanilla essence
3 eggs
85g (3 oz) caster sugar
125g (4½ oz) crème fraiche
   or soured cream

TO FINISH
400g (14 oz) strawberries
3 tablespoons redcurrant
   jelly

Preheat the oven to 170°C/325°F/Gas Mark 3. For the base, mix the digestive biscuits and butter thoroughly and press evenly into a 24cm (9½ in) cake tin with a removable base. Bake for 10 minutes.

Beat the cream cheese until soft and then beat in the remaining filling ingredients in order. Spoon into the crust and smooth down lightly. Bake at the same temperature until just set, about 25-35 minutes. Cool and chill for 2 hours before unmoulding.

Halve the strawberries (or slice thickly if they are enormous). Put the redcurrant jelly into a small saucepan with 2 teaspoons water. Heat gently, breaking the jelly up, until it is quite dissolved. Brush over the surface of the cheesecake. Now arrange the strawberries in overlapping concentric circles, cut sides up, over the top. Reheat the redcurrant glaze a little, then brush generously over the strawberries. And now it is ready to serve at your pleasure.

Cherry Clafoutis Ⓥ

The clafoutis is the French version of the batter pudding, and a very fine thing it can be too. At its best a clafoutis is chock-a-block with juicy, lightly cooked fruit encased in a sweet, light, eggy batter. If you've had less than appetising clafoutis in cheap restaurants in France (made usually with too much flour and not enough egg), try making it yourself. It is an easy pudding to run up at home, and can be made with all kinds of different fruit. Cherries are the classic, but try it too with blueberries, peaches, blackberries, apricots and so on. This is an extra eggy version, verging on a baked custard, that we particularly like. If you want to head more towards the classic clafoutis, use only three eggs and increase the flour by 30g (1 oz).

SERVES 6

500g (18 oz) dark red cherries
60g (2 oz) plain flour
a pinch of salt
85g (3 oz) caster sugar
4 eggs
600ml (1 pint) full-cream milk
3 tablespoons Kirsch*, brandy or other hooch
30g (1 oz) flaked almonds
icing sugar

Preheat the oven to 190°C/375°F/Gas Mark 5. Pull the stalks off the cherries and if you are a cook of great virtue and patience, stone them too. I don't, on the premise that this would be to deprive my children (not to mention the adults) of the pleasure of playing 'tinker, tailor, soldier, sailor'. Spread the cherries out in a buttered, shallow ovenproof dish, approximately 25 x 20cm (10 x 8 in) or a little larger.

Sift the flour with the salt then stir in the sugar. Make a well in the centre and add the eggs. Now start whisking the flour into the eggs, gradually adding the milk at the same time, to make a smooth batter. Pour over the cherries, then spoon the Kirsch or whatever booze you've chosen over the batter and finally scatter with almonds. Bake for 40-45 minutes, until handsomely browned and puffed up. Serve hot or warm, dusted lightly with icing sugar.

Banana White Chocolate Custard ⓥ

Banana custard is a good, old-fashioned nursery pudding that can send grown men (and women) into ecstasies. Well, it does the job for William, anyway. This variation is perhaps even more devastating, what with the addition of sweet, creamy white chocolate. Not for grand occasions, then, but perfect for those times when you crave comfort food and a taste of nostalgia.

SERVES 4-6

4 bananas

CUSTARD
110g (4 oz) best-quality
   white chocolate with at
   least 25% cocoa
   butter/solids

3 egg yolks
30g (1 oz) caster sugar
20g (¾ oz) plain flour
450ml (15 fl oz) milk
150ml (5 fl oz) single cream
½ teaspoon vanilla extract

To make the custard, break the chocolate up into small pieces and place in a bowl. Cover with clingfilm and microwave on medium power for 2 minutes. Stir, then return to the microwave for 1 minute on medium power. Let it stand for 1 minute, then stir again. Or melt the chocolate in a bowl over simmering water, but take great care not to overheat it.

Beat the egg yolks with the sugar until pale and thick. Add the flour and beat in smoothly. Bring the milk and cream up to the boil. Pour about two-thirds of this into the egg yolk mixture, whisking constantly. Then pour the rest into the chocolate, whisking constantly. Rinse out the pan and pour both mixtures and the vanilla extract back in. Bring up to the boil, stirring continuously. Let it simmer for about 1 minute.

Peel and slice each banana into four to six individual bowls, or one single serving bowl. Pour the custard over the bananas, then leave to cool. Serve lightly chilled or at room temperature.

Pouring Custard Ⓥ

Call it what you will – *crème anglaise* if you are feeling chi-chi, egg custard if you want to be more prosaic – there is nothing like a straight, properly made custard for adding that wonderful finishing touch to all manner of puddings, from the homely to the stately. Take it gently, don't overheat, and the rest is easy.

MAKES ABOUT 300ML (10 FL OZ)

300ml (10 fl oz) milk or milk and single cream mixed
1 vanilla pod, or ¼ teaspoon vanilla extract

3 egg yolks
15g (½ oz) caster sugar

Put the milk and cream (if using) into a pan with the vanilla pod, if using. Bring gently and patiently to the boil. Meanwhile, beat the egg yolks lightly with the sugar. Take out the vanilla pod, then pour the hot milk into the egg yolks, stirring constantly. Pour back into the pan, and stir over a low heat until the mixture has just thickened enough to coat the back of a spoon. Don't expect it to thicken dramatically – we're talking something just a little bit thicker than single cream, which should take no more than 5 minutes.

Strain the custard into a cold jug or bowl, and stir in the vanilla, if using. Serve immediately if using hot, or leave to cool and thicken a little more.

Stand-Your-Spoon-Up-In-It
Bay or Vanilla Custard ⓥ

This is so thick that it is verging on *crème pâtissière*, or confectioners' pastry cream. It is just perfect as a basis for fruit fools (see page 197), but it is also very good spread (while still warm) in sweet pastry cases as a base for strawberries or other soft, seasonal fruit.

MAKES ABOUT 450ML (15 FL OZ)

3 egg yolks
30g (1 oz) caster sugar
45g (1½ oz) plain flour
300ml (10 fl oz) full-cream
  milk
150ml (5 fl oz) single cream
1 vanilla pod, or 2 bay
  leaves

Beat the egg yolks with the sugar. Add the flour and beat in smoothly. Put the milk, cream and bay or vanilla pod into a saucepan and bring slowly to the boil. Pour while hot and steaming into the eggs, whisking constantly.

Return the mixture to the pan (leave the bay or vanilla pod in there for the time being) and bring up to the boil, stirring continuously. As soon as it has thickened, strain into a bowl. If not using immediately, rub a knob of butter over the surface to prevent a skin forming.

Sage and Onion Bread ⓥ

A fabulous loaf, that goes particularly well with cheese. I came up with the idea when I was working on menus for a British food promotion in the Philippines, and it went down there almost as well as it does here.

MAKES 1 LARGE LOAF OR 2 SMALLER LOAVES

310g (11 oz) brown bread flour
310g (11 oz) white bread flour
1 sachet easy-blend yeast*
2½ teaspoons salt
45g (1½ oz) butter

250g (9 oz) halved and thinly sliced onion
1 heaped tablespoon caster sugar
3 tablespoons chopped sage
a little milk or lightly beaten egg to glaze

Mix the two flours with the yeast and salt. Add enough water to make a soft dough. Knead vigorously for 5-10 minutes until smooth and very elastic. Cover the bowl with a damp cloth and leave in a warm place until doubled in bulk.

Meanwhile, caramelise the onions. Melt the butter in a heavy-based saucepan, add the onions, stir, then cover and turn the heat down low. Leave to sweat gently for about 30-40 minutes, stirring once in a while, until the onions are very tender (they shouldn't brown at this stage). Now uncover and add the sugar. Raise the heat slightly, stir and cook for a further 15 minutes or so, until lightly caramelised. Draw off the heat.

Knock back the dough, knead briefly, then flatten out and spread the onion mixture over it. Sprinkle on the sage, then roll up the dough and knead for a further 3-4 minutes, until the sage and onion are mixed more or less evenly through the dough. This is a squelchy, slippery business, but persevere. Either leave as one piece, for a large loaf, or divide into two and form into smaller loaves. Place each loaf on a greased baking tray. Cover with a damp cloth and leave to rise until doubled in bulk. Brush with milk or lightly beaten egg.

Preheat the oven to 230°C/450°F/Gas Mark 8. Bake the loaves for 10 minutes, then reduce the heat to 200°C/400°F/Gas Mark 6 and bake for 15 minutes (10 minutes for smaller loaves), until the loaf sounds hollow when tapped underneath. Cool on a wire rack.

A Plain White Loaf Ⓥ

There are disappointingly large areas of the country where it is impossible to get halfway decent bread. I know, because I live in one of them. Supermarkets do their best but, to be frank, even the best loaf in the world suffers miserably by being wrapped in plastic and left out on the shelf. Still, all hope is not lost, for making a good plain white loaf is a doddle. This is not to belittle the art of the skilled master baker: the basics are easy to get to grips with, but the subtleties and in-depth knowledge take years to acquire.

   You must start with high-quality, strong white bread flour. If you can lay your hands on organic bread flour from a small independent miller who knows his grains, then you are flying. To make life simpler, use one of the easy-blend, or quick-bake yeasts, and then all you require is a bit of patience. If you happen to have a sturdy mixer (of the Kenwood or Kitchen Aid type), then you can let the dough hook do all the work of kneading for you. Some processors claim to be able to handle it, but I've overworked and destroyed the motors of several in attempts to get them to knead bread dough.

MAKES 1 LOAF

500g (18 oz) strong white
   bread flour
2 teaspoons salt

1 teaspoon granulated or
   caster sugar
1 sachet easy-blend yeast*

Mix the flour, salt, sugar and yeast. Add enough water, around 300ml (10 fl oz), to mix (it's much easier with your hands) to a soft, but firm dough. Now knead vigorously for 5-10 minutes until the dough is silky smooth and elastic. If the dough is a touch sticky when you start, just keep sprinkling it with more flour as you knead, until it stops sticking. If the dough is very hard to work and on the dry side, sprinkle a few drops of water over it as you knead until it becomes easy to handle.

Now return the dough to the mixing bowl, cover with a damp cloth and leave in a warm place (but not hot – you don't want to kill the yeast) until doubled in bulk. That takes anything between 1 and 1½ hours.

Grease a 450g (1 lb) loaf tin. Punch the dough down and gather it up into a ball. Knead again briefly. Form into a thick sausage shape and lower it into the tin. Cover again with a damp cloth and leave to rise again in a warm place. Preheat the oven to 220°C/425°F/ Gas Mark 7. When the dough has risen handsomely above the rim of the tin (but before it overflows and flops down the sides), it is ready to bake.

Place in the oven, then quickly throw about 30ml (1 fl oz) cold water on the hot base of the oven. Quickly close the door before the steam escapes – this will produce a better, sturdier crust. Bake for 10 minutes, then turn round so that it browns evenly, throw another 30ml (1 fl oz) water on the base of the oven and bake for a final 10 minutes. The bread is done when it slides easily out of its tin with the minimum of encouragement, and sounds hollow when tapped on the base. If it sticks, return to the oven for 3-4 more minutes and try again.

Cool on a wire rack and make sure everyone admires it thoroughly before slicing.

A Light Brown Loaf Ⓥ

Have you even been subjected to the kind of brown bread that could easily double as a doorstep? If not, then count yourself lucky. Brown bread is not as easy to make well as white, but there are a couple of tricks that can guarantee a light, moist loaf that you can be justifiably proud of and will not sit like a brick in your stomach. The first is the addition of some fat that is solid at room temperature. Butter works well, and lard is fine unless you are vegetarian. Vegetable shortening is possibly the most effective, though hardly in keeping with the organic frame of reference.

The second trick comes in the form of a crushed Vitamin C tablet. Choose the type that is soluble and crush it to a powder in a mortar or strong bowl. Avoid blackcurrant-flavoured tablets (they stain the bread); if absolutely unavoidable, orange-flavoured ones will not ruin the taste of the finished article. For more detailed bread-making instructions, see the method for the white loaf.

MAKES 1 LOAF

30g (1 oz) butter, chilled and diced
500g (18 oz) wholemeal bread flour
2 teaspoons salt

1 x 500 or 1000mg Vitamin C tablet*, crushed
2 teaspoons caster sugar or honey
1 sachet easy-blend yeast*

Rub the butter into the flour, then add the salt, crushed Vitamin C tablet, sugar or honey and yeast. Mix, then add enough water to form a soft, but not sticky dough. Knead vigorously for 5-10 minutes, until it feels smooth (bar the knobbly bits of bran) and elastic. Return to the bowl, cover with a damp cloth and leave to rise until doubled in bulk.

Punch down the dough and gather up into a ball. Knead again briefly. Shape into a ball and place on a well-floured baking sheet. Rub a little more flour lightly over the top then slash a cross in the top. Cover again with a damp cloth and leave to rise until doubled in size. Meanwhile, preheat the oven to 220°C/425°F/Gas Mark 7. Put the loaf in the oven and then quickly, before you close the door, spatter the floor of the oven generously with water. Close quickly and bake for 10 minutes. Turn the loaf and throw a little more water on the floor of the oven to create a second blast of steam. Bake for another 10 minutes, until browned. If it is done, the loaf should detach itself easily from the baking sheet and will sound hollow when tapped on the bottom. Cool on a wire rack.

Pitta Bread ⓥ

Making your own puffed-up Arab bread is really rather exciting. And there's no scary technique to it, either. They enter the oven as flat as a pancake and, somehow, quite magically and mysteriously, they puff up in the heat.

Arab flat breads come in many sizes and forms and these are no exception. Though I've called them pitta breads, I actually prefer to make them thicker and a little breadier than what is usually sold here under that name, without losing the essential pocket in the middle, in which to carry a cargo of something suitably delicious. If you need ideas, then how about sliding in a wedge of goats' cheese with diced tomato, shredded lettuce and pitted olives, topped with a spoonful or two of thick yoghurt flavoured with crushed garlic and mint. Or fill with cream cheese, honey and stoned cherries (a rather good concoction patented by our children). Or just look at what's in the fridge, and start from there.

MAKES 8

150g (5 oz) strong wholemeal flour
350g (12 oz) strong white bread flour
1 sachet easy-blend yeast*

1 teaspoon caster sugar
2 teaspoons salt
1 tablespoon extra virgin olive oil, plus a little extra

Mix the two flours with the yeast, sugar and salt. Now add the olive oil and enough water to form a soft, but not sticky dough. Knead the dough vigorously for 5-10 minutes until smooth and elastic. Pour a little extra oil into the mixing bowl, return the dough to it and turn to coat in oil. Cover with a damp cloth and leave to rise, about 1-1½ hours, until doubled in bulk.

Punch down and knead again briefly. Divide into eight balls. Spread out a tea-towel and dust lightly with flour. One by one, roll out the portions of dough, so that they form ovals of about 5mm (¼ in) thick for breadier, doughier flatbreads, or about half that thickness for larger, thinner flatbreads. Lay each one on the floured cloth and when they are all done, cover with a damp tea-towel. Leave to rise for another half an hour.

Preheat the oven to 230°C/450°F/Gas Mark 8. Oil two baking trays and place them in the oven to heat through. When they are good and hot, lay three pitta breads quickly on each one, sprinkle them quickly with a touch of water, then quickly close the oven door. Bake for 6-8 minutes, until puffed up and smelling of mouth-watering, newly baked bread. Cool on wire racks. Store in an airtight container if not using immediately.

Popovers Ⓥ

An American breakfast-time treat, these are almost like miniature Yorkshire puds, but not quite. They puff up wildly in their cases, and are crisp on the outside and soft, eggy and moist inside. Eat them warm from the oven with butter and jam.

MAKES 9-12, DEPENDING ON THE SIZE OF THE TINS

2 eggs
225ml (8 fl oz) milk
130g (4½ oz) plain flour

1 tablespoon melted butter,
  plus extra for greasing
¼ teaspoon salt

To make the batter, just pile all the ingredients straight into a large bowl, and start whisking them together. The blissful thing about this is that you positively don't want to end up with a smooth batter! So, don't overdo matters. Just whisk until the batter is fairly evenly mixed together.

Spoon into the muffin tin, filling each hole no more than two-thirds full. Bake for 10 minutes, then reduce the heat to 180°C/350°F/Gas Mark 4 and bake for a further 10-15 minutes, until puffed up like uneven balloons and enticingly browned. Turn out and eat while still warm.

Orange Shortbread Ⓥ

Shortbread is a never failing delight – to nibble on with tea or coffee, or as an accompaniment to creamy fruit fools and other puddings. It's one of my great stand-bys; it is phenomenally easy to make, and deeply seductive to both children and adults.

To get a really crisp, short, crumbly shortbread, I replace some of the flour with either cornflour or rice flour. Much as I love plain shortbread, I think this orange zest version is possibly even better, and it goes brilliantly with lightly cooked fruit – try it with rhubarb and ginger.

MAKES 12 PETTICOAT TAILS

finely grated zest of 2 oranges
170g (6 oz) plain flour
100g (3 oz) cornflour
90g (3 oz) caster sugar
180g (6 oz) unsalted butter

Preheat the oven to 180°C/350°F/Gas Mark 4. Put the orange zest in a bowl with the flour and cornflour. Add the sugar, then work in the butter to give a soft dough. Alternatively, just put everything in the bowl of the processor and process until the mixture forms a ball. Roll the dough into a smooth sphere.

Place the dough on a baking tray, then either press it out with your fingers, or roll with a rolling pin, to form a circle about 1cm (½ in) thick. Prick all over with the tines of a fork and crimp the circumference prettily. Bake for 25-30 minutes, until the surface is lightly coloured. Take out of the oven and cut straightaway into twelve wedges, then leave to cool on the tray. When cold, break up into 'petticoat tails', and eat.

Chocolate Shortbread Ⓥ

To make chocolate shortbread, leave out the orange zest, and replace 30g (1 oz) of the cornflour with cocoa. Mind you, orange and chocolate shortbread is something of a winner too; for that one keep the orange zest in *and* replace 30g (1 oz) of the cornflour with cocoa.

Torta Caprese Ⓥ

This, my friends, is a cake to die for. Intensely chocolatey, rich and dastardly, it is just divine. There's no flour in it at all, just an awful lot of ground almonds, which keep it moist, and an awful lot of chocolate. It comes from the island of Capri, but is made and appreciated from mainland Naples down to Salerno, and probably far beyond. If not, it deserves to be.

For absolute perfection, top it with a big spoonful of crème fraîche, thick Greek yoghurt or some beaten mascarpone.

SERVES 8-10 (AT A PINCH)

200g (7 oz) dark chocolate
4 eggs, separated
175 (6 oz) caster sugar
1 teaspoon vanilla extract

250g (9 oz) ground almonds
200g (7 oz) butter, melted
 and cooled until tepid
icing sugar

Line the base of an 24cm (9½ in) cake tin with non-stick baking parchment and grease the sides. Preheat the oven to 180°C/350°F/Gas Mark 4.

Process the chocolate until finely chopped, but still retaining a little texture. If you don't have a processor, chop the chocolate finely with a large knife. Beat the egg yolks with the sugar and vanilla until the mixture is pale and thick. Fold in the chocolate, the almonds and melted butter. Whisk the egg whites until they form soft peaks and fold into this gorgeous chocolatey goo. Spoon into the prepared cake tin, and bake for about 50-60 minutes, until just firm to the touch. Leave to cool in the mould, then turn out. Dust the surface with icing sugar before serving.

Walnut or Brazil Nut Fudge Ⓥ

Every now and then I give in to the urge to buy fudge. Heaven knows why, because it is nearly always a disappointment. Most commercially produced fudge is vile, and has very little to do with the genuine article. Not only do the wretched manufacturers contaminate what should be one of the most divine, sweet and rich confections with margarine and other cheap fats, but they shoot wide of the crumbly, sandy, melting texture that is the birthright of real fudge. The only answer is to make it oneself, by far the best option, reserved for the occasional major treat or, perhaps, just perhaps, for presents for very dearly beloved friends and family.

MAKES ABOUT 675G (1½ LB)

500g (18 oz) granulated sugar
200ml (7 fl oz) double cream
60g (2 oz) unsalted butter

a pinch of salt
110g (4 oz) shelled walnuts or Brazil nuts, very roughly chopped
1 teaspoon vanilla extract

Butter an 18 x 18cm (7 x 7 in) tin. Put the sugar, cream, butter and salt in a roomy heavy pan. Stir over a moderate heat until the sugar and butter have completely dissolved, brushing down the sides from time to time with a brush dipped in cold water.

Bring the mixture up to the boil and boil gently, stirring every once in a while, until the mixture reaches soft ball stage. In other words, when a drop of the hot, creamy syrup forms a soft sticky ball when dropped into a glass of cold water – this may take as little as 7-8 minutes, but even so, don't try to rush this stage or you will more than likely burn the base of the pan.

As soon as the mixture reaches that critical soft ball stage, whip it off the heat, add the nuts and vanilla and start beating energetically until it thickens and starts to crystallise. It can take what seems like forever, but persevere. Now work quickly (this is not the time to answer the phone or mop up spilt drinks or respond to any other distractions), tipping and scraping it out immediately into the oiled tin. Smooth down and leave to cool. Cut into squares and store what isn't eaten immediately in an airtight container.

My Bircher Muesli Ⓥ

This recipe for a fresh muesli has strayed a fair way from the Swiss Dr Bircher-Benner's original, but it retains, I think, the essence of it. We make it for Sunday morning breakfasts, when we have time to linger a little. It tastes delicious and healthy, and is just what you need to face the day ahead.

SERVES 2

2 heaped tablespoons
  rolled oats
3 tablespoons milk or water
2-3 tablespoons Greek-style
  yoghurt or fromage frais
1-2 tablespoons clear
  honey

1 apple, grated
fresh fruit (1 peach or
  1 banana, blackberries,
  strawberries or
  raspberries, etc.)

Soak the oats in the milk or water for at least 20 minutes. Mix in the yoghurt, honey and grated apple. Divide between the two bowls and top with fresh fruit, cut up if large.

Granola ⓥ

Granola is that crisp morning cereal with clusters of grains and nuts and seeds in it. The joy of making your own is that you can tailor it to your very own tastes. I've used a mixture of large rolled oats and wheat flakes, but you could also add rye or barley flakes. Then there are the nuts and seeds and dried fruit. The options are endless, so just use my quantities to guide you.

MAKES ABOUT 550G (1¼ LB)

4 tablespoons sunflower oil
2 tablespoons clear honey
2 tablespoons dark muscovado sugar
1 tablespoon lemon juice
225g (8 oz) large rolled oats
60g (2 oz) wheat flakes
30g (1 oz) sesame seeds
45g (1½ oz) almonds, finely chopped
45g (1½ oz) hazelnuts, finely chopped
30g (1 oz) desiccated coconut
60g (2 oz) raisins
60g (2 oz) dried papaya, chopped*

Preheat the oven to 140°C/275°F/Gas Mark 1. Place the oil, honey, sugar and lemon juice in a large pan, and stir over a gentle heat until melted and evenly mixed without letting it boil. Take off the heat and add all the remaining ingredients except for the raisins and papaya. Stir and mix until evenly coated. Spread the mixture on two baking trays lined with non-stick baking parchment. Bake in the preheated oven for an hour, stirring frequently, until crisp and golden brown. Cool, stirring occasionally to break up lumps. Now mix with the raisins and papaya, and store in an airtight container until breakfast-time. Serve with milk and/or yoghurt and fresh fruit. Alternatively, sprinkle over creamy puddings.

Banana and Strawberry Cinnamon Milkshake ⓥ

When the sun shines down hell for leather, when some small one just won't contemplate eating fruit of any kind, when you just fancy a rich, slurpy treat... whizz up an icy, thick, fruity milkshake. This is something that we all love every now and then, and if you keep a stash of good-quality organic vanilla ice-cream in the freezer, you can adapt this milkshake to whatever fruit you have hanging around (but not kiwi, papaya or pineapple which will all instantly curdle the milk, bringing a nasty bitter underflavour in their wake).

SERVES 4-6

3 bananas, peeled and
  roughly sliced
250g (9 oz) strawberries,
  hulled
175g (6 oz) good-quality
  vanilla ice-cream

1 teaspoon ground
  cinnamon
300ml (10 fl oz) milk

Put all the ingredients in a liquidiser and liquidise ferociously but briefly until blended. Distribute and drink quickly, while still thick and icy.

Lemonade Ⓥ

This is the perfect thirst-quencher for a hot day. Present it in a big jug with lemon slices, ice cubes and sprigs of mint or borage flowers floating about on the surface, and everyone will greet it like a long-lost friend.

SERVES 4

4 lemons
caster sugar to taste

ice cubes
a few sprigs of mint

Slice the ends off the lemons and discard. Cut the rest of the lemons up roughly and put into a processor with any juice that has squeezed out under the knife blade. Add about 110g (4 oz) caster sugar and 300ml (10 fl oz) water. Process to a mush, then tip out into a sieve set over a bowl. Press down (but don't try to rub the lemon mush through, or it will be horribly bitter) to extract the last few drops of liquid, then return the contents of the sieve to the processor, with 60g (2 oz) sugar and another 300ml (10 fl oz) water and repeat the whole process.

Pop the debris back into the processor, add 150ml (5 fl oz) water, and about 30g (1 oz) caster sugar and process one last time. Strain again, pressing down to extract the last few drops of fragrant juice, then discard all the debris in the sieve. Taste the lemonade: if it is still too sharp, add more water and then stir in a little more sugar. Serve chilled.

Blackcurrant or Redcurrant Jelly Ⓥ

This is the easiest and quickest jelly recipe I know, and the jelly it produces has a rich, intense flavour. The basic recipe comes from my mother's *Fruit Book*, and though she also includes other methods of transforming currants into jellies and jams, this is the one I return to again and again. The yield is not enormous – for each 500g (18 oz) of fruit and sugar, yield is approximately 350-380g (12-13 oz) – but the flavour is so good that I don't think you'll mind. You will also need a stash of sterilised jars waiting in the oven (see page 239).

Pour enough water into the base of a large preserving pan to just cover the base. Tip in both the currants, which do not need to be stripped from their stalks, and the sugar. Stir over a moderate heat until the sugar has dissolved, then bring up to the boil. Boil for 8 minutes, then draw off the heat. For a really sparkling jelly but the lowest yield, tip into a jelly bag and let the juices drip briefly (they still need to be hot when spooned into the attendant jars). For a less perfect looking, but fine tasting, jelly of slightly greater quantity, tip the cooked blackcurrants into a sieve and let the juices pour through into the bowl below.

Either way, pour the hot, molten jelly into warm sterilised jars, then cover, seal and label in the usual way.

Gooseberry and Elderflower Jam Ⓥ

Gooseberry jam is one of William's favourites, and luckily our two gooseberry bushes are prolific fruiters, so we can make enough to give away and keep us going right through the year. Even if you have to buy them (and around mid to late June they should be widely available, particularly from farmers' markets), it still pays to turn your hand to a spot of jam-making, especially when creamy white elderflowers are in full bloom. They add a particular, muscat flavour to the jam that makes it even nicer.

Before you pour in the water, however, consider the weather. If the three or four weeks before have been horribly, miserably wet, then you will only need the lower quantity, as the gooseberries themselves will produce more. On the other hand, in your average British on-off June weather, you will need the full amount.

MAKES ABOUT 3KG (6½ LB)

2kg (4½ lb) gooseberries
300-450ml (10-15 fl oz)
  water

15 elderflower heads Ⓦ
2kg (4½ lb) sugar
a knob of butter

Top and tail the gooseberries, and place in a preserving pan, or a very large, heavy-based saucepan, with the water. Heat up and simmer gently for some 20 minutes, stirring frequently to prevent sticking.

Meanwhile, wrap the flowers up in a square of muslin (or possibly a J-cloth rinsed out in boiling water). Pile the sugar into a big heatproof bowl, and warm it through in a low oven.

Draw the pan off the heat when the gooseberries are very tender. Stir in the warm sugar, the butter and the elderflowers in their muslin. Keep stirring until the sugar has dissolved then bring up to the boil. Boil hard for about 10 minutes until setting point is reached (see below). Extract the bag of elderflowers and discard. Ladle the hot jam into hot sterilised jars, seal and label in the usual way. Store in a dark, dry cupboard.

To test for a set Before you begin making the jam or jelly, stash three or four saucers in the fridge. Start testing for a set fairly soon after the mixture, with the sugar in, has started to boil hard. Just drip a few drops on to one of the chilled saucers. Cool for a minute or two, then nudge one of the drops with your finger. If it wrinkles on the surface, then your preserve has reached setting point and is ready to pot up. If the drop remains very runny, then continue boiling for about 5 minutes more and try again.

To sterilise jam jars Wash jars thoroughly in soapy water, then rinse well. Without touching the insides, turn them upside down, and leave to drain and dry on a rack in the oven set to 110°C/225°F/Gas Mark ½ for at least half an hour, or longer. Unless otherwise indicated in the recipe, fill the jars straight from the oven, while they are still hot.

Raw Onion Chutney Ⓥ

This raw onion chutney, an old favourite that first appeared in my book *Eat Your Greens*, makes a fine invigorating accompaniment to a curry like the one on pages 144-5.

SERVES 4-6

1 large red onion, finely chopped
1 heaped teaspoon ground cumin

¼-½ teaspoon cayenne pepper
½ teaspoon sweet paprika
2 tablespoons lemon juice

Mix all the ingredients together. Taste and add a little more cumin or cayenne if needed.

Carrot and Mint Raita Ⓥ

This is a quickly made, soothing accompaniment to spicy dishes. Though it comes from the stable of Indian cooking, it runs well alongside chilli-heated dishes from other parts of the world.

SERVES 4

1 tablespoon black mustard seeds
1 large carrot, grated
2 tablespoons shredded mint

310g (11 oz) natural yoghurt
a little salt

Dry-fry the mustard seeds in a small heavy pan until they start to pop and jump. Tip into a bowl and leave to cool, then mix with all the other ingredients.

Harissa Ⓥ
(Moroccan Chilli Relish)

I have yet to come across a really good organic chilli sauce. I dare say one will happen along pretty soon, but in the meantime, I'm more than happy with this fiery concoction that packs an inflammatory punch. It is a North African speciality, traditionally served with couscous. Not that its uses stop there. Pep up soups, stews and tomato sauces with a small slurp (go gently at first, you can always add more) or make a mayo with attitude, flavoured with a touch of harissa and finely chopped spring onions.

MAKES ENOUGH TO LIFT THE ROOF OFF A CROWD OF MOUTHS...

110g (4 oz) medium-hot, fresh red chilli peppers, seeded
4 garlic cloves, roughly chopped
1 teaspoon coriander seeds
1 teaspoon cumin seeds
1 teaspoon caraway seeds
2 tablespoons chopped fresh coriander leaves
¼ teaspoon salt
4 tablespoons extra virgin olive oil

Chop the peppers roughly and place in the processor with the garlic. Dry-fry the seeds in a small pan over a moderate heat until they turn a shade darker, scenting the kitchen. Cool then grind to a powder. Add to the chillies with the coriander and salt. Process until finely chopped, scraping down the sides. Keep the blades whirring as you gradually trickle in the olive oil.

Scrape out and store in a small screw-top jar in the fridge, pouring a thin layer of olive oil over the surface to exclude the air. It will last for several months as long as you make sure the layer of oil is renewed every time you dip in.

Chicken Stock

Home-made chicken stock makes such a big difference to soups, sauces, risottos, pilafs, stews and all kinds of savoury dishes. You can make it fairly speedily in a microwave, but even if you don't, it begs precious little attention as it burbles away on the stove. If you don't have the carcass of a fresh bird to hand, you can use the bones left after a roast, or buy say, four or so chicken thighs or eight wings to replace the carcass altogether.

MAKES ABOUT 750ML (1¼ PINTS)

the carcass and, if available, giblets (excluding the liver), and scraps of skin from 1 chicken
1 onion, quartered
1 carrot, quartered

1 celery stalk, quartered
1 bay leaf
3 parsley stalks
1 large sprig of thyme
8 black peppercorns

To cook in the conventional way, place all the ingredients in a large pan and cover generously with water. Bring to the boil and simmer for 2-3 hours, occasionally skimming off any scum that rises to the surface. Add extra boiling water if the level drops severely.

Strain and cool. For absolutely perfect stock, chill overnight in the fridge, and then lift off any fat that has set on the top of the stock.

To cook in the microwave, put all the ingredients into the largest microwaveable bowl that you have. Cover with boiling water, then cover tightly with clingfilm and place in the microwave. Microwave at full power for 25 minutes, then leave to stand for 30 minutes before straining.

Vegetable Stock Ⓥ

There is no one basic recipe for making vegetable stock. The crucial thing is to include a good variety of vegetables (peelings and trimmings are fine) so that no one flavour dominates, and the depth of flavour is strong enough to support the dish the stock will be used for. Take this as a model and build your own recipe.

MAKES 750ML-1 LITRE (1¼-1¾ PINTS)

2 onions, quartered
2 leeks, trimmed and
  quartered
2 carrots, halved
4 celery stalks, quartered
1 medium potato, cut into
  big chunks

2 garlic cloves, chopped
2 tablespoons extra virgin
  olive oil
2 bay leaves
6 parsley stalks
2 sprigs of thyme
1 small sprig of rosemary

Put all the vegetables into a processor and process until chopped.

Heat the oil in a large pan. Add the vegetables and herbs, and stir to coat well. Cover and sweat over a low heat for 15 minutes, stirring occasionally to prevent burning. Add 1.5 litres (2½ pints) water, bring to the boil and simmer for 30 minutes. Strain, squeezing as much liquid as possible out of the vegetables.

The Organic Cook's Compendium

This is by no means a comprehensive list of all the organic ingredients on offer. If it were, it would be long out of date by the time the book hits the shelves. Instead, we've listed ingredients (mainly) where there is something distinct and particular differentiating organic from non-organic, and a few others which can never be totally organic for very good reasons. The compendium is intended to act as a handy, quick reference section aimed, primarily, at the cook. For more detailed enlightenment turn to the relevant chapters.

Anchovies: Since anchovies swim in shoals in the deep blue sea, they are classed as a wild product, so cannot be labelled organic in the EU. The best-quality fish will be packed in olive oil (rather than vegetable oil), and that, of course, could theoretically be organic.

Apricots, Dried: Organic dried apricots are brown and very, very sweet – almost like fruity toffee – and altogether quite different from the common-or-garden dried apricot. The reason for the difference is sulphur. Usually, apricots (and many other dried fruit for that matter) are dusted with sulphur to prevent discoloration and deterioration.

This yields the familiar bright orange, tart/sweet dried apricot. Without the sulphur they darken as they dry and their sweetness intensifies. If you are using organic apricots in a recipe written for non-organic apricots, you may want to add a little lemon juice to make up for the lack of acidity.

Bacon: Bacon is, of course, processed, preserved pork and the raw material, the pig, will have to have been raised according to organic Standards, and duly certified for it to be called organic. There has been some controversy about allowing sodium nitrate and nitrite to be used as a 'curing aid' in the production but this really reflects the need for there to be a system in place that produces a consistently healthy and bacteria-free product. However, polyphosphates are not allowed. That's the stuff that is responsible for increasing the water content of bacon and results in the irritating spitting and the white gloop in the frying pan. Organic bacon is no-spit, no-gloop bacon.

Bread: As yet there is not enough organic yeast around to make all the organic bread required. To get round this, non-organic yeast is permitted in 'organic'

bread since it is considered a processing aid rather than an agricultural ingredient. A bit of a fudge, if you ask us. Still, a small one, which will, it is hoped, eventually change. Naturally leavened sourdough breads use natural airborne yeast for the starter. Organic bread flours are widely available and are as variable as conventional product. Sadly, experience has taught us that much of the mass-produced organic bread sold in supermarkets is every bit as dull as non-organic. To get really good organic bread, you will either have to track down a right-minded, skilled baker, or roll up your sleeves and start baking your own – see the recipes on pages 219-229.

Butter and Cream: Organic cream and butter have no chemical or antibiotic residues. It is known that pesticides can accumulate heavily in fats, so organic dairy products have enormous appeal. Natural (rather than the denatured, processed fats from milk, which are found for example in long-life milk) actually contain high levels of unsaturated fatty acids, which are good for you. Organic butter and cream can be pasteurised or unpasteurised (see milk below).

Carrots: Remember when we were all told to peel and cut the tips off carrots (non-organic ones, of course) before cooking or eating them raw? This was due to the build up of harmful chemicals used in controlling carrot-root fly. Organic carrots are free of toxic synthetic chemicals, so you can eat them skin, tips and all. Hurray.

Cheese: The comments on dairy fats sited in the entry for butter and cream apply equally to cheese. Look out for both pasteurised and unpasteurised organic cheeses. The latter will usually taste far better. And be warned, just because cheese is made from organic milk doesn't mean it is going to taste brilliant. If it is mass-produced (and here I'm thinking in particular of some organic Cheddars), it will still taste mass-produced. Search out the best, organic farmhouse cheeses from small producers, who put heart and soul into them. Incidentally, rennet from either vegetable or animal sources may be used but doesn't as yet have to be organic.

Chickens: All organic chickens are free range, though not all free-range chickens are organic. No use of growth-promoting hormones, or industrialised intensive levels of farming are allowed under organic standards although there is a need to implement a consistent policy on permitted flock size. Even so, there are organic chickens and organic chickens – in other words they vary enormously in quality of flavour and texture. For the best of all worlds, search out locally produced, healthy looking birds, rather than pasty white flabby ones, wrapped in too much packaging.

Chocolate: Yipidee-do-da! Organic chocolate is just fab, fab, fab, and can hold its own against the finest non-organic chocolate, no problem. All of the organic dark chocolate I have come across has been high in cocoa solids (at least 70 per cent) which makes it brilliant for cooking. Organic white chocolate, too, is very pure so far, made with cocoa fats, not cheap vegetable fat, which again, makes it perfect for cooking, if you don't guzzle it down first.

There is also a more serious and compelling reason for buying organic, and Fairtrade chocolate. A recent television documentary estimated that at least 40 per cent of the chocolate eaten worldwide was produced using slave labour. Such suspect social conditions are issues addressed under *The Standards*. Though it may seem a minor issue in comparison, it is also worth noting that conventionally produced chocolate has been shown to have high levels of residual chemicals. Particularly worrying is the level of the organo-chlorine Lindane, that can cause breast cancer.

Citrus Fruit: Organic citrus fruit is widely available and, reassuringly, will not have been sprayed with fungicides. It is often unwaxed, which means that it will dry out more quickly than non-organic waxed fruit. Store it in the fridge and don't expect it to last for weeks. It is best to buy just what one needs and use it up as soon as possible. Don't be put off by splashes of green on oranges and lemons – this is not necessarily a sign that they are not ripe, just that the night temperature where they are grown has not fallen low enough to trigger the natural colouration mechanisms of the fruit. At least you will know that it hasn't been dyed! Green lemon zest, by the way, is a delicious flavouring for liqueurs, puddings and the like.

Coconut

If you are very lucky, in the right place at the right time, you may find organic fresh coconuts. Failing that, it is possible to track down organic coconut milk, coconut cream and desiccated coconut.

Eggs: All organic eggs are free range, chemical and antibiotic free. Not all free range eggs are organic though. Reminisce as we may about the sunshine yellow of egg yolks of old, these days it pays to be wary of over-bright yolks, as canny non-organic egg-farmers have caught on and introduce artificial colouring into the chicken feed. The yolks of organic eggs tend to be paler due to the lack of such colouring in the bird's diet.

Fish, Farmed: Organic fish means primarily organic salmon and trout. Supplies of organic sea bass and cod will be appearing soon. Organic salmon is coloured with naturally derived substances and no synthetic chemicals are used in the farming process. It is still difficult to practise anything other than monoculture and there are concerns about the effect that fish farms have on the local environment.

Fish, Wild: EU rules now mean that wild fish cannot be called organic. If you want to be sure that the fish you buy is fished in a sustainable way, then look out for eco-labelled fish, certified by the Marine Stewardship Council.

Flour: A wide variety of organic flour is available. In terms of use, it can be used just as non-organic flour, with the glorious advantage that it will taste of something interesting! Organic flours will vary much more in flavour according to provenance – buy them if you can from a good miller such as Shipham Mills, or Marriages.

Fruit:
No preservatives and growth suppressants are allowed anywhere near organic fruit, which means that it must be consumed more quickly than non-organic. We have become used to piling up non-organic fruit in a fruit bowl, safe in the knowledge that it has a longish shelf-life. It is only a small matter of adjustment, to buying smaller quantities that will be used up speedily. There is increasing evidence that organic fruit has higher levels of beneficial phytochemicals than conventionally farmed equivalents.

Game:
Is, for the most part, semi-wild so cannot be labelled as organic.

Herbs:
Absorption of chemicals and pesticide residues on herbs is similar to lettuces and salad crops, or in other words, more than most of us would care to know. For all but the most common herbs, the best solution is to grow your own, in the garden, on the window-sill, in a pot by the back door. Some herb growers (such as Jekka McVicar) are now growing only organic herbs, and will be able to provide pots of organic herbs, ready to plant on. Failing that, the better supermarkets are increasingly stocking organic herbs of the most common varieties.

Honey:
All organic honey has to be free from pollution, which is something of a tall order in this country, as bees can travel miles to collect their nectar. This inevitably means that all organic honey has to be imported, mainly from Argentina, with Mexico and Australia following hot in their footsteps.

Lettuce and Salad Crops:
What with their tender leaves and relatively vast surface area, lettuces and other salad crops are bound to absorb considerable amounts of pesticides and chemicals when exposed to them. My natural instinct is, therefore, to head straight for organically produced lettuces of all sorts, where good old-fashioned dirt, grit

and possibly the odd bit of wild life are the only irritants. And of course, you can by-pass these by buying ready-washed and prepared salads in neat plastic bags. Be aware, however, that even organic ready-to-use salads are packed with generous helpings of added nitrogen, oxygen and/or carbon dioxide to prolong shelf-life.

Milk:
As well as having no growth hormones, or residual chemicals, organic milk is derived from cows fed with relatively high levels (minimum 60 per cent) of grass, hay or silage rather than concentrates. The result is that it has higher levels of CLA, or conjugated linoleic acid which helps prevent cancer and heart disease.

Mushrooms:
Non-organic mushrooms and the straw upon which they grow may have been sprayed with chemical pesticides, watered with chlorinated water, sterilised with formaldehyde, fumigated with methyl bromide, bleached etc., which makes organic mushrooms that much more attractive. There is now a wide range of organic mushrooms available, including shiitake (pronounced *shee tah kee* by the way) and oyster mushrooms which are cultivated according to methods that avoid these chemicals. Beware also of using mushroom compost on your garden, which can have high levels of chemical residues.

Mushrooms, Wild:
Cannot be organic in the EU, despite occasional misleading labelling, since they pop up, willy nilly, in woods, entirely of their own volition. Tracking down and picking and, perhaps, drying, do not count as cultivation.

Oil, Olive:
Organic extra virgin olive oil tends to come from less intensive olive-growing areas and is often very high quality. Like conventional extra virgin olive oils they vary enormously in flavour, texture and aroma, so taste before buying if possible, and choose accordingly.

Oils, Other:
There's a bit of a treat in store for you here if you buy cold-pressed organic oils. They tend to have bags more flavour than equivalent non-

organic. Look out in particular for organic cold-pressed sunflower oil which is deliciously nutty, and makes a brilliant dressing, as well as being good for cooking.

Pasta:
Conventional wheat (semolina or durum) pasta is likely to have some degree of pesticide residues. If you want to avoid these, opt for organic. Either way, you get what you pay for. Cheaper pastas tend to be stickier and flabbier, while more expensive ones have a much better texture, and the sauce clings with enthusiasm.

Pepper and Peppercorns:
Somewhat by default, I am told, many peppercorns are grown virtually organically, or at any rate without pesticides and unnecessary chemicals. The good thing about certified organic pepper is that you can also be sure that it hasn't been irradiated.

Peppers, Red, Yellow and Green:
Bell or sweet peppers from Spain were temporarily banned in the EU due to high levels of pesticides. Many of these are grown in the hothouses of Almería, Spain, where controls on pesticide use were lax. The situation has now been tightened, but organic peppers avoid all this. As a general word of warning, even some of the mass-produced organic vegetables from Holland seem to be particularly tasteless.

Rice:
Conventionally grown rice is treated with a high level of pesticides, and there are increasing concerns about the working conditions of rice workers worldwide. Organic rice is now widely found in all forms, from risotto rices through to the finest basmati.

Salmon:
With lower stock densities and no toxic chemicals used in rearing organic salmon, there are clear pluses, but in some organic salmon there is a paler colour that you may find off-putting. This is as a result of using only natural by-product from prawns as a colouring agent, which is wholly laudable. Try to convince yourself that pale pink is a good colour for salmon, smoked or fresh, and eventually you'll come to appreciate it.

Salt:
The Soil Association did certify some sea salt but has decided against certifying it any more as it isn't really an agricultural product. You may see sea salt with herbs certified where the herbs are organic.

Spices:
A wide range of organic spices is available. Irradiation is not allowed as a preserving method.

Spirits:
Organic gin, vodka, Cognac, grappa, Calvados and whisky are all now being made, and sold. Hooray. There's nothing quite like a good g & t at the close of a tough day. But hold on, what about the t? Phew, it's all right – there is such a thing as organic tonic water, so we're on safe ground here.

Sugar:
Although you wouldn't necessarily know it in your average supermarket, there are organic granulated, caster, muscovado and Demerara sugars. If you can't find any organic icing sugar, whizz organic caster or granulated sugar in an efficient processor, or an electric coffee or spice grinder. Lime is the only additive used in making organic sugar.

Vegetables:
Organic vegetables may taste better than non-organic, but not necessarily, since there are so many variables. Organic veg and fruit tend to have a lower water content than non-organic. In theory this should mean a more concentrated flavour, but not necessarily a better one. Flavour is also affected by variety, soil, climate, freshness and storage, etc. When these all come together you are on to a winner.

Vinegar:
Most types of vinegar, from cider and wine to balsamic, are now being made organically.

Wine:
The quality of organic wine has improved enormously over the past decade or so, and it can now hold its own beside conventially produced wines. And the really good news is that organic wine is less likely to give you headaches (hurray), due to the absence of sulphites used in wine-making. Now there's something to celebrate – pour me another!

Yeast:
See Bread above.

Appendix

Many of the issues relating to organics are complex and involved. This section contains a list of some of the key players in the organic world, with web-links and contact numbers to help you follow through any ideas or queries that you may have. You can quite easily spend hours surfing the web chasing up sites that can tell you just about all you need to know about prions, BSE and all the gloomier things we have confronted in our food over the past few years. Some of the sites are informative; a few even amusing. They may help you to see why going organic is so much more than just avoiding eating pesticides. Information rules!

Main Representative Organisations

IFOAM

For individual national IFOAM offices, contact their head office at:
c/o Okozentrum Imsbach, D-66636 Tholey-Theley, Germany
Tel: 06853 91 98 90 Fax: 06853 91 98 99
E-mail: HeadOffice@ifoam.org
Website: www.ifoam.org

Organics in the UK

Organic food labelled in the UK will have one of the following numbers on the label which indicates who has certified them as organic. As well as acting as certifiers, the representative bodies below all act as pressure or trade groups, with the exception of UKROFS which is the Government body attached to MAFF, the Ministry of Agriculture, Fisheries and Food, working as the ultimate authority on organics UK.

UK 1: United Kingdom Register of Organic Food Standards (UKROFS)

c/o MAFF, Room G47, Nobel House, 17 Smith Square, London SW1P 3JR
Tel: 020 7238 5915
Fax: 020 7238 6148

UK 2: Organic Farmers and Growers Ltd (OF&G)

50 High Street, Soham, Ely, Cambs CB7 5HF
Tel: 01353 722398 Fax: 01353 720289
Website: www.organicfood.co.uk
Originally set up in the mid-1970s as an organic food marketing co-op.

Certification Office
The Elin Centre, Lancaster Road, Shrewsbury SY1 3LE
Tel: 01743 440512 Fax: 01743 46148

UK 3: Scottish Organic Producers Association (SOPA)

Suite 15, Software Centre, Stirling University Innovation Park, Stirling FK9 4NF
Tel: 01786 458090 Fax: 01786 45809
E-mail: contact@sopa.demon.co.uk
Set up in 1986 to support the development of organic production in Scotland. Operates an inspection scheme using UKROFS standards.

UK 4: Organic Food Federation (OFF)

1, Mowles Manor Enterprise Centre, Etling Green, Dereham, Norfolk NR20 3EZ
Tel: 01362 637314 Fax: 01362 637980

UK 5: Soil Association Certification Limited

Bristol House, 40-56 Victoria Street, Bristol BS1 6BY
Tel: 0117 9290661 Fax: 0117 9252504
E-mail: info@soilassociation.org
Website: www.soilassociation.org
Responsible for by far the biggest, and best-known, organic certification scheme in the UK – its symbol is the one you are most likely to come across. It is a membership organisation with charitable status and has around 6,000 members, each of whom receive a quarterly magazine called *Living Earth*.

UK 6: Biodynamic Agricultural Association (BDAA)

Painswick Inn Project, Gloucester Street,
Stroud, Gloucester GL5 1QG
Tel/Fax: 01453 759501
Website: www.anth.org.uk

Organics in Ireland

UK 7: Irish Organic Farmers and Growers Association (IOFGA)

Harbour Building, Harbour Road,
Kilbeggan, Co. Westmeath, Ireland
Tel: 0506 32563 Fax: 0506 32063

Organics in Australia and New Zealand

AgriQuality

Head Office, 33 Lambie Drive, PO Box 98905,
South Auckland Mail Centre, Manukau, New Zealand
Tel: 09 262 7350 Fax: 09 262 7370
Website: www.certenz.co.nz

The Biological Farmers of Australia Co-operative Ltd

1st Floor, White Horse Building, 456 Ruthven Street,
Toowoomba, Qld 4350, Australia
PO Box 3404, Toowoomba Village Fair, Qld 4350, Australia
Tel: 07 4639 3299 Fax: 07 4639 3755
E-mail: bfa@icr.com.au

National Association of Sustainable Agriculture Australia (NASAA)

PO Box 768, Stirling, South Australia 5152
Tel: 08 8370 8455 Fax: 08 8370 8381
Email: enquiries@nasaa.com.au
NASAA is Australia's premier organic certifier and certifies
organic production and processing in Australia, Japan, Nepal,
Samoa, Papua New Guinea, Sri Lanka and Indonesia to
Australian (AQIS) and international (IFOAM) standards.

The Soil and Health Association of New Zealand Inc.

PO Box 36-170, Northcote, Auckland 9, New Zealand
Tel: 09 480 4440 Fax: 09 480 4440
Website: www.soil-health.org.nzç

Organics in Canada

Ecological Agriculture Projects

McGill University (Macdonald Campus), Ste-Anne-de-Bellevue
QC, H9X 3V9 Canada
Tel: 1514 398 7771 Fax: 1514 398 7621
E-mail: info@eap.mcgill.ca

Organics in South Africa

Organics Group Limited – OAGL

Organic Farm and Garden Supplies (Pty) Ltd
12 Hibiscus Street, Durbanville, South Africa
(Reg. No. CK94/04709/07)
Tel: 021 975 3166 Tel/Fax: 021 975 6950

Biodynamics

Biodynamic Agricultural Association (BDAA)

See previous

The Biodynamic Farming and Gardening Association in Australia Inc.

PO Box 54 Bellingen, NSW 2454, Australia
Tel/Fax: 266 55 8551

Demeter Scheme Co-ordinator

17 Inverleith Place, Edinburgh, EH3 5QE
Tel: 0131 624 3921 Fax: 0131 476 2996
Website: www.anth.org.uk

Emerson College

Pixton, Hartfield Road, Forest Row, E. Sussex, RH18 5JX
Tel: 01342 822238 Fax: 01342 826055
E-mail: info@emerson.org.uk
For US/Canada see also: www.biodynamics.com

Food Miles

SUSTAIN, The Alliance for Better Food and Farming,
94 White Lion Street, London N1 9PF
Tel: 020 7837 1228 Fax: 020 7837 1141
E-mail: sustain@sustainweb.org
Website: www.sustainweb.org

Genetic Engineering, GMOs and Gender Benders

See: www.eawag.ch/courses/eedc/abstracts.html
An article by Michael Pollan, originally published in the *New York Times*, on Sunday 25 October 1998 called 'Playing God in the Garden', is available from the Soil Association. I found the following websites particularly useful:
Natural Law Party Canada: www.natural-law.ca/genetic/
The Union of Concerned Scientists: www.ucsusa.org
The National Centre for Biotechnology Education:
www.ncbe.reading.ac.uk

NGOs and Pressure Groups

Non-governmental organisations can play a big part in letting us know what really is going on, especially when it comes to food production and agriculture.

Friends of the Earth

26-28 Underwood Street , London N1 7JQ
Tel: 020 7490 1555 Fax: 020 7490 0881
Website: www.foe.org.uk
Or worldwide: www.foe.org

Greenpeace

Canonbury Villas, London N1 2PN
Tel: 020 7865 8100 Fax: 020 7865 8200
E-mail: (questions about Greenpeace and its campaigns)
info@uk.greenpeace.org
(supporter inquiries): supporter@uk.greenpeace.org
(comments and questions about website):
editor@uk.greenpeace.org
Website: www.greenpeace.org

WWF

Panda House, Weyside Park, Godalming, Surrey GU7 1XR
Tel: 01483 426 444 Fax: 01483 426 409
Website: www.panda.org
Scotland office
8, The Square, Aberfeldy, Perthshire PH15 2DD
Tel: 01887 820 449 Fax: 01887 829 453

Pesticides

Pesticide Action Network UK

Eurolink Centre, 49 Effra Road, London SW2 1BZ UK
Tel: 020 7274 8895 Fax: 020 7274 9084
E-mail: admin@pan-uk.org
Website: www.pan-uk.org

Other Organic Organisations

Compassion in World Farming

Charles House, 5A Charles Street, Petersfield, Hampshire GU32 3EH
Tel: 01730 264208/268863 Fax: 01730 260791
E-mail: compassion@ciwf.co.uk
Website: www.ciwf.co.uk

Elm Farm Research Centre (EFRC)

Hamstead Marshall, Newbury, Berks RG15 0HR
Tel: 01488 658298
E-mail: efrc@compuserve.com
An independent organisation researching organic agricultural systems. Has a network of farm advisers, operating through the Organic Advisory Service (OAS), who assist farmers with farm conversion and who provide advice and support afterwards.

The Farm & Food Society (FAFS)

4 Willifield Way, London NW11 7XT
Tel: 020 8455 0634
A vigorous little pressure group, set up and still run by the indefatigable Joanne Bower, that has been agitating since the mid-1960s for more humane treatment of livestock.

Green Network

9 Clairmont Road, Lexden, Colchester, Essex CO3 5BE
Tel: 01206 546902 Fax: 01206 766005
The brainchild of Vera Cheney who runs the organisation.
Concerns cover many issues but it has been especially
prominent in campaigns against pesticide misuse and the
threat posed by genetically modified organisms (GMOs).

The Henry Doubleday Research Association (HDRA)

Ryton Organic Gardens, Coventry CV8 3LG
Tel: 02476 303517 Fax: 02476 639229
Website: www.hdra.org.uk
Europe's largest organic organisation, aimed primarily at
consumers and organic gardeners, with a wide range of
activities. It has 24,000 members who each receive a
quarterly magazine, *Growing Organically*, access to free
gardening advice, plus free admission to the two organic
demonstration gardens HDRA runs – at Ryton and at Yalding,
near Maidstone in Kent – and to a further eight national
gardens. HDRA is a registered charity whose patron is the
Prince of Wales.

National Federation of City Farms

The Green House, Hereford Street, Bedminster, Bristol BS3 4NA
Tel: 0117 923 1800
E-mail: farmgarden@btinternet.com
The co-ordinating voice for the sixty or so city farms and
community garden projects that exist throughout the UK and
which almost exclusively employ organic methods.

Willing Workers on Organic Farms (WWOOF)

19 Bradford Road, Lewes, East Sussex BN7 1RB
Tel: 01273 476286
An opportunity for people to do voluntary work on organic
farms and smallholdings in return for free board and lodging.
Website: www.organicfood.co.uk

Index

Note: Page numbers in **bold** refer to major text sections, those in *italic* to illustrations. Recipes are in **bold** text, with non-vegetarian recipes in ***bold-italic.***